PRAISE FOR
NAMASTE MOTHERF*CKERS

'This is an absolute book.'
Dawn French

'Who needs lots of long dead philosophers when you've got Cally Beaton bursting with life.'
Kirsty Wark

'Immediately gripping and real – much needed.
I LOVE THIS BOOK.'
Helen Lederer

'For women, life is in two acts; the trick is surviving the interval. But once you get through menopause, it's the best time of your life. Cally's gutsy, hilarious, kick-ass book will teach you how to age with mischief, audacity and sass, and how never to pass your amuse-by date.'
Kathy Lette

'If you've ever met a woman over 40, or ever plan to, read this so you don't piss us off.'
Angela Barnes

'This excellent book delivers empathy, peace of mind and hard-won advice with a side order of Cally's trademark sweary feel good factor. Plus: way less effort than yoga.'
Viv Groskop

'A charming, witty guidebook for anyone who's ever felt like an invisible imposter.'
Deborah Frances-White

'A hugely inspiring story of one woman's refusal to go gentle into that good night (or anywhere) interwoven with a wise and witty guide to midlife – brava!'
Helen Russell, author of *The Year of Living Danishly*

'Hilarious, furious, fabulous – she IS woman. Hear her roar!'
Louisa Young

Author photo by Natasha Pszenicki

Cally Beaton is a comedian, keynote speaker, awards host, business leader, podcaster, writer and entrepreneur. She has held senior management positions at some of the biggest media companies in the world. Early in her career she headed an independent television production company that was bought by ITV and Cally became the youngest and only female member on the board. She left to set up an award-winning creative consultancy, Road Trip Media, and went on to do a ten-year stint as Senior Vice President at the US studio giant ViacomCBS. If you want someone to blame for bringing *South Park* and *SpongeBob SquarePants* to the world, you need look no further.

In 2021 she launched her hit podcast *Namaste Motherf**kers* with a star-studded roster of celebrity guests, including Miriam Margolyes, Philippa Perry, Sally Phillips, Deborah Meaden, Kirsty Wark, Omid Djalili, Susie Dent, Sir Grayson Perry, Esther Rantzen, Paloma Faith and the Reverend Richard Coles.

Her popular Instagram reels have amassed over 100 million views and counting.

*Namaste Motherf*ckers* is her first book.

NAMASTE MOTHER F*CKERS

cally beaton

NAMASTE MOTHERF*CKERS

a modern manifesto for keeping cool when you're a hot mess

Copyright © 2025 Cally Beaton

The right of Cally Beaton to be identified as the Author of
the Work has been asserted by her in accordance with the
Copyright, Designs and Patents Act 1988.

First published in 2025 by Headline Home
An imprint of Headline Publishing Group Limited

1

Apart from any use permitted under UK copyright law, this publication may
only be reproduced, stored, or transmitted, in any form, or by any means,
with prior permission in writing of the publishers or, in the case of
reprographic production, in accordance with the terms of licences
issued by the Copyright Licensing Agency.

Illustrations on pages iii, 11, 43, 73, 99, 127, 151, 183, 211, 243, 265 © Chris Lincé 2025
Illustrations on pages 50, 86, 176, 191, 194, 207, 224 by Jason Cox 2025
Prayer hands illustration © Shutterstock
Cartoon on page 28 © Jason Adam Katzenstein, *The New Yorker*
Cartoon on page 231 © Damian 'Damo' Clark

Cataloguing in Publication Data is available from the British Library.

Hardback ISBN 978 1 0354 2051 3
ebook ISBN 978 1 0354 2052 0

Designed and typeset by EM&EN
Printed and bound in Great Britain by Clays Ltd, Elcograf S.p.A.

Headline's policy is to use papers that are natural, renewable and recyclable
products and made from wood grown in well-managed forests and other
controlled sources. The logging and manufacturing processes are expected
to conform to the environmental regulations of the country of origin.

Headline Publishing Group Limited
An Hachette UK Company
Carmelite House
50 Victoria Embankment
London EC4Y 0DZ

The authorised representative in the EEA is Hachette Ireland,
8 Castlecourt Centre, Dublin 15, D15 XTP3, Ireland (email: info@hbgi.ie)

www.headline.co.uk
www.hachette.co.uk

To Jake and Ella.

You've taught me everything,
apart from how to live without you.

Author's note on language

I was born into a world that was binary – you were gendered male or female, and your sexuality was gay or straight (ideally straight – definitely not queer). Women in my generation were still being encouraged to go to university to meet a suitable husband (I came out with a 2:1 and, to this day, no husband). Thankfully, the world has moved on in the intervening half-century. I identify as a cis woman, and this book comes from my lived experience as such. My intention in writing it is that there will be much with which you will identify, however you identify.

Contents

Introduction 1

Part One
THINK ABOUT IT

1. INVISIBLE MY ARSE
Challenging midlife female stereotypes 11

2. THE (VERY) ODD ONE OUT
Standing out and belonging 43

3. MAKE THE EDIT
Getting your voice heard 73

4. THIS TOO SHALL PASS
Leaning into tricky emotions 99

5. LESSONS FROM AN AUTISTIC ZOOKEEPER
Be more bonobo 127

Part Two
DO IT

6. REINVENTION
With age comes power 151

7. SAY YES! BUT ALSO SAY NO!
Making good decisions 183

8. PERFECTIONISM
You learn more from a bad gig than a good gig 211

Part Three
LET'S GET PERSONAL

9. GLOW THE FUCK UP
Growing older, bolder and more beautiful 243

10. HERE ENDETH THE MANIFESTO
Empty nest and beyond 265

Acknowledgements 295

References 298

Index 301

Introduction

This book is not – and I repeat *not* – a luxury item. It is not about success, redemption nor vagina candles, but it has radical reinvention and possibility at its heart, combining human life hacks with life lessons from the natural world. It is my conviction that reinvention is an essential and recurring theme in people's lives in the twenty-first century – and that, as the years go by, reinvention isn't necessarily about downsizing. Instead, it can be about taking everything you've done to date along with you and going bigger, and bolder, ensuring that what you do next is the best you've done yet.

I've known for the longest time that this is a book that needed to exist, and one that I needed to write. It's a book that started out as an ember somewhere in my (no longer very fertile) innards, and has since become an unignorable blaze in my heart and soul. But I didn't know where to begin.

And then, something happened. I was ghosted for the very first time. Ghosted. At fifty-five. He was sixty-three (probably still is; he didn't actually become a ghost). For a minute I felt very modern, like one of those jilted Gen Z or millennial daters one reads about. I'd been aired, orbited and breadcrumbed before, and now I'd been ghosted. The night before we'd been at the theatre, holding hands, laughing, whispering in each other's ears while watching *Crazy for You* – ironically – then afterwards kissing and walking, arm in arm, across movie-perfect Waterloo Bridge. The next morning, gone. Just like that. I was baffled. Then hurt. Then, as the days rolled by, I became untethered and vulnerable. If it wasn't for social media, I'd have been calling around hospitals. Thanks to Twitter (I still refuse to call it X – I miss the little bird) I could see that he was tweeting nonchalantly about things like the cricket, which didn't seem the sort of thing you'd make your focus in your final hours in intensive care.

So there it was, the latest version of something I've been grappling with for years: invisibility. He disappeared in an instant, as if I had dreamed him, and in doing so erased me – out of mind and out of sight. Overnight I'd reached my sell-by date. I never even got my goodbye. Having managed to avoid being ghosted during the dating decades since splitting up with the father of my at-the-time young children, it pulled me up short. I'd become invisible to him, and it brought into sharp relief how invisible and irrelevant I sometimes felt to the wider world, and also to myself.

When I'm having one of those days when I'm channelling 'I am woman, hear me roar', I'm all about invisibility on women's terms and for women's benefit. Would that playing Helen Reddy on a loop could be enough to keep a midlife woman – or, indeed, any woman – consistently empowered (although she herself is pushing eighty and still roaring, by all accounts, so fair play). But the reality is that the midpoint in a woman's life can be a right old bloody drag; such a drag that the peak age at which women die by suicide is in their early fifties – an oestrogen-deprived version of the heartbreaking men-in-their-twenties mental-health epidemic.

Menopause happens to over 50 per cent of the population, and if it was the other just under 50 per cent – you know, blokes, captains of industry, leaders of society, wagers of war – I reckon there'd have been a bit more done to help by now. Having not been talked about enough for decades – centuries, even – now you can't move for books, podcasts and articles about it, and it's doing for hormone awareness what salted caramel did for desserts.

After a recent gig, where I'd done a bit of menopause material – menerial – an audience member came up to me. We were having a rollicking good chat until he said . . . could he just ask, not that he's got anything against female comics talking about periods or menopause or sex or whatever – or, indeed, against female comics full stop – but how did I think his mother and grandmother coped with menopause without needing to talk about it all the time? Having briefly toyed with slapping an oestrogen patch over his still-open mouth (but they're very hard to come by, so why waste one?), I responded by explaining that we'd all coped with lots of things in the past, like dentistry without anaesthetic, or passive smoking in public spaces, or dying in car accidents without seatbelts. And how did he know they'd 'coped', when women were routinely being locked in institutions and given everything from Valium to hysterectomies when all they actually needed was HRT? And if, for generations, men had been having their willies removed because of anxiety, depression and an inability to regulate their own body temperature, then I think we'd all feel able to agree that it's a pretty good thing it's finally on the agenda now. Yes? Right. Are we going for that drink or what?

No idea why I'm single.

Last month, I was offered the chance to join a workshop at my GP surgery about what to expect in perimenopause. I mean, it's brilliant they're offering this kind of thing, but I can't help noticing they're . . . er . . . ten years too late? Is this what NHS waiting lists have come to? Perhaps they're mistaking me for some kind of Benjamin Button of female hormones – I'll be working my way back to antenatal classes by the time I'm sixty. Next stop, a hip replacement for someone who's already dead. Either way, I doubt there's a midlife woman reading this who hasn't at some point been misdiagnosed, misunderstood or dismissed by her GP, in a way that simply doesn't happen to men. (And sadly, there aren't many younger women who won't also have had this experience.) This is medical misogyny – and we'll be returning to it later.

We may think, or at least hope, that equality is just across the horizon, but books like *Invisible Women* by Caroline Criado-Perez remind us that we are living in what is indubitably a man's world, not least because those who built it were mainly men: men who didn't sufficiently – or often even slightly – take gender differences into account. Smartphones are too bulky for us; buildings are too cold for us. When I used to skydive, parachutes were too big for us, and I daresay they still are. Cars are still designed around the body of 'Reference Man', meaning that although men are more likely to crash, women are more likely to be seriously hurt. I wish there was a suit that could be built around the body of a 'Reference Midlife Woman' so that men could walk a day in our shoes. Like Billy Connolly said: 'Before you judge a man, walk a mile in his shoes. After that, who cares? He's a mile away and you've got his shoes!' Midlife women across the land would be willingly donating our shoes if only it meant we could see strides towards our needs being met – at work, at home and in the world at large.

Like all females born in the 1960s, it was inevitable that I would come hard up against invisibility (if one can indeed come hard up against literally nothing – physics never was my strong point), and the fact that you don't get to choose when you're invisible and when you're not. One of my earliest memories is of hiding from my brother behind the sofa when I was nearly two: *You can't find me!* At twenty-two months older than me, my brother could – mainly because my face was hidden behind the sofa, while the rest of me was very much sticking out. At nearly four, he knew more than me about most things, including that I was crap at hide-and-seek. (Later that day, we played a game that involved him pushing me down a steep hill in a wheelbarrow. I ended up smashing my head into a wall, then one of our goats did a poo on the kitchen floor; welcome to growing up in the 1970s. And to males pushing me around.)

I didn't realise it until decades later, but invisibility would go on to define much of my life. (Wheelbarrows and shitting goats, less so.) My brother went on to become a physicist, by the way. I'd get him to mansplain the viability of coming hard up against invisibility, but I'm too hot and too tired and I can't be arsed.

Here's the thing – being a midlife woman is nothing if not a series of contradictions, and for all its limitations, invisibility is also a superpower – right up there with teleportation and being able to fly. My solo show the year I turned fifty was called *Invisible*, inspired by the words of French author Yann Moix (at the time aged fifty himself) about women over forty-nine being 'invisible' going viral. No one likes to be underestimated, and no one likes to have their story written for them. So I wrote my own story – and never had I been more visible. It doesn't matter whether it was a hit or a flop; it was my show, in my words, performed to my audiences.

Despite all this, midlife is a time not for compromise and resignation, but for empowerment and ambition – and that's why I knew I *needed* to write this book. And you *need* to read it! OK, you are reading it. I'll calm down.

What you're about to read is empowering but also practical. It's my own story of unexpected midlife reinvention, what led up to it and what has happened since, and it challenges at every turn the age-old narrative that women become invisible when they cease to be fertile. Allow me to reassure you

– it's not a smug, redemptive story inviting you to be more like me. I'm not one of those climbed-up-Everest-on-one-leg-in-a-tweed-suit types; this is more the still-don't-know-what-the-fuck-I'm-doing-but-if-I-can-do-it-so-can-you school of self-help. Don't worry, you'll be fine. Or as fine as any of us can hope to be.

This is also a book about defying the bullshit expectation that midlife women at best maintain (looks, careers, relationships), and at worst decline. Not sure now's the time for a quote from an old (dead) white guy, but hey – in the words of Frank Sinatra, 'The best is yet to come'. For balance, my daughter bought me a brilliant T-shirt for my birthday, and on it, it just says in big letters: 'My weight is not the most interesting thing about me'. What a brilliant, feminist thing to have on a piece of clothing. I'd wear it more, but it makes me look fat.

I have written this book partly as a memoir, but more importantly as a stereotype-defying manifesto. It's about my experiences of life in the boardroom, then of treading the boards, and throughout it all being a single parent. And it includes nuggets of wisdom, with perhaps the wisest of all coming from my autistic zookeeper son, who has spent the past two decades sharing feminist case studies from within the animal kingdom. In fact, he's taught me pretty much everything I need to know; apart from how to be a single parent in an empty nest, with him and his little sister now fledged.

First, we'll take on the boardroom. After more than two decades of senior management positions at some of the biggest media companies in the world, sitting in male-dominated groups like Sigourney Weaver in *Gorillas in the Mist* (only more males and less handsome), I have stories to tell. Loath as I am to use the phrase 'pale, male and stale' – sometimes it just slips out – that was the world I inhabited. Thank goodness I traded it in for comedy, where the gender balance is . . . well, pretty much exactly the same, actually.

Before I went from holding court to playing court jester, from the front of planes to the back of Megabuses, my side hustle during the boardroom years was coaching, training and public speaking. What people want from coaching or an inspirational talk is a) an amnesty on pretending everything is OK, b) to be reassured that 'it's not just me', and c) words and thoughts that can turn into meaningful actions. (It's the same with comedy, if you replace c) with 'having a laugh'.) So here, I'll be sharing my all-time favourite takeaways for free (well, you did buy the book). No pressure to do them unless you want to; life's hard enough. But they're here if you want them. And I promise you, they bloody well work.

Thirdly, I'll be sharing lessons from the animal kingdom. As humans puzzle over the glass ceiling and how to get more women into leadership and empowered positions, could it be possible to look to the natural world for solutions? The answer is yes. My son has introduced me to some of the world's strongest females – often in person, despite my protests. Thanks to him, I know the natural world is full of gender stereotype-busting females whose stories I will tell, from orcas to bonobo apes (who, frankly, make Germaine Greer look like an amateur).

And finally, there is a sprinkling of *Bake Off*-worthy gorgeousness atop it all, in the form of exclusive nuggets from my conversations with celebrities, experts and national treasures over a couple of hundred episodes of my podcast, *Namaste Motherf**kers*. Each episode ends with three questions:

1. What would you pick as your namaste motherf*cking life-changing moment?

2. What's your favourite joke?

INTRODUCTION

3. What bit of life advice would you give to anybody listening?

I've picked the very best of these to share with you, as well as some extra interviews done especially for this book.

You'll laugh, you might cry (when you read Chapter 4, you'll see that's a good thing) and, as part of a collective of women going through similar things, you'll feel lighter (emotionally, not physically – we're not into beach bodies around here, unless your beach body is the exact same body you have at this very moment, blobbed out reading this).

Last but not least, my intention is for this book to resonate far beyond these pages with tips, tricks and takeaways in every chapter. Think of it as a road map to help you get out of your own way.

*Namaste Motherf*ckers* is about presenting our authentic, imperfect selves to the world and being the narrators of our own messy stories. If you're still wondering if this book is for you, then – unless you're living in a remote yurt without a mum, daughter, sister, female friend/partner/neighbour – I'd say it will have more than passing relevance. Join me in this celebration of and for the female of the species: invisible no more.

part one

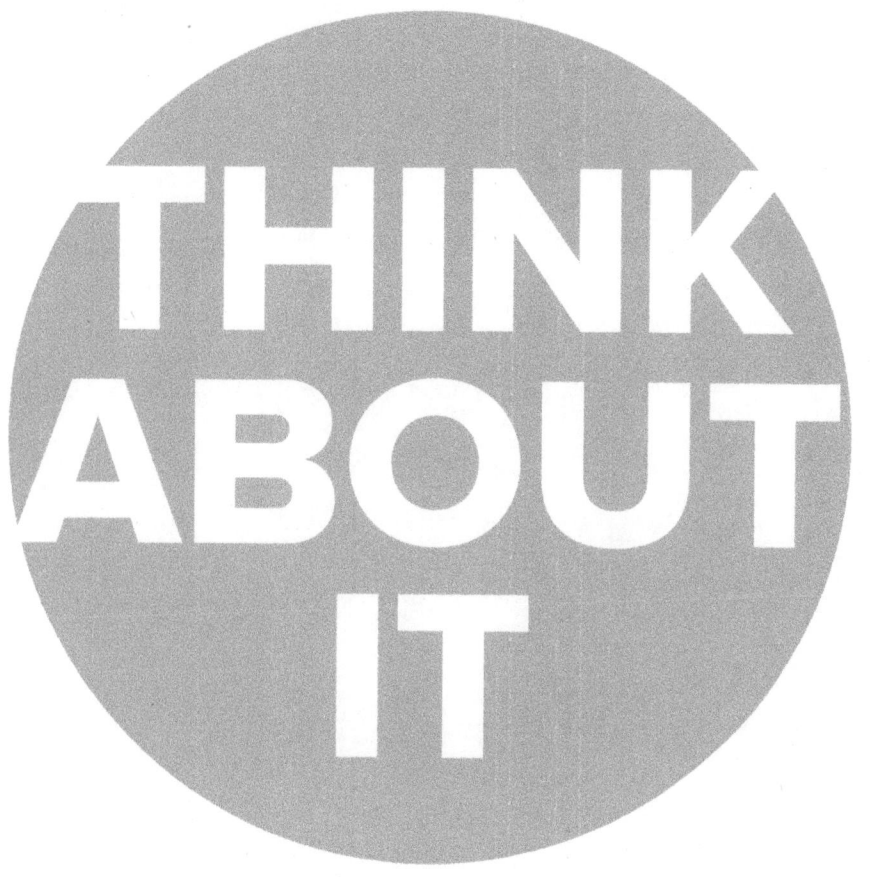

part one

1
INVISIBLE MY ARSE

CHALLENGING MIDLIFE FEMALE STEREOTYPES

'If you fell down yesterday, stand up today.'
H. G. Wells

invisibility
/ɪnˌvɪzɪˈbɪlɪti, ˌɪnvɪzɪˈbɪlɪti/
noun
1. The fact of something or someone being impossible to see
   'the bits of gold in the sand were small to the point of invisibility'
2. The fact of being ignored, not noticed, or not considered

Source: https://dictionary.cambridge.org/dictionary/english/invisibility

---

> If female dragonflies aren't up for a shag, they fake sudden death. Not a headache – actual death. Talk about invisibility as a superpower.

Fact from fiction

I'm an invisible midlife woman, and I use it as a superpower – but it's also really shit. Debilitatingly shit. This chapter – indeed, much of this book – is about standing up and standing out, even when all you feel like doing is lying down. Before we go any further, some invisibility facts:

> Invisibility is nothing new. It's been a recurring literary conceit as far back as Plato's *Republic*, continuing through Shakespeare's *The Tempest*, Tolkien's *Lord of the Rings* and *Harry Potter*, not to mention its popularity in comic strips and movies.

> Invisibility has helped us build cultures and wage wars. While researching this book, I discovered that British secret agents used semen as invisible ink during World War One on the advice of MI6 director Mansfield Smith-Cumming, who adopted the motto: 'Every man his own stylo.' Gosh.

> By way of a semen palate-cleanser, I also found out that during World War Two, spitfires were painted pink to camouflage them against the clouds at dawn and sunset. I think those two facts just about balance things out in terms of taste and common decency.

> The word 'camouflage' came into play in 1917. It comes from the Italian verb *camuffare*, 'to dress up for a masked ball'. Humans and other animals had been doing it long before 1917 – not so much because of going to masked balls, more because they wanted to survive.

Invisibility is the supreme form of camouflage, and animals will go to extreme lengths to achieve it. I asked my son for some examples of undercover animals and he told me about the Indian grass mantis (looks like a blade of grass), the dead leaf butterfly (looks like a dead leaf) and the Vietnamese mossy frog (you've got the hang of this now). Then he told me about another frog, the glass frog, which relies on transparency for camouflage, which it achieves by sending red blood cells temporarily out of circulation and hiding them in its liver. That's one hell of a thing to pull off when you're only a couple of centimetres long. I'm five foot six and a half, and some days it's all I can do to change my pants.

A couple of other bits of invisibility trivia: in the Air Guitar World Championships (an actual thing), one of the rules is that the guitar must be invisible (fair); and there's no such thing as a chemical that makes your pee visible in swimming pools. So piss away (good midlife mantra in any situation).

From the boardroom to treading the boards

Pinning down invisibility is like trying to catch a cloud. It's hard to notice the lack of a thing, like when something stops hurting and you don't realise until a while after the pain is gone. I don't think I'd realised how invisible I'd become, not least to myself, until a series of unexpected events led to me becoming very visible indeed.

Nowadays, I make a living out of writing and talking. I quit my board-level job to make my side hustle my main hustle, in a radical midlife pivot that is so far working out OK, although for every moment in the sun, there are many more in the shade.

Until 2018, I was a senior vice president at ViacomCBS, one of the biggest US Studios. Sexy, right? Yes and no. I got to sit at the front of planes, drink champagne on yachts and hang out with A-listers. The bottom line is that I was there for the bottom line. Responsible for millions of dollars of revenue, I ran a business that made hard cash out of TV and film content. It was me, albeit not as a lone wolf, who brought *South Park* and *SpongeBob SquarePants* to the world. I sat in creative meetings for all the Viacom brands, among them Comedy Central. I was the boring businessperson, there to make money out of hit shows, and make sure they were global hits. Like all international TV execs, I went to Cannes twice a year – not to the film festival, but to the TV festivals MIP* and MIPCOM†; nothing like an acronym to suck the glamour out of things. Sometimes I would be accompanied by talent from our new shows: Kevin Hart, Amy Poehler, Ben Stiller, Stephen Colbert and, the life-changing one, Joan Rivers.

It was watching Joan Rivers on *The Carol Burnett Show* in the seventies that taught me that a) women could be funny and b) women could front TV shows. She was a comedy icon and one of my heroes and, therefore, it was a great privilege to get to know her a bit before she died (would have been weird if it had happened afterwards, admittedly). One night over dinner, she told me two things.

The first she shared when she found out that I, like her daughter Melissa, was in the throes of online dating. 'Here's the thing you need to know,' she said. 'The odds are good, but the goods are odd.'

And then the second, as we were talking about a group of male TV executives who had 'heckled' me as I was introducing her earlier that night: 'Why don't you try stand-up?'

---

* Marché International des Programmes

† Marché International des Programmes de Communication

To which I replied, 'I'm forty-five. I'm a single parent of two kids, one of whom has special needs. I have a massive day job. It's too late. That ship has sailed.'

She just looked me square in the eye and said: 'I'm eighty-one. You'll look back one day and realise you were in the thick of it and think, "Why didn't I?"'

Two weeks later, she died. Two weeks after that, I did my first-ever stand-up gig. And three years after that, I jettisoned the day job to become a full-time comedian, writer, broadcaster and speaker. Yup, you heard right: I gave up a board-level job with a secure income and share options to become a full-time comedian and performer, just before a global pandemic shut down all live venues. If you want business advice, don't look to me.

I won't be doing loads of clanking name-dropping, by the way. That's not to do with modesty, more that I'm so shit at knowing who anyone is I'm the worst name-dropper ever. Once, on a flight back from Cannes to London, I had a seat next to a middle-aged man in a dad jumper, dad trousers, dad shoes. We got talking and it turned out he was an actor, so I asked if he'd been in anything I would know. He looked hesitant, so I said, 'Oh, *that* kind of actor. So, what's your actual job?'

When we disembarked at Heathrow, a couple of colleagues who'd been on the same flight came racing over, asking me what he was like.

'Who?' I said.

'John Hamm,' they said.

I'd never watched *Mad Men*. Until that night when I got home and binged it. Sigh.

Another time, I was meeting the author Kathy Lette in a London hotel bar one evening. I managed to know who she was, and when I arrived she had someone with her and asked if I'd mind if her friend Carly joined us for dinner, as she'd just arrived from Australia and was jetlagged and hungry. We had a lovely chat, Carly and me. She asked me about being a performer and whether I get nervous onstage, and I told her it's never too late to get out there and let yourself be seen and heard. We got as far as finishing our mains before I clocked Carly was actually Kylie. I'd missed that I was having dinner with Kylie Minogue – and I'd given her some performance tips. Look, she wasn't wearing make-up or hot pants. It was an easy mistake to make. And I'm a bit of a twat. Never mind *me* being invisible; it seems A-listers are invisible to me.

Back to my namaste motherf*cking life-changing decision to switch careers. Wasn't I brave? No – definitely not brave. I'm not a fearless person, and I'm not a flawless person. (A pelvic floorless person, maybe.) It is estimated that one out of ten women quits their jobs due to menopause. I just happened to quit one job for another in a way that looks like a ninja-level carpe-diem move. It's true I *did* seize the day, but only because of the very long, dark night that had preceded it.

Picture the scene. Forty-seven. Glittering career working for one of the biggest and best media companies in the world. Proud single mum of a sixteen-year-old and a nineteen-year-old, one doing their GCSEs, the other their A levels. It's hard, looking back, to know when exactly the wheels started to come off. My best guess is that it had been a slow train crash taking place over a period of about fifteen years.

I split up with my kids' dad twenty years ago, and we have gone on to enjoy a blended family set-up so well-functioning it's almost annoying to those less fortunate. He's a good man, and I love his partner and their son like one of my own; which is lucky, because he's the brother of my own. My two children have always lived with me, and that's been our household, (wo)manned by we three Beaton musketeers.

Now, what felt like out of nowhere, the empty nest was looming uncomfortably large. Soon there would be just two musketeers – and within sight on the not-too-distant horizon was the prospect of just one. I found this idea unexpectedly and intolerably painful. I thought I'd dodged the empty-nest bullet by having had a successful and fulfilling career all those years. Turns out I was entirely wrong about that.

My first solo comedy show was in 2017, and was called *Super Cally Fragile Lipstick*. The title and the poster were the best things about it. The show itself? A bit meh. How I wish I'd saved that title for a show that deserved it. It had some good things about it, sure, and some funny things in it. The problem, as well as being too new to stand-up to be trying an ambitious Edinburgh debut, was it was a show about falling apart under a faux glossy mask of having life sorted, while I was falling apart under a faux glossy mask of having life sorted. It should have been vulnerable and heartfelt and award-winning. Instead, I was in too much of a mess to know how to be authentic. Tragedy + time = comedy. There just hadn't been enough time.

I remember exactly how I was feeling that year: running a comedy side hustle alongside an overwhelmingly massive day job, all underpinned by increasing empty-nest despair and burnout. I didn't know much about depression at the time and had no idea that was what was happening. It wasn't just feeling sad, it wasn't low mood; it was what fast became full-on, life-threatening depression. Though I'm at risk of mixing my transport metaphors, the wheels came off the bus and I crashed.

I was lucky enough – really very lucky indeed – to have private health insurance through my job that got me a period of intensive outpatient treatment at a leading psychiatric hospital. I literally don't know how I'd have survived without it. I feel guilty writing about this, knowing that I was afforded the life-saving support I needed when most people are battling to have the bare minimum of their mental-health needs met. It's a resource the majority of us will need access to at some point in our lives. I was in group therapy by day, and by night I was back home, helping the kids with their GCSEs and A levels. I never told them. I've only told them now because I want to write about it. It felt like a shameful secret that should be kept. Turns out if you hold shame up to the light, it dissipates.

During my outpatient treatment, I was diagnosed with bipolar disorder and given a cocktail of medication. It's not uncommon for women to get diagnosed as being bipolar in midlife. Sometimes it's an erroneous diagnosis when what's really going on is hormonal, and in other cases it is an accurate diagnosis, decades delayed due to the fact that women are extremely skilled at 'masking' – until the point when their hormones strip that mask away. It turns out that in my case, that diagnosis was not correct. Perimenopause was confused with a mental health disorder, and bipolar medication offered in place of HRT. I had about six weeks off, sneaking in and out of the psychiatric hospital like a cat burglar, and then I went back to work, medicated and thinking I was cured. Turns out, I wasn't.

I've mentioned slow train crashes and wheels coming off buses, but it was a car crash that changed everything, at a time when, far from planning my own death, all I was planning was a mini-break: a mini-break that rendered me invisible, ghosted by the world.

Adventures in invisibility

It's hard at any age to find the right person, or even the person who's alright for a bit, and that doesn't get easier with time. Then there's the whole 'dirty weekend' debate. You're not even allowed a dirty weekend now; they're called 'mini-breaks' instead. I'm in my fourth decade of dirty weekends. I should get some kind of certificate. You used to have to make an effort for a dirty weekend. Nowadays you've got the internet and budget airlines. You can have a dirty weekend in Prague for fifty-two quid. I've had dirty weekends in Nuneaton. Part of the challenge is working out where you can go that neither of you has been before – somewhere that hasn't got memories of shagging, break-ups, make-ups or mental breakdowns (often all on the same mini-break). That's how, with my then-boyfriend – let's call him Will – I ended up going to Iceland.

Three hours after leaving Heathrow, we got off the plane in Reykjavík. Reykjavík airport is beautiful: floor-to-ceiling glass, blond wood, snow-capped desolation as far as the eye can see. It was all just perfect. Perfect, that is, until, out of the blue, Will finished with me. At first I thought he was joking. He wasn't. The last thing you want to hear when you're invisible is, 'I don't want to see you anymore.' He dumped me at Arrivals – not even Departures. Who does that? I'd been dumped in one of the most sparsely populated places on Earth. There's only one place worse to be dumped than Iceland the country, and that is Iceland the shop.

There's no big reveal coming about Arrivals dumping guy, by the way. He didn't have a secret double life; he wasn't an undercover agent or a modern-day Clark Kent. He wasn't having an affair with Björk. Turns out he was having an addiction-fuelled crisis of his own. If this was a movie, he would be the guy who gets killed off in the opening scene – just so the rest of the movie can happen. He's dead. He's gone. It's my movie now. (He's not dead; he lives round the corner from me and is on social media. A lot.)

After spending twenty-four hours crying in the mini-break hotel on my own, it was time to get adventurous, to make my way out of the city and discover exciting Icelandic things. Most people have their own version of 'What would Beyoncé do?', or, if you're from the nineties, 'What would Madonna do?' My guiding female icon is from longer ago. It's weird, isn't it, how many iconic figures in history and science and exploration are men? Female adventurers have always had to do more than just discover new continents and conquer space. Female adventurers have always had to *not* make it. Take Amy Johnson or Amelia Earhart: both more famous for their deaths than for their ahead-of-their-times piloting skills. Or Emily Wilding Davison, as famous for dying after being hit by King George V's horse as for her actual suffragetting. We probably wouldn't even know that Marie Curie discovered radioactivity if she hadn't died from radiation poisoning. And if you didn't manage to die spectacularly, you at least had to pretend to be a man. Charlotte, Anne and Emily Brontë each took male pen names; in fact, the only Brontë sibling who made it to adulthood and didn't pretend to be a man was Branwell Brontë, who was an actual man, and who actually couldn't write for shit.

All of which brings me to Fanny Bullock Workman, who lived from January 1859 to January 1925 and should be really famous because she was called Fanny. Bullock. Workman. Fanny was an American cartographer, explorer, writer and champion of women's rights and suffrage – and she was also one of the first female professional mountaineers. She set several altitude records, and was the first-ever woman to lecture at the Sorbonne and join the Royal Geographical Society of London. The very definition of a triple threat. In short, Fanny Bullock Workman was a bloomin' legend and decades ahead of her time. So, when in doubt, I channel Fanny (don't start).

What would Fanny do? I thought.

Six hours later, I was a long way north of Reykjavík and it was snowing – I mean, *really* snowing. I started to realise I'd bitten off more than I could chew. I'm normally a good driver, but I wasn't prepared for the snowstorm that hit. Conditions got rapidly worse and, out of nowhere, I found myself facing completely the wrong way in the snow, the car spinning and spinning like a bottle at a teenage birthday party. And then it started to slide – uncontrollably and in ultra slow motion – off the road, nose-first into the tundra. I was fine, but the car was buggered, I had no phone reception and, worse still, no idea where I was. It was a long time since I'd passed through the last town. What a moment to realise I was too old to die young.

I left everything in the car and started walking. It was well below freezing and, in terms of outerwear, I was less Bear Grylls, more 'Bear with me, I'm having a bit of a breakdown'. I didn't know this when I started walking, but I was actually very close to a place called Hellnar, in the far west of the country – so close, in fact, the walk would barely have registered on a Fitbit. Hellnar is the place where Jules Vernes' *Journey to the Centre of the Earth* begins: a tiny, remote village at the foot of a volcano, perched on a peninsula, looking out to sea across hundreds of miles of nothingness towards Greenland. It's considered one of Earth's mystical energy centres, like Stonehenge or Machu Picchu or Kim Kardashian's moon cup. And the people of Hellnar took me in.

And so I didn't die not young. I survived. Iceland didn't conquer me; I conquered Iceland. That night in Hellnar, everything changed. Two weeks later, I was back in London. Two months later – and three years after that life-changing chat with Joan Rivers – I quit my job. My radical, fearless and empowering reinvention came about not out of bravery, but out of mental collapse and near-death necessity. The Iceland crash was a wake-up call, a metaphor showing that what I was doing was killing me. Just as in the animal kingdom, it was adapt or die.

Anuvab Pal – 'If you want to go into comedy, please go do something else first. Catch fish, sell drugs, work for Her Majesty's tax department, build broad-gauge railways. You know, stitch shoes, along with other small children in third-world countries – anything, do anything. People always talk in minutes of material. I think if you've lived a life, you've got material. If you're a murderer, I think you have a set already. You have a great set.'

When I set out, like many comics, my goal was *Live at the Apollo*. The year after the pandemic, I was lucky enough that that happened; I was the first fifty-something new face to be booked to appear on the show. Arguably, at fifty-six, I've never been more visible. I will not go gentle into that good night, I decided. I might go mental, but I will never go gentle.

If invisibility can save you or cost you dear, then part of having it as a superpower is choosing carefully the times when you wish to don your invisibility cloak and the times when you wish to be visible. Not that I'm kidding myself we always get to decide, but the sweet spot is surely selective visibility. In the natural world, spiderwebs are visible to birds, who fly around them, but not to insects, who fly into them. Flower petals have evolved to attract bees by reflecting a blue halo that is visible to bees but not to humans. As someone who learned to drive on the winding roads of rural Dorset and now travels the country for gigs, I'm aware of the invisibility of roadside deer. My parents still live in the West Country, and just this weekend, my dad ran into a cow in the New Forest. Both are doing fine, by the way, Dad and cow, but I can't believe my dad hit an actual cow just when I'm writing about female invisibility.

The age of invisibility

I've got a fair idea of what invisibility feels like to me, so I decided to do an online search: 'Do men feel invisible?' The first result I got was the age at which male invisibility occurs:

sixty-four (very prescient of the Beatles back in 1967). For women, the average age at which invisibility occurs is fifty-two. I then searched: 'Do women feel invisible?' and two things came up. The first, results confirming that women stop being noticed in midlife. The second, advice for beating the age odds, largely along the lines of how to stay attractive to men when you're in your fifties, by using anti-ageing skin remedies and silk pillows and neck irons and lord knows what else.

But if you do not wish to massage the juice of a camel's scrotum on to your crow's feet, there are other ways.

Signs of invisibility

Underestimated, ignored, talked over, not taken seriously – being invisible is a bit like the auto sensor in the toilet not working. There you are, pants down. You stand up expecting to get a reaction and instead . . . nothing. Being a midlife woman can feel a lot like having your pants down, waving your hands and your bum about, the world refusing to see you. I used to have a fair chance of an upgrade just by locking eyes with the right person at check-in. Nowadays, electronic passport gates spend longer looking at me than human ones.

While writing this, I put a post out on social media asking for experiences that had led people to feel invisible, whether funny or serious. Some of what came back was depressingly relatable; some was laden with hope, defiance and joy. The comments were from all comers – young, old, short, tall, diverse gender identities and nationalities. Invisibility casts its net wide. Some themes came up repeatedly, including: being in a wheelchair, turning forty (or fifty, or seventy – oddly, no one said sixty), not being the good-looking one in your twenties or thirties, redundancy, going grey, being with a more attractive companion or family member, being short, not being served in shops, bars and restaurants. (There were so many medical ones that I'm covering them separately in Chapter 3.)

There were some comments about disappearing once married, others about being invisible when not married. Lots of people talked about the invisibility that comes with becoming a mother (no one mentioned it happening when becoming a father) – although not getting cat-called while pushing a buggy or dragging screaming toddlers up the street came up as a positive. Women who were not mothers in friendship groups where others were, found this diminished their visibility. And lots of women mentioned a weird thing of automatic doors not opening, as seen in *Drop the Dead Donkey* back in the nineties. *Plus ça change.*

One person wrote that if all crimes were performed by women in their fifties, none would ever be solved as there would be no eyewitnesses. A couple of years ago, I was in John Lewis buying garden furniture, because I'm nothing if not middle class, and I lugged all this bulky stuff over to the till only for the assistant to tell me she was going on her break. So I struggled with it over to another till by the door. A security guard came over, said, 'I'm so sorry, madam, let me get the door for you,' and offered to help me to my car with it. Turns out that for the perfect heist you don't need to be George Clooney with a floor plan of the casino; you just need a National Trust car sticker and a womb that's turning to dust.

There were some one-offs, like becoming invisible after shaving off a goatee (from a bloke, but to be fair could go either way). One person wrote that she was sitting in the garden one night, hot and sweaty and dismayed at her own invisibility, and a hedgehog walked over her foot. I love that woman.

The weight of invisibility

And then there's the depressingly reliable relationship between invisibility and a person's weight. Someone commented that for the past twenty years, she has weighed between 220 and 270 pounds, and at the same time as getting many unsolicited comments about her weight from strangers, people regularly walk into her with a: 'Sorry, didn't see you.' Someone else described weight as an 'invisibility switch – lose weight, now you see me; gain weight, poof – I'm gone!' Others said the same, with one sharing that when she weighed 250 pounds after having four kids, she was invisible; she dropped 100 pounds and was suddenly visible, then put back on 50 pounds, and became invisible again.

I'm still on my own journey with weight and eating issues, and anyone who listens to Jess Fostekew's podcast *Hoovering* will know there aren't many women who aren't. Two to three stone overweight in my teens and early twenties, I lost weight in my mid-twenties, and soon after got a job at MTV, back when it was staffed by people who were almost exclusively young and cool. It was a job that changed my life and put my TV career on its trajectory. I sometimes wonder if I'd have got that job had I looked and/or felt as I had a year earlier. I'll never know, of course, but I do wonder.

Invisibility and sexism

A whole lot of the comments were about the sexism involved in anything to do with cars or home improvements. Women were routinely ignored or talked over when buying a car, with the salesperson instead addressing the man they were with. The same thing happened with tradespeople only addressing the man in the house or asking women to check with their partners. I relate. My personal experience of this includes someone coming to give me a quote on a new kitchen a few years back and saying, 'Lovely tiles; your husband's spoiling you.' I thanked him and said if ever I met my husband, I'd tell him.

Some women shared stories of estate agents addressing information to the man they were with, or answering women's direct questions by replying to the man present.

Along similar lines, there were numerous examples of bank managers and financial advisors explaining things to men and ignoring women, even if the discussion was regarding joint money, or in some cases money belonging solely to the woman. This happened to my mum a few years ago. She was eighty and had inherited some money from her parents' estate. She went to get investment advice, and my dad drove her to the appointment. The financial advisor refused to engage with her, preferring to discuss everything with my similar-aged dad, whose money it was not. They didn't even have a joint bank account.

Sexism cuts both ways. There were tales from men of buying clothes with their wife or partner and being spoken over, as if they weren't there. One man said: 'I've never felt so invisible as when my wife and the shop assistant were deciding which suit I should wear. I was fifty-three and three-quarters at the time.'

Second only to those comments about medical encounters that we'll be looking at later were comments about the workplace: stories of women being talked over, having their ideas appropriated by others, or being assumed to be admin support. I'll be getting into this in more depth, but these stories seem to be more to do with being a woman in general than with being a midlife woman in particular. They reminded me of the *New Yorker* cartoon on the next page where there's a woman sitting across the dinner table from a man with the caption: 'Let me interrupt your expertise with my confidence.'

"Let me interrupt your expertise with my confidence."

Women in STEM deserve a book in their own right. Actually, there is the brilliant *Lessons in Chemistry* by Bonnie Garmus, in which the outstanding protagonist Elizabeth Zott battles sexism in the field of science in the 1950s. Reading the comments under my post, I wondered if much has changed since that era.

A female pharmacist shared stories of customers asking her male 'boss' (not actually her boss, but a colleague) to come and advise them instead. Women working in construction and engineering spoke of being ignored or talked over, and of having second opinions asked of men less experienced than them. One woman wrote: '[I was] standing in my hi-vis and safety boots in front of the foreman for a new office refurbishment programme I was overseeing on behalf of my client. I'm nearly six feet tall, bright copper hair, a woman of some substance and I carry myself with confidence. It's fair to say I'm conspicuous in almost all situations. Three times, the foreman wondered out loud where the "client's bloody project manager" was. Three times, I quite clearly said, "I'm right here." In the end, I walked up to the whiteboard, wiped off the foreman's "plans for the day" and replaced that with my name and job title.'

Rage against the invisible machine

The reality for women at this midpoint in our lives is that our fertility is on the wane and we are supposedly invisible. Even meno queen Davina McCall has described menopause as making her feel 'frightened and invisible'. If Davina McCall's invisible, frankly, most of us are fucked. Only we're not. Or at least, I don't believe we have to be.

Invisibility is no joke; it couldn't be more dangerous. It leads to emotional and psychological difficulty, job loss, financial instability, divorce, mental and physical ill health and, at its worst conclusion, death.

It's hard not to rage against societal and patriarchal assumptions and limitations, fuelled by a cocktail of hormones, real and synthetic. I'm so jacked up on HRT I sometimes worry that if I brush against a bloke on the tube, he'll grow a pair of tits. When talking about invisibility as a superpower, I'm not suggesting trading in anger. But we have a choice. We can either become so overwhelmed by the painful stuff that we become inert, a state which each and every one of us will inevitably inhabit at times. Or we can decide to lean into the pain and harness this conferred invisibility, reframing it as a means of allowing us a freedom that is hard won.

Things change. I used to think nothing of driving a couple of hours to get to a rave; now it's a garden centre. I conform to some midlife female stereotypes (cat, herbal teas, Pilates), but defying negative midlife stereotypes is a lifeline. I get regular reminders from my work as a stand-up that women's experiences of midlife vary. I sometimes chat to women my age in the audience and, as with all crowd work, you never know what you're going to get. One time in the Trinity Theatre in Tunbridge Wells, I asked an audience member how she was finding being in her fifties, and she looked as if she was going to cry. I asked what was wrong and she said: 'Brain fog, people, vaginal dryness.' Then another woman at the back of the theatre shouted out: 'I'm moist!' By way of menopause bingo, I thought, she's winning.

I had a bit of material I used to do, inspired by something someone said to me after a gig. It led me to write this (tip: it works better performed out loud as a rant than in one's own head – try saying it to yourself in a mirror or on the bus or while you're having a mammogram):

THE STATS

Someone came up to me after a gig last week and said, 'I didn't know women could be funny.' And it *is* funny, isn't it, that we as women earn 85 per cent of men's salaries, and we make up 15 per cent of company directors and 5 per cent of world leaders – yet we do 70 per cent of the cleaning, 80 per cent of the washing, 90 per cent of the childcare. And society demands that we have 1 per cent body fat and 0 per cent body hair, despite paying 20 per cent more for exactly the same razors because they're pink. It also demands that we're 100 per cent up for performing sexual favours, even on a school night, on 50 per cent of the sleep we need, with only 50 per cent of the people in the bed achieving orgasm – and in about 5 per cent of the time they promise. And as we lie under our 30 per cent of the duvet, we can take a moment to remember that we, as women, are 75 per cent more likely to get depressed – no shit – despite being reminded throughout 100 per cent of our childhood that we'd be so much prettier if we'd just smile . . . I think it's fair to say that if women didn't have a pretty awesome sense of humour, there'd be a fuckload more murders.

Women my age grew up with many -isms, including casual sexism. I learned early on, as did the millions of others whose stories we increasingly get to hear, that I was expected to smile, flutter and laugh along with jokes, and that above all I was not to be a spoilsport by actually telling lecherous, boundary-crossing men to piss off. From a young age, my internal people-pleaser did battle with my inner rebel, and that battle only intensified as time went by. I charmed. I raged. I wanted men to want me. I hated the ways in which men wanted me. And I hated how much I wanted them to want me.

No one has said, 'Go on, give us a smile,' to me in at least a decade. Amen to that. I used to have material about being a bad feminist because of how a bit of me felt insulted when I hit the age when I was no longer cat-called – but I dropped it, because, as the proud owner of a daughter in her mid-twenties, the things I see and hear her going through are no joke.

What I've discovered in my mid-fifties is that when you are no longer being desired in the same way or even seen at all, you get the chance to observe. I've always been a world-class eavesdropper, and it's no coincidence I worked on some of the world's first reality shows (MTV's *Real World* and *Road Rules*, which laid the foundations for *Big Brother* and all that followed, and for which I can only apologise). But what about a job at the top of the eavesdropping tree? A spy!

The hidden power of invisibility

I had the big-brained Helen Fry on the podcast to talk about her book *Women in Intelligence*, a history of women in British Intelligence across the two world wars. It's well known that by 1945, the majority of Bletchley Park employees were women, but until now we knew less about the other roles played by women across the two wars. Her book contains many stories never told before. I love the fact that Winston Churchill didn't know that his own daughter Sarah was working undercover for Operation Torch. It all tumbled out in a parent/child conversation in the early hours one morning. (A lot worse came tumbling out in early-morning parent/child conversations in our house, but hey ho.)

It was Helen's groundbreaking research that uncovered the fact that Edith Cavell was definitely a spy, a subject still open to debate up until that point. Not just any old spy, but a spymistress, with her own extensive network of male and female spies. And then there was her age:

> One of the things [I hadn't realised] when I started the book was Edith Cavell's age. We always think of her as a nurse, and I assumed she was in her twenties. But she's forty-nine when she faces the firing squad – utterly determined that she has to face her fate, and wouldn't have changed a single thing in her life. She'd have done it all over again.

Edith was a forty-eight-year-old British nurse living in Belgium when World War One broke out. She decided not only to stay on and continue to work as a nurse, but also to go undercover. She set up one of the most effective spy networks of all time – and she did it all while perimenopausal! Being a nurse wouldn't have helped much back then, as I'm pretty sure HRT patches didn't exist. Even in 2025, Brexit's knock-on effect on HRT production means my oestrogen patches rustle like crisp packets and are so big you can see them from space. Any resources that could have gone into women's health during the world wars instead went into condom production and promotion, with ads like the one shown opposite.

It was a 'poor boob' who ultimately betrayed Edith. A man in her network gave her away, leading to her being imprisoned and shot at dawn in a desolate Belgium field. It doesn't get more invisible than that. But her legacy was very visible

Surgeon Sage Says—

Only a poor boob pays his money, loses his watch, gets the syph, and brags that he's had a good time.

indeed, for it was Edith who went on to inspire the generation of female spies that followed.

Many other women, of Edith's age and older, were getting their groove on in midlife at the time. Belgian aristocrats were a big part of Edith's support network, and there's one whose story Helen is researching further. Thérèse de Radiguès was nearly fifty at the start of World War One and successfully ran a whole intelligence section for the British, while having German soldiers billeted in her castle. Not only did she get away with it, but in World War Two, at the age of seventy-five, she did it all over again. She got arrested once towards the end of the war, feigned dementia, got out and went right back to running her spy network. The thing about Edith and Thérèse and all the other women whose stories are now being told is that they were hiding in plain sight, afforded invisibility by the simple fact that they were female. Some male spies even disguised themselves as women to help them go undetected (a sort of reverse Brontë sisters approach).

At the peak of our invisible power

Midlife women may often be missed by society as a whole, but we remain not only visible but also valuable to our peers; in fact, we become increasingly so. Kirsty Wark and I talked when she came on the podcast about her groundbreaking 2017 BBC documentary *Let's Talk About the Menopause*. Kirsty herself went into hard menopause due to a hysterectomy in her late forties, and talks in the documentary about menopause happening in the prime of life, when women are often at the peak of our careers and our powers.

Dr Grace Lordan, economist and behavioural science professor at the London School of Economics, talked to me about her research into the combination of pleasure and purpose being what is most likely to provide fulfilment in our lives. When I think about what drives me forward during this life phase, it is indeed a combination of pleasure and purpose, coupled with identity. The irony is that for many midlife women, it's only as the outside world is questioning our visibility that we are finally becoming visible to ourselves. With some of the trappings of younger womanhood stripped away, we can start to see what's what.

Deborah Meaden – 'Just work out what matters. We spend way too long on stuff that just doesn't matter. And what matters is different for everybody. But just make sure you know what it is. Otherwise, one day you wake up and think, I don't really know what I care about. I don't really know what I do. I don't really know what I love. Work out what matters.'

If you've got five minutes to spare (four minutes and fifty-seven seconds, to be precise), search: 'Inside Amy Schumer – Last F**kable Day'. It's a sketch in which Amy Schumer happens upon Tina Fey, Julia Louis-Dreyfus and Patricia Arquette celebrating Julia's last fuckable day. She jokes that she can't believe Hollywood let her stay fuckable right through her forties and into her fifties, assuming there must have been a clerical error. Amy asks, 'What about men? When do they have their last fuckable day?' And oh, how they laugh – because Hollywood men stay fuckable forever. Julia is fine with it, because she doesn't have to keep a perfect figure and can grow her pubes out. Good times.

There are women who crack Hollywood post-fifty, more often behind the cameras than in front. Women like Katherine Bigelow and Jane Campion, but the list is not long. And then there are women over fifty who have been in the business for years and go on to occupy midlife space that inspires and delights us, like Kate Winslet in *Mare of Easttown*. And then there are women like Helen Mirren, who still looks good in a red bikini at seventy-four, although she's contributed rather more to the world than that.

I spent my boardroom years sometimes as much unheard as unseen, and once you get over the outrage (you never get over the outrage) there are advantages to be found. I got used to having my ideas appropriated by others, to having to position myself carefully to be heard, to having to hold my feelings close for fear of saying what I was thinking and being dubbed an over-emotional woman. On occasion, it suited me not to be heard. I would lay out something I was planning to do and it would get glossed over, barely acknowledged, and therefore not resisted. I didn't have to fight as hard to get my own way, because my own way was so frequently underestimated. I often thought of that quote from Admiral Grace Hopper, also, in my opinion, worthy of her own Netflix series: 'It's easier to ask forgiveness than it is to get permission.' I was able to introduce initiatives and manage my team and my business my way. This was, admittedly, partly by virtue of being in London when the head office was in New York – I thoroughly recommend a geographical gap of at least three and a half thousand miles if you must have a boss – but it was also partly down to no one paying much attention. I worked really hard to be good at my job, and most of what I did worked. And on the occasions when it really, *really* worked, I became highly visible and much celebrated just for a moment or two before everyone else was ready to take credit for it and I went back into the shadows again. No wonder I got mental fatigue and gave it all up to become a clown.

Comedy is not well paid, but public speaking is, and so between them I make a living. I do many corporate events, from hosting awards (what I don't know about plumbing/landscape gardening/accountancy/construction isn't worth knowing, depending on the night) to keynote and after-dinner speeches. When Baroness Ayesha Hazarika came on the podcast, she talked about how, when she arrives at a venue to give a speech, people often seem to worry for her and expect her to be out of her depth. Have you seen her CV? I have the same thing. People at venues rarely expect me to be the speaker, particularly on the after-dinner circuit, which is overwhelmingly male. I am mistaken for everything from the event's organiser to someone's plus-one or the venue point person. Ayesha and I agreed that the capacity to over-deliver once you've been passed over unseen and underestimated delights us. We could spend a long time trying to talk people into taking us seriously, but nothing would get close to the luxury of having the chance to show them. A couple of weeks ago, as I waited to go onstage, I was reassured by a man next to me, who told me not to be nervous. He even gave me a bit of advice on mic technique (none of which was solicited). I asked him if he did much public speaking, and he said yes, a couple of times a year. This is my living. I do it a couple of times a week. Shut up! By the time I came offstage, he had.

It's not just the corporate world. I've arrived at comedy venues and had to argue with whoever's on the door about the fact that I'm a comedian. I was doing tour support for Micky Flanagan at a London theatre a couple of years ago, and couldn't get past the person on the door; she sent me to the back of the queue, making me do the walk of shame past everyone who was shortly going to see me onstage. I had to call Micky's manager to come and get me. If there's a trend for menopausal women trying to blag free entry to comedy gigs by pretending to be on the bill, then a) I'm not aware of it, and b) bloody good for them. Let them in.

I'll say it again: invisibility is a superpower. Just look at Banksy. Oh, you can't. Research suggests that it's the superpower we most dream of, with 37 per cent of those surveyed wishing for it. The ability to read minds comes in second at 29 per cent, followed by the ability to fly at the speed of light in third place at 20 per cent.[1]

Things may not be changing at the speed of light, but they are changing. In *Cracking the Menopause*, Mariella Frostrup talks about menopause having historically been a kind of 'living death'. Things aren't exactly perfect for us now, but they are hopefully better than that.

People find a new sense of self and freedom as they age, leading to a term I recently heard for the first time: 'gerontolesence', referring to a type of second adolescence for those aged fifty to seventy-five. In the US, women like this are dubbed 'queenagers'. Course they are. It's taken this queenager half a century to start to have a clue who I really am, and I've earned that knowledge. The power and wisdom of midlife women is hard won and merits more than being a well-kept secret. Vulnerability and strength are intrinsically linked, and together they give us agency. When thinking about change, it's alright – advisable, even – to start small, but that doesn't mean we can't dream big. I was talking to a friend about dreams and told him a recent one I'd had of being in prison – it was actually a hospital to begin with, but then all the nurses gradually changed to prison guards and there I was, no visible way out. He said that was funny, because his wife's dreams are always about driving off cliffs with no power to stop, *Thelma and Louise* style (much as I love both him and his wife, he's no Brad Pitt), while his are about freefalling with neither plane nor parachute, yet feeling completely safe in the knowledge he'll have a soft landing. Talk about patriarchal privilege, even in sleep.

The contents of this book do not just concern my own matriarchal prison break, but yours too. I believe we can be motivated and equipped to defy limiting expectations and be the authors of our own imperfect stories. Bryony Gordon's life advice on the podcast was: 'Stop dismissing yourself. Stop dismissing your feelings. Stop dismissing your wants, your needs.' Midlife women are supposed to vanish quietly and quickly from society once they are no longer fertile and, if they're mothers, once their kids have grown and flown. Well, here's my battle cry: I demand the right to be a mother and a fucker, motherf*cker.

Fancy stopping me? You'll have to find me first.

DO TRY THIS AT HOME

If we're serious about change, we need to re-educate ourselves to see the unfamiliar on the horizon not as a threat, but as an opportunity. This is the very opposite of what enabled us to survive as a species, so no wonder it feels unnatural. If we're feeling too comfortable, chances are what we're doing isn't working as well as it might. We don't need to be uncomfortable all day every day, but building up the muscle to be able to walk towards, rather than away from, discomfort and try new things is a must. The takeaways in this chapter help increase visibility, agency and pleasure for those of us not willing to be erased. It's easy to notice all the things we can't do, but what about the things we can? The takeaways in each chapter will build on what's come before until, by the end of the book, you will have such a range of techniques that you will be a fully paid-up self-help bore and everyone will hate you. As with all the takeaways in the book, it's better to write them out rather than just think about them. All the ideas and techniques work independently of each other, so just pick the ones you fancy – no pressure.

Build your own spy network

Putting your head above the parapet without allies or cheerleaders is tough, and everyone needs their own personal boardroom, whether it's made up of colleagues, friends, family, peers or experts. Firstly, write down the roles you have in life; in my case, that's mother, daughter, comedian, speaker, writer, friend, sister, etc. Then, next to each of those roles, write down your allies and supporters. Do you need more? Do you have too many in some roles and not enough in others? Which of your roles need more support? What would that support look like? What are one or two actions, however small, you can commit to? It's fine to ask for advice and support – in fact, it's essential – and on page 69 we'll look more closely at how to make meaningful connections with people and create an optimal support network.

Stop, look, learn

We can't change or control other people or indeed many situations; all that is within our gift is our own response to things. Whenever you're in a situation where there's a feeling of invisibility or a lack of agency, the first thing within your gift is to notice exactly what's really going on. Ask yourself: Where am I in this? What's happening, internally and externally? Am I muting myself? What is my real opinion? Where is my agency? Is what I'm doing helping or hindering me? What part of this situation is within my control? What can I let go of in order to free up some space to do things differently? Is there anything, however small, I can do differently? At this point, it's more about getting into the habit of being curious about your own response to things and noticing the details, than it is about taking action. Often the very act of stopping to take stock will give you the answers anyway.

Reframe

Reframing is really helpful when it comes to existing or future situations where visibility and agency are at stake.

If you find yourself following a train of thought or path of action that's not getting you where you want to be, then it's good to look at alternatives; to replace what's not helping you with new things that might. There are lots of ways to do reframing, but here are the basics:

> Pick a situation that hasn't gone as you wished it to or something that has caused you to be stressed or anxious; the more recent the example, the better.
>
> Write down as much about it as you can remember, and how you reacted practically, emotionally and physically, in as much detail as you can.
>
> Now think about alternative responses you wish you had had, practically, emotionally and physically, and write those down.
>
> Finally, visualise that situation and reverse it by replacing the reaction you had with the response you wish you'd had.

You can use this technique to think about how you would like to reframe future situations too.

LAST WORDS

The last words in each chapter go to my podcast guests, with a selection of their jokes and life advice. The joke in this chapter is based on Jenny Eclair's true story, which she told onstage as part of her last tour show:

> 'My mother was in her very late eighties, and she got an iPad when she became a widow. It was quite difficult to get her on board with the technology. And, living 250 miles away, I had to give her these iPad lessons over the phone, and they'd always start like this:
>
> Me: "OK, have you switched it on?"
> My mother: "Yes."
> Me: "What can you see?"
> Mother: "A naked man."
> Me: "A naked man? What's he doing?"
> Mother: "He's got a vegetable up his bottom."
> Me: "He's got a vegetable up his bottom? What did you put in the Google search engine?"
> Mother: "Interesting things to do with aubergines."'

The first piece of life advice comes from Kerry Godliman, and also, by coincidence, involves vegetables:

> 'Be kind to yourself. Eat your vegetables. Don't be a cunt.'

And where else to end a chapter about being invisible than with the words with which Rosie Jones left listeners:

> 'Never apologise for being you.'

2
THE (VERY) ODD ONE OUT

STANDING OUT AND BELONGING

'Because true belonging only happens when
we present our authentic, imperfect selves to the world,
our sense of belonging can never be greater than
our level of self-acceptance.'
Brené Brown

belonging
/bɪˈlɒŋɪŋ/
noun
> Secure relationship; affinity
> 'a sense of belonging'

Source: https://www.collinsdictionary.com/dictionary/english/belonging

> Male seahorses may never help their offspring with homework, go to parents' evenings or drop them off at ballet. But they do outdo humans on one count: male seahorses are the ones to undergo pregnancy and give birth.

Back to school

Nobody dropped *me* off at ballet. There was no need; I got my not-belonging credentials in early. As a little girl, I was ginger, knock-kneed and overweight – and I wore industrial-strength glasses. I was a sort of curious devil child of Ed Sheeran and Matt Lucas. Both my parents were teachers, and when I was eight they sent me to the school where they both taught, which was not a recipe for blending in – because, you see, my parents taught at a boys' school. There were more than two hundred boys in that school, and I was the only girl. The bullying wasn't bad – if I was teased it was more for being ginger and the offspring of teachers than for being a girl – and I'm a decent cricketer and rugby player. But there was one day which I'll never forget, and that was the day when I heard that I hadn't got the female lead in the school play. You may be laughing more than I did about that.

That was my first experience of not fitting in: being a little girl in a boys' prep school. I suppose there were a couple of other things that didn't help, experiences that shaped me even earlier than that. At the first school I went to, the local primary where, usefully, my parents did not teach, three of us wanted the part of Mary in the nativity play – of course we did. For reasons that beggar belief, it was decided the class would hold a Mary vote. Just like Brexit, only without AI interference or lies on buses. I got the fewest votes – I suspect by a margin of rather more than 4 per cent – and was cast as a sheep. Like all good sheep, I was a non-speaking sheep. I suppose, being a sheep, I should have felt the ultimate sense of belonging, but I couldn't even get that right.

The other happened on my very first day of primary school, when I wet myself in the Wendy house. I had to wear spare knickers from the lost-property drawer and wait in the Wendy house while my dress dried on the radiator. I was really good at reading by then, and I watched through the Wendy house window as my classmates kept getting all the words on the spelling cards wrong, unable to join in, my only contribution the smell of warm wee drifting from my drying dress and into their nostrils. To be fair, it's gone pretty much full circle, and if I spent much time in a Wendy house now, there's a good chance I would do a bit of a wee. And I think my spelling's got worse since then, with the advent of first spellcheck, then menopause.

Nativity sheep and Wendy houses aside, I was happy at that first school. Then we moved counties, from Buckinghamshire to Dorset, and I became a) a teachers' kid, and b) a private school kid. It wasn't just my gender and my staff-child status that set me apart. It was being at a prep school where most of the pupils came from money and privilege. They were a worldly bunch with their expensive belongings and sophisticated ways. Some of them lived abroad, while I had never been on a plane. They knew about life. I did not. Wrong gender, wrong status, wrong weight. There's a scene that would be pivotal in setting up my not-belongingness in a movie version of my childhood, and that's the one with eleven-year-old me standing on a diving board in front of my whole class, in what was at the time a bang-on-trend 1970s denim-effect halter-neck swimming costume. As I walked along the diving board, the teacher pointed out to my entire class how closely I resembled a sack of potatoes. The other kids laughed while I pretended to laugh and managed not to cry. It sounds like an anxiety dream, but it was actually just a school swimming lesson. There's no good time to be fat-shamed, but that was a rotten time.

The first joke I ever wrote was this: 'I came out of the tube and a bloke outside called me a fat cunt. So I went up to him and I said: "You must never, ever call a woman fat."'

Crap bit of stand-up, but I think you can see where it might have come from . . .

My brother was less unhappy than me, maybe because, as a boy without glasses, he 'only' had the teachers' kid and ginger bits of not fitting in, reducing his not-belonging by 50 per cent compared with mine. I liked knowing my big brother was there and didn't want the time to come when he would leave for a new school; little did I know he would throw a curveball and nearly die on the last day of his last term.

He'd had a nagging pain in his leg most of that summer term, which our family GP had diagnosed as malingering. Turns out it was something with a couple more syllables and rather more seriousness – osteomyelitis. Osteomyelitis is a rare bone-marrow disease with a current mortality rate of one in five: back then, it was considerably higher. He spent the summer of 1980 in hospital, while I stayed at a friend's house on the other side of the country. No one told me they feared he was going to die; I just knew. Several weeks of treatment and rehab later, he survived. He had the good grace not to disappear completely, but he did disappear from the school, leaving me a lone and lonely sibling.

By the time it was my turn to be in my last year at that school, I was thirteen, a boarder (my parents sleeping in a house at one end of the school drive, me in a dormitory at the other) and very into *Jackie* magazine. I wanted more than anything to be like one of the girls in *Jackie*, going to a local school with my local friends, and being into local boys and discos and clothes. I tried to negotiate a transfer from private to state education, but my negotiation skills, although sufficient to make me stand out in later life, were not sufficient to clinch this important deal.

Instead, a scholarship took me to a third-rate public school (we had no money for fees, so in hindsight I could have just flunked the scholarship exam). I properly hated that shitty school, and that school hated me. Despite no longer being the only girl, my not-belonging had reached dizzying heights. As well as becoming terrible at sports (let's blame diving-board day, and the fact the boys' school didn't have a netball court), I was now a weekly boarder in a school where most students stayed there at weekends, and a scholar where most were from families who could afford to pay full fees. And I didn't look right (I was still overweight and had not yet got into fashion). In case I didn't already feel like enough of an outsider, I was sent to Coventry (is that still a thing?) for a whole term. For a period of twelve weeks, literally no one spoke to me. Actually, one girl did once, but then no one spoke to *her*, so she stopped. In the end, I stopped eating – fully stopped eating – in order to get someone to notice how unhappy I was. Finally, I was taken out of that school and sent to the local comprehensive. Result! I ended my hunger strike, started eating again, and life at last had more than a passing resemblance to the pages of *Jackie* magazine – and by then *Just Seventeen*, too, which felt just around the corner.

> As a kid, I was so bad at life I became really good at music. There was a piano in the school hall at my boys' school, a beautiful Steinway grand, which I would play every day for hours and hours. It was a musical trapdoor into my own world: an escape from not fitting in. My very first love affair was with the piano. A few years later, I found my second love: an actual boy, a boy named Nick, who made me mix-tapes, wrote lines from Shakespearean sonnets on my school books, and made my heart sing.

> As my social life picked up, my piano playing died down, until by sixteen it had pretty much ground to a halt. I still didn't fit right in, but I didn't stand right out either.

Finding your tribe

When we don't fit in, our instinct, deep-rooted in our lizard brain, is to do everything we possibly can to camouflage ourselves in order to survive, even if that means turning down the dial on who we really are to almost nothing. That primal instinct to belong, to not stand out, is fierce, and rooted in life and death. There's nothing more unnatural than what I do for a living – standing in rooms facing the wrong way. Our limbic systems may not have moved on, but the world has, and not being exactly the same as the next person is where our value lies. If you think about why someone hired you to do a job, it's probably because they didn't already have a *you*. Yet within a matter of months, if not weeks, we take on the behaviours of those around us, trying to fit in with our tribe at all costs. Instead of doing things that might be effective because they're different or unique, we opt for doing what everyone else is doing, which isn't good for morale or identity. Nor is it good for business.

In 1943, psychologist Abraham Maslow introduced his famous 'Hierarchy of Needs', a model based on the fact that people are motivated to fulfil basic survival needs before moving on to other, more complex and ultimately fulfilling needs (shown overleaf).

Maslow was way ahead of his time in focusing on what makes people happy; most psychologists in his era were concentrating on using psychoanalysis to address problem behaviours. Maslow's premise was that as soon as the most

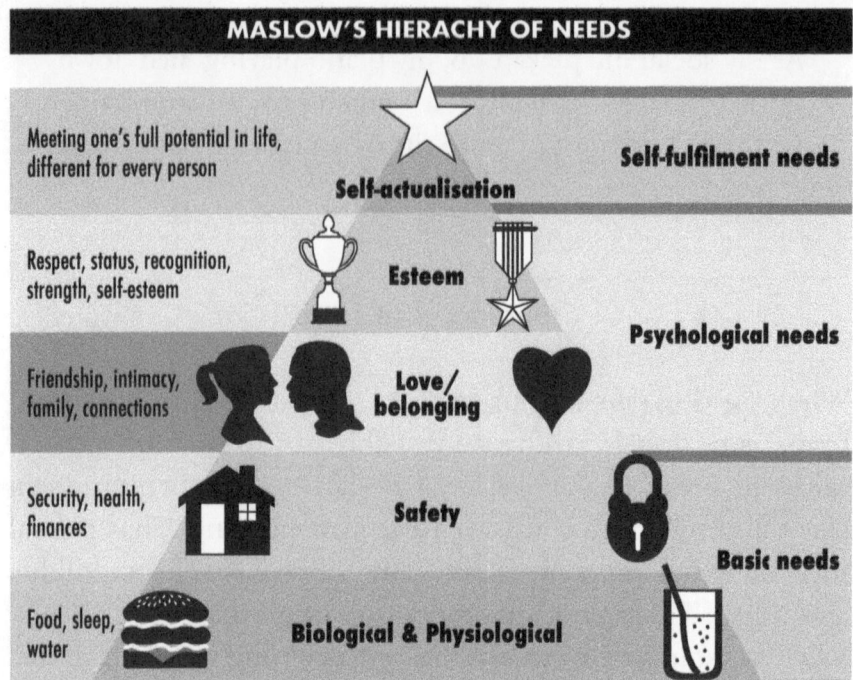

basic needs of safety, food and water are met, humans look to things like love and belonging. He split human needs into 'deficiency needs', arising due to deprivation, and 'growth needs', coming from a desire to grow as a person. Esteem and self-fulfilment needs are at the top of Maslow's pyramid, and these include the need for appreciation and respect. As we move up the pyramid, it becomes increasingly important to be valued by others and have our efforts recognised. It's a basic part of the human psychology to want to belong to a tribe.

I talked to Professor Matthew Williams, author of *The Science of Hate*, about tribalism, or 'groupness'. When I asked him about the difference between intense dislike and hate, he linked it to something that happens at the extreme end of not-belonging:

> Intense dislike I would usually ascribe to a relationship between a person and another person. It could be within

your family – you're in intense dislike of your father or your brother, or it could be your husband or wife. It could be your neighbour. It could be intense dislike of that President, but it's one on one. Hate is somewhat different; it's not so much that interpersonal connection; it's more to do with a person's perception of another group that they think that person belongs to. They're thinking of a person as belonging to another group. So they say, "Well, you're whatever the negative stereotype is, because of your membership of that group that I think you're from, which is different from my group." So we get this "in group, out group" dynamic going on. The in group is us, and the out group is them. And that's what drives hate.

And then he told me about the 'Salah Effect', which is a joyous thing:

Mo Salah joined Liverpool Football Club in 2017, in the midst of a string of terror attacks. Mo is Muslim, and the anticipation is that he's not going to get a very warm reception. But it turns out he's very good at football and he performs exceptionally well. An academic from Stanford University decided to test whether the arrival of Mo Salah at Liverpool actually had an effect on hate crimes on the streets in Merseyside and hate speech on social media. And indeed, they found that while all around the country, hate crimes against Muslims were increasing, in Merseyside they'd actually gone down. This was attributable to the success of Mo Salah and his public portrayal of Muslimness on the pitch, because every time he would score, he would celebrate by praising Allah, and he would celebrate his successes with reference to his Muslim identity. And what ended up happening – you wouldn't believe it – but fans would start to sing 'Praise to Allah' in the stands of Anfield and in the pubs in Merseyside. And this chanting had a huge effect on reducing anti-Muslim prejudice in Merseyside. So what it shows us is that we can undo negative stereotypes with positive portrayals of minorities.

I'm not sure stadiums are going to start chanting 'women are funny' any time soon, but it's good to know we might undo the negative stereotype that 'women aren't funny' by positively portraying that we, in fact, are. Here's the thing. If a female comedian isn't funny, audiences leave the gig thinking women aren't funny. If a male comedian has a bad gig, it's unlikely that 'men aren't funny' is what will be extrapolated. When you're the privileged majority, you are seen to represent yourself; when you are marginalised in any way, you are seen to represent anyone like you.

Tough love

Not belonging feels uncomfortable and can be dangerous, but there are those who opt not to fit in. We link many human instincts and behaviours to the animal world, and there are some animals that don't need to belong. Polar bears, for example, prefer to be alone unless they're eating or mating. I feel much the same, to be honest. And then there are moose which, unlike most deer, don't travel in herds. I guess when you're six feet tall and weigh in at more than a thousand pounds, you're probably OK to go it alone. At five foot six and a half, and not quite a thousand pounds even after Christmas, I'm less confident without my tribe. Moose calves stay with their mothers for their first year, and then go off on their own. This is in stark contrast with human calves, who stay with their parents until they're, say, thirty and even then only leave if their parents can provide them with their first property or in some other way pay them to go. At least polar bears and moose, while solitary, stick around to raise their young for a bit. Female tortoises just dig a hole in the ground, lay their eggs, and fuck off. The tiny, weeny little tortoise hatchlings are left to fend for themselves from the get-go and only 2 per cent make it. I mean, there's being solitary, and then there's being a crap parent.

The mouldy vagina tribe

Despite it catching on when I was a young person, I never did catch chlamydia. I do, however, remember going to the pharmacy not long after I'd moved to Amsterdam in the early nineties because I thought I had thrush. I didn't know the Dutch for thrush, so I tried my best to explain it. First of all, the pharmacist was insistent I had an STD. I was insistent I did not. She then asked if I had mould on my vagina. No, I did not! Turns out, thrush in Dutch is *'schimmelinfectie'* – mould or mildew infection – and she went on to say loudly in front of the whole queue: 'Half the people in here have a vagina, and half of them will have had mildew on it.' Every day's a school day. Bottoms up, and welcome to Holland.

How did my mould-free vagina and I end up in the Netherlands? In 1987, I had gone to Goldsmiths in London to study drama. I went because I thought I could act, but within a couple of weeks I realised that, alas and alack, I could not. I set my hat at working in telly instead. In my third year at Goldsmiths, I did a dissertation on children's television, less because it was my genre of choice, more because the only person who replied to the fifty or so letters I sent out was the wonderful Anna Hume, then Head of Children's Programmes at the BBC. If I'd wanted a strong female role model at the age of nineteen, I could have done a lot worse than Anna. She got me shadowing a couple of BBC children's dramas (one written by Andrew Davies, soon to go on to great things), due to which I had enough on my CV to be able to get a job as a runner when I graduated. My first job was at a children's cable channel called The Children's Channel – simpler times – and it was there I met my kids' Dutch dad.

It was fortuitous meeting him, not only because we went on to have the best kids in the world, but also because it led to me accidentally moving to the format capital of the world just before the TV format boom hit. I did a stint working for a Dutch production company that went on to become part of Endemol right before *Big Brother* launched, and a couple of years later, back in the UK, that job led to me being asked to head up the international division of a successful game show production company. I enjoyed working at the production company – relatively small-scale and dynamic as it was – but then we caught the eye of Carlton Television, part of ITV, and they acquired us. Next thing I knew, I had my first experience of boardroom life, and to say I didn't fit in was an understatement. People talk about 'bringing your whole self to work'; without realising it, that's what I'd been doing in the years prior to this acquisition. When you are doing something where you just slot in, you tend to take it for granted. But when you stand out like a ginger sore thumb, things change.

Pale, male and stale

The view changed. The literal one got better, as Carlton TV's HQ was 1 Knightsbridge, with spectacular views across Hyde Park. The metaphorical view was less impressive, as I was now in a forest of privately educated white men. My knee-jerk reaction was to assimilate the behaviour of those around me, admitting to no one, least of all myself, that I felt afraid or exposed. I was an undercover woman, acting like a man.

I've since discovered the ultimate undercover woman, journalist Norah Vincent, who conducted an eighteen-month experiment in which she went undercover as a man called Ned (because that's what men are called). She integrated into traditionally male-only venues, like a bowling league and a monastery, to discover what it is men talk about when women aren't around. She found out lots of things, which she wrote about in her 2006 book *Self-Made Man: My Year Disguised as a Man*. I like to think maybe she uncovered the truth about the fact that when we ask men what they're thinking and they say, 'Nothing,' what they're actually thinking is . . . nothing.

No one should have to act like a man in order to belong, especially when male role models in 2025 include Donald Trump, Kanye West and Andrew Tate. That wonderful triumvirate, united in the opinion that a good way to exert power over a woman is to say you wouldn't have sex with them. That's a bit like telling someone you're not going to burgle them and expecting them to be disappointed. Most women have had this lovely type of unrequested feedback levelled at them at some point, and on behalf of all of us, I'd just like to say that rather than being an insult, it's more of a massive relief. So thank you.

A froth of mansplainers

There are many clubs to which I do not wish to belong – the Garrick Club, for example – but I'd like it to be my choice. It's like a wedding you don't want to go to, but you still want to be invited to so you can say no. I'm not sure what the collective noun is for men-only member's clubs (a few spring to mind), but thanks to my son, I know some of the glorious collective nouns for groups of animals. There are the classics – a pride of lions, a murder of crows, a crash of rhinos – and then there are others, like a tower of giraffes, a flamboyance of flamingos, a kaleidoscope of butterflies, a fluffle of bunnies, a loveliness of ladybirds, an exaltation of larks, an implausibility of wildebeest, a charm of finches, a dazzle of zebras, a fever of rays, a shitload of dung beetles (OK, I made that one up), a memory of elephants, a bloat of hippos (or menopausal women) and a blessing of unicorns. Apparently, groups of vultures have different names, depending on what they're doing; if they're flying together it's a kettle, if they're perched together it's a committee, and if they're feeding together, it's a wake. In one social media post, I wondered what the collective noun for mansplainers might be. 'A wank of mansplainers,' I suggested. The comments that came back were a delight. Here are some of my favourites:

> an insecurity of mansplainers
>
> a tedium of mansplainers
>
> a 'well, actually' of mansplainers
>
> a monotony of mansplainers
>
> a bother of mansplainers
>
> a whataboutery of mansplainers
>
> a merkin of cockweasles (I salute this person)
>
> . . . or just a bunch of knobs

All of this got my male trolls into a right old froth. Wait – a *froth* of mansplainers! We've got it.

The land of opportunity

Women pay a heavy price for not belonging, and those early boardroom years cost me dear. It was during my time in senior management at ITV that I found myself the single parent of two young children. Something had to give with all that overcompensating, and sadly it was the very most important thing. Their dad moved out when they were three and five (much more my fault than his), and there we were: three discombobulated musketeers instead of our nuclear Anglo-Dutch family. Now I didn't even know how to belong in my own home. Human beings are a social species, and it's in our wiring to need to belong. No wonder we all have such a hard time with a solitary lifestyle. The current loneliness epidemic was described in 2023 by the World Health Organization as a 'global public health concern', as bad for people's health as smoking fifteen cigarettes a day.[2] Terrible outlook for solitary chain-smokers.

It's not irrational when we're without our tribe to feel exposed, unprotected and under threat. After a couple more unhappy, tribeless years, I left ITV and set up my own little creative consultancy – which was all well and good until I realised I'd ended up in a life where I was on my own at home and on my own at work. It wasn't quite on the 'girl in a boys' school' level of not-belonging, but I did need to find my tribe. And that's when I hit upon the genius idea of working for Americans.

I saw a job at MTV advertised in *Broadcast Magazine* – the only job I've ever applied for from a newspaper ad – and, it being the pre-email era, off I wrote. A couple of London job interviews later, and I was flown out to New York to meet the President of MTV in their iconic offices at 1515 Broadway, overlooking Times Square. That was my first time ever setting foot in New York City, and as I walked out into the November sunshine after my interview, I looked up at the towering electronic billboards of Times Square. One of them had an MTV ad running on it and I stood on that Manhattan pavement, praying to the gods of Beavis and Butt-Head that I would get the job. And, dumbass, I did.

I was based in London, working for the New York HQ, shuttling back and forth across the Atlantic at a frequency for which I can only apologise now we know what we know. Sorry, Greta – truly, I am. Over in the States, they don't get ginger like we do over here; I don't know if they've been vaccinated or something, but I think they thought I was a royal or a Weasley, and they seemed to love me. My 'otherness' was working in my favour.

Broken rungs and glass ceilings

I'm writing this chapter during International Women's Week in March – incidentally, one of my busiest weeks of the year, so let's never fully smash the patriarchy or it'll screw up my March earnings. I was chatting to a taxi driver on the way to a speech I was giving. It was at a breakfast for female lawyers, a sector still male-dominated at partner level, with only 37 per cent of partners being women.[3] The taxi driver asked me what I was going to talk about. I asked him if he was aware of the glass ceiling; he was, so I told him that now people are talking more about the 'broken rung' being the greatest obstacle to women in their careers. For every 100 men promoted from an entry-level position to manager, only 87 women are promoted, leading to a broken rung on the ladder, with women falling behind, never to catch up.

'A broken rung on the ladder?' he asked.

'Yes,' I said.

'What you need's a bloke to fix that,' he said.

See? Men can be funny.

But he was right, in a way. Male allyship has been shown to be a major trend in accelerating women's equality; in fact, you could argue it's impossible without it. Two explanations are sometimes rolled out to explain the broken rung: the first is that women are not asking for promotions, and the second is that they're more likely to step away from work. As it turns out, neither is true. Women ask for promotions as often as men do, and they are no more likely to leave their place of work. The real reason is depressing and is best summed up as women being hired for what they have already done, men for what they can become. Social scientists call this 'performance bias'. It's one thing to increase women's representation at the top, but unless the broken rungs are fixed lower down the ladder, it's a sticking-plaster solution. I wasn't gifted in woodwork class at my boys' school, but even I know you can't mend a ladder with a plaster. Because of the broken rung, in a typical company, men end up holding 60 per cent of manager-level positions, while women hold just 40 per cent. As a result, there are fewer women to promote to director. The number of women decreases at every level thereafter. When Tim Davie took over from Tony Hall as the seventeenth Director-General of the BBC in 2020, his appointment was widely criticised, the role going as it did to a white, male, privately educated Oxbridge graduate. The shortlist of four was fifty–fifty male and female, yet Davie won out on credentials. The women in that top-tier field in media still had not had as clear a run up the ladder as the man who ultimately got the job.

Keep your wing women close

There are two points at which we women are lost from the workforce – pregnancy and menopause (and a third waiting in the shadows, as we're the ones still statistically most likely to become carers for elderly parents). What an irony that there is a mass exodus of women in midlife, just at the point when, as Kirsty Wark pointed out in her documentary, they are at the very peak of their powers.

It's not just enough for us to help ourselves. We need help from others. It's pretty hard to put your head above the parapet and get as uncomfortable as this book is asking you to get unless you have allies; you need your wing people in place. My wing women have had my back throughout my adult life, on everything from the school run to online dating. Back in the early days of *Guardian* Soulmates, long before the apps – I'm nothing if not an early adopter – I'd always tell a girlfriend where I was going on my date, in case anything went wrong, then I'd call or text when I got home safely. One time, I texted my friend Sarah that I was meeting my date at the RFH at 7.30pm. I got home a couple of hours later from an underwhelming date and checked in with Sarah to mark myself safely home. She asked why I'd been meeting at the Royal Free Hospital anyway? RFH: Royal Festival Hall. FFS, Sarah.

That first unhappy, male-dominated boardroom experience had taught me the importance of allies and the odds against your survival without them. You can't rely on what you're given; it's better to grow your own personal boardroom, a robust network of people around you whom you can trust. You only need one or two strong allies in your professional life, and the rest of them can be made up of any number of friends, family or partners who may or may not have anything to do with your line of work. Growing your network might sound a bit *Apprentice*-like (although don't let's slag off the show, as they always book me for *The Apprentice: You're Fired*), but really it's about human connection, as creative as it is corporate. Andy Warhol said: 'Human beings are born solitary, but everywhere they are in chains – daisy chains – of interactivity.

Social actions are makeshift forms, often courageous, sometimes ridiculous, always strange. And in a way, every social action is a negotiation, a compromise between "his", "her" or "their" wish and yours.'

Skipper of the first all-female round-the-world yacht crew, Tracy Edwards, told me about the necessity of pushing allyship and belonging to the limit aboard her fifty-eight-foot yacht, *Maiden*, back in 1989:

> Team spirit was very good and became stronger and stronger. All of a sudden, people who weren't necessarily allowed to step up stepped up and were incredibly able. Towards the end, we didn't need to talk to do any of the manoeuvres we did. We thought each other's thoughts before we were even doing them. I didn't feel the need to speak. It was just closeness.

It was in part due to my conversation with Tracy that I realised I've lived my adult life largely on the basis of 'lead or leave', but rarely 'belong'. I've fairly naturally occupied leadership positions and been willing to flex my elbows sharply enough when necessary to avert the frequent land grabs that are a fact of senior management life. Yet – and I'm not proud of this realisation – in rooms where I've had to muck in as a member of a team, I've tended to ostracise myself and leave. Not because I think I'm better than anyone else; the opposite, in fact. So fundamental is my conviction that I don't belong, I'd rather get in there first with a bit of self-sabotage and leave early rather than risk being rejected if I stay.

The impostor conundrum

Plato said you should debate ideas, not people, and you can't argue with Plato, especially now he's been dead for over two thousand years. Our need to belong links directly to the degree to which we feel like an impostor. Impostor syndrome was first written about by two female psychologists, Pauline Rose Clance and Suzanne Imes. They developed the concept, originally termed 'impostor phenomenon', in their 1978 founding study focusing on high-achieving women.[4] They noticed that: 'Despite outstanding academic and professional accomplishments, women who experience the impostor phenomenon persist in believing that they are really not bright and have fooled anyone who thinks otherwise.' Impostor syndrome can be summed up as comparing our insides with other people's outsides.

Despite the consistent external validation the women they surveyed received, they lacked internal acknowledgement of their accomplishments. When asked about their success, some participants attributed it to luck, while some believed that people had overestimated their capabilities. They discovered that the women in the study experienced symptoms of generalised anxiety, lack of self-confidence, depression, and frustration related to the inability to meet self-imposed standards of achievement: the link between perfectionism and impostorism. Reminds me of the joke about the perfectionist who walks into a bar. Apparently, it wasn't set high enough.

Impostor syndrome is less a fear of being found out; it's more about an individual with an incapacity to internalise their own success. My impostor syndrome has been raging about writing this book – not helped by the fact that when I started this bit about impostor syndrome, I didn't know whether it was spelled with an 'e' or with an 'o' so I had to google it. Then, to write that bit, I had to google whether it should be written as 'spelt' or 'spelled'.

For a long while, impostor syndrome was thought to be a phenomenon affecting mainly females, but research has since shown that the majority of people suffer from it to some degree. If you're reading this thinking, 'Brilliant! I'm in the minority who don't!', then there's a good chance you're either a narcissist or a psychopath. So why not run for President? Go on! Please God, go on.

One could argue that real frauds and bullshitters are the least likely to feel like impostors. The opposite of impostor syndrome is expert syndrome, and Welsh philosopher and mathematician Bertrand Russell once said: 'The trouble with the world is that the stupid are cocksure and the intelligent are full of doubt.'

I've come up hard against expert syndrome many times on the comedy circuit – someone who, in the green room beforehand, exudes such confidence I think they must be the next Sarah Millican and I've just somehow missed them. Then they go onstage, stink the place out, and I think, 'Ooh, that was awkward.' And they come back to the green room as if they've just nailed a Peter Kay stadium appearance. Part of me thinks, 'Lucky them'; another part thinks I'd never be good at anything if I was them, as it's my hale and hearty inner critic who pushes me on. I don't subscribe to the idea of ridding ourselves of the feeling that we are impostors, nor to the idea of banishing our inner critic. It's more about accepting our inner critic camping out in our head, a bit like accepting a teenager not cleaning their room or saying thank you for ALL THE THINGS YOU DO FOR THEM. While allowing ourselves to run with self-doubt and impostorism, we can still make a conscious decision to be brave, turning the volume on ourselves up, not down.

Before any big speaking engagement, a part of me is thinking, 'This will be the one where I'm found out; there's obviously been some kind of booking error. I shouldn't even be here.' Instead of telling myself not to be stupid, that of course I'm good enough to be there, I just try to notice it and not give myself the anxiety of fighting it on top of everything else. A couple of years into doing stand-up, I got booked for the Women of the World Festival at the Royal Festival Hall (or maybe it was the Royal Free Hospital, you'd have to ask Sarah). It was the biggest gig I'd done to date, with an audience of around two and a half thousand, and as I got mic-ed up I could see the auditorium through the wings. Suddenly I felt very small indeed, and the stage looked very big indeed. So I noticed it, accepted it, tried not to let it blow my skirt up, took a couple of breaths and walked out there, small as I was, planting my feet on the ground and occupying my own space. And it went OK. Actually, it went better than OK.

I know we shouldn't be feeling too sorry for him, what with everything he touches turning to gold 'n' all, but Richard Osman told me he's always felt like an impostor:

'That impostor syndrome thing is interesting, because obviously, I always felt that. I'm shy – an alpha introvert. I can command a room when I need to, but also I prefer to watch from the corner. Maybe because my eyesight is terrible, I couldn't fully engage. I've always had to be more of a spectator, because I'm a bit frightened of the world. I have a tank, which drains. Sometimes I just want to go home and watch the snooker, just be me, sit with my partner and the cat.'

Last time I just wanted to retreat home and be with the cat (but not the snooker) was just last week. I was about to give an after-dinner speech and a bunch of women came into the loos as I was finishing my wee. They were talking about the night, and one of them said: 'I just hope the speaker's not shit and we can hurry up and get pissed.' That was my opener sorted, but I did almost miss my own speech, waiting for them to leave before I could exit the cubicle.

There's a lot of 'fake it till you make it' type advice out there, which is exactly what I did during those ITV years, but honestly, I think that's bollocks; just because it rhymes doesn't make it self-help. It's one thing to style it out a bit now and again when you have to, but ultimately the bigger the gap between your real self and the self you are projecting, the more trouble you're in. Over my decades of coaching, a significant and common stumbling block I often witnessed was people's limiting beliefs, arising in part from comparing themselves with the glossy, external version of others – all exacerbated, of course, by social media. People sometimes say they feel they know me because of how genuine and vulnerable my Instagram reels are, but while certainly authentic, they're also the sixty seconds in any given twenty-four-hour period that I choose to share. A fragment of my real self.

Maya Angelou famously said: 'I have written eleven books, but each time I think, "Uh oh, they're going to find out now."' The problem with impostor syndrome is that no amount of brilliance will sort it. The better we get at things, the more likely it is we'll be surrounded by people who are also better at things. In comedy, we're always comparing ourselves to the person next up the greasy pole. One thing that helps is for successful, influential people to be more open about their insecurities, but that of course only works if they are willing to acknowledge that they have them. When we see people we respect struggling or admitting they don't know what they're doing, relief floods in. We start to feel very differently if we get a glimpse inside other people's heads, which is why I'm such a fan of group therapy. (Seriously, I can't get enough of it. My name's Cally and I'm a hot mess.)

French philosopher Michel de Montaigne said: 'There is as much difference between us and ourselves as there is between us and others.' Attempting to stay as close to one's authentic self as possible is a noble objective, but it's tricky when I am never me, and you are never you. We are constantly changing. Our opinions change as the world around us changes. Our interests and passions and circumstances change, and we're always morphing into the next thing. All we can really hope to do is have an awareness of those different versions of ourselves, and find a way to keep them connected so we don't become 'split'. Wanting to do whatever the next thing is as well as we can doesn't make us impostors. That makes us human.

If you are an impostor, rejoice! You're one of us, you do belong and it's a great club to be in. Lots of really cool people are in it. Tina Fey once said: 'The beauty of the impostor syndrome is you vacillate between extreme egomania and a complete feeling of: "I'm a fraud! Oh God, they're on to me! I'm a fraud!" So you just try to ride the egomania when it comes and enjoy it, and then slide through the idea of fraud.' Even David Bowie's 'Changes' was a nod to impostor syndrome.

Being a comedian is the closest I have come to belonging. I am not unique in saying that the very things that made me stick out in the real world help me fit in when it comes to comedy. Admittedly, I've traded in one male-dominated environment for another: only 27 per cent of the comedy circuit is female, which is still marginally better than the 20 per cent of board seats worldwide currently held by women. I sometimes MC all-female comedy nights, and never have I referred to it being a women-only line-up – on the basis that I don't suppose there's been an all-male comedy night in history where that fact was mentioned.

Growing up

After a childhood where I was at once too visible and not visible enough, I'm starting to find my place in the world. It's only taken me just over half a century. At fifty-six, I'm getting better at owning my space, knowing what I think, and valuing whoever the hell it is I am. I'm even getting better at calling things out. I was at airport security a couple of weeks ago and a man in the queue, gesturing in my direction, said to the woman he was with, in what I can only assume he thought was a quiet voice: 'I'm glad you don't do that to your hair.' They realised I'd heard, so we all had a laugh about it, and I said: 'I'm glad I don't share a bed with a man who says things like that!' And she said, 'He's my brother.' How we laughed.

I wish someone had told me when I was younger that no one knows what they're doing and everyone thinks they're going to be found out, although I probably wouldn't have heard them, because I'd have been so busy worrying about whether whatever I said in reply would be good enough. Here's my advice: stop comparing yourself to others and run your own race. (I could have just said that and left out all the rest, but they said each chapter had to be a few thousand words.) Each of us has the right to want to be ordinary enough to fit in and extraordinary enough to stand out. That's not too much to ask.

DO TRY THIS AT HOME

From impostor to disruptor

Developing a sense of self-worth, belonging and bravery is less about external factors and more about befriending your inner critic. Courage and confidence come from taking risks and working hand in hand with impostorism, not trying to ignore or eliminate it. Before deciding what to do about it, the first thing is to notice it. Ask yourself, what exactly is it you're thinking and believing about yourself? And what is happening as a result? No need to change a thing; just allow yourself to be curious rather than judgemental about what's going on. Is what you're worried about based on fact or fear? Unless it's 100 per cent factual, best waft it away like a fart. Then use the following technique by way of a circuit-breaker next time impostor syndrome kicks in and threatens to interfere with something you're going to do:

- Ask yourself: 'Who am I comparing myself to? And how is that helping or hindering me?'

- Now ask yourself: 'What is the evidence that I can do it, however big or small? What qualities do I have that mean I might be OK having a crack at this?'

- Next, pick one thing you're good at or enjoy that is unrelated to the thing about which you're feeling like an impostor – this could be walking the dog, being a friend, going to the cinema, anything at all – and focus on it. Notice how it feels thinking about that. Swim about in it a bit, and let it be the last thing you think about right before you do your impostor thing.

- Do the thing!

- After the thing, give yourself at least one compliment for what you just did, as if your favourite person was by your side saying it to you, making sure you put self-care over self-criticism.

A non-wanker's guide to networking

The first rule of belonging is not to go it alone. Following on from building your own spy network in Chapter 1, remind yourself where in your life you would like more allies, narrowing it down as specifically as possible. It might be in one area of your life – for example, work – or it might be to do with one specific aspect of that part of your life – like having to give presentations at work. Now write these four headings at the top of a piece of paper: 'strong', 'weak', 'lateral', 'dormant' (not doormat, as autocorrect tried to do for me). Next, list all the relevant allies and connections you can think of, putting each of them in one of these columns, before asking yourself these questions:

- STRONG: 'What more could I be doing with my strong connections?' Relationships can't just be transactional, and if you're only in touch with someone when you want something, then you're not doing it right. Make contact with people before you need something from them, and think about what you're willing or able to do for them too.

- **WEAK**: 'Which of my weak connections can be made stronger? How?' And if there are any that can't, which there will be, stop worrying about them and put your energies elsewhere. Give it up.

- **DORMANT**: 'Who have I lost touch with?' This is the quickest and most often forgotten-about way to bolster your wing people: identify the people you haven't kept up with, but you wish you had. What small, daily steps can you take to breathe life back into this part of your network?

- **LATERAL**: 'Who else might I meet?' A good network isn't the people you know, it's the people you don't know yet. Every conversation you have is useful, whether or not it leads to anything concrete or bolsters your network. It might not open a door, but each serendipitous connection you make at least opens a bit of your mind.

> *'Be kind, for everyone you meet is fighting a hard battle.'*

This quote is sometimes attributed to Plato and sometimes to Philo (and even to people not beginning with 'P' and ending in 'o'). Whoever said it, I would like to add to it: 'and remember to be kind to yourself'. Take a look at this list:

kind

good listener

hard worker

loving

honest

intelligent

resilient

creative

loyal

able to connect

Write down a minimum of three of these ten things that apply to you; if you have more than three, great. Now think about yourself in relation to each quality you have picked. How does it feel taking a moment to notice it? How and why do you value this quality in others? And in yourself?

You can take this idea a step further. Gratitude journaling is widely recognised as one of the few quick-fix self-help techniques that actually works. It helps retrain our cynical modern-day brains to filter in the positive, rather than being eclipsed by the negative. Each night, I do a twist on traditional gratitude journaling (writing down three things, however small, for which you're grateful at the end of each day). After I've written my three grateful things, I write three things I like about myself, and then lastly three things I'm proud of having done that day. Your own struggle may be much harder than you realise; after all, you have nothing to compare it to. So be kind.

LAST WORDS

The other thing that helps when you're stressing about impostorism, or indeed about anything, is taking a step back and allowing yourself to have a sense of humour about it. Here's a joke, picked by Laura Lexx when she came on the podcast:

> 'A man walks into a bar with a huge lizard on his shoulder, and says to the barman: "I'll have a pint for me and a pint for my mate, Tiny."
> The barman pours the pints and sets them down, and says: "Look, mate, I've just got to ask – why have you called that enormous thing Tiny?"
> And the bloke says: "Because it's my newt."'

The world's not short of white men talking to each other, but I do love the *Chatabix* podcast, and I had its hosts, David Earl and Joe Wilkinson, on the podcast. David's life advice was:

> 'No one knows what they're doing. I wish I'd known that earlier. I thought everyone knew what they were doing.'

And a last bit of advice, this time from Viv Groskop:

> 'Everybody else has not got this. We all think we're missing a trick and there's some secret to things that we haven't found out yet or other people are living some amazing life that is somehow eluding us. Nobody has really got the life that you want, and nobody has got the life that you think that they have. So stop looking at them and just look at yourself; figure it out and do what you need to do.'

3
MAKE THE EDIT

GETTING YOUR VOICE HEARD

'We've learned that quiet isn't always peace
and the norms and notions of what just is
isn't always justice.'
Amanda Gorman

voice
/vɔɪs/
noun

1. the sound or sounds produced through the mouth by a person speaking or singing
   'we could hear voices in the next room'
2. a particular attitude, opinion or feeling that is expressed; a feeling or an opinion that you become aware of inside yourself
   'the voice of reason/sanity/conscience'

Source: https://www.oxfordlearnersdictionaries.com/definition/american_english/voice_1

> Female Barbary macaques are noisy fuckers (literally). They make a racket during sex for two reasons: to attract *other* potential mates, and to make their partners climax more quickly so they can go find more. Go, Barbary macaque! She has shit to do!

Panel show panic

I got my first panel show booking, an episode of *QI*, when I was relatively new to stand-up, about a year in. After the initial excitement of the invite, the terror set in. I was sure it was too early. I just wasn't ready. I was going to get found out. My agent at the time explained that you couldn't just say no to these things and expect to be asked back next time. It was shit or bust, and I needed to say yes. I panicked. I called some people. I watched loads of old episodes of *QI* on iPlayer. I panicked some more. Then I said yes, and the panic really took hold. Then I was given some brilliant advice by *QI*'s creator John Lloyd: 'There are five panellists on set. You are the fifth. You don't need to be Alan or Sandi or either of the others – all of their seats are already taken. The only person whose voice *QI* viewers have yet to hear is yours. All you need to do is be your fifth of the pie. Don't wait to have the cleverest or the funniest thing to say. Get your voice heard from the start and keep being heard. Make sure you make the edit.'

'Make the edit' is something I want women everywhere to hear. Quite simply, if you don't use your voice, there is no chance it can be heard, and stand-up has been significant in helping me find mine. People sometimes say comedians are brave. We are not. Firefighters are brave. Underwater welders are brave. Eating a curry before going to Pilates is brave. I am the opposite of brave. I'm the sort of person who is so scared of everything, I pretend to be scared of nothing. I've jumped out of planes and off bridges. I've ridden motorbikes. I've posted a no-make-up selfie on Instagram, with only a little bit of make-up. I've taken toddlers on long-haul flights. I'm the sort of person who, after giving birth, genuinely apologised for getting blood on the floor. I'm the sort of person who'll go onstage, night in, night out, because I find the twenty-three hours when I'm not onstage really difficult. Tonight I'm doing an after-dinner speech, and I feel nervous – not so much about the speech as about the dinner. Business dinners with people I don't know hold about as much appeal for me as a smear test, albeit more dignified and with the plan to keep my pants on.

Do take it personally

It's ironic that the thing that got me into stand-up was a trip to Cannes, when with the benefit of hindsight I realise how much I hated those twice-yearly trips to Cannes. (It *is* hard being me, thanks for noticing.) A few years have passed since the last time I had a boss or a place on anyone's payroll, and that time and space has given rise to the realisation that those trips took one hell of a toll. I think I understand why. I never liked the networking bit, and I found the whole being 'on' 24/7 thing soul-destroying. You would have had no clue as to my inner awkwardness and growing existential despair, because I was great at masking, which I did in the form of radical overcompensation. I didn't just make the edit; I *was* the edit. I remember regaling Amy Poehler over dinner with a tale of shitting myself on a transatlantic flight (you'll have to wait until Chapter 9 for the full story). I made a Hollywood A-lister piss herself at a story of me shitting myself. I was a work-dinner rock star. Until I got back to my hotel room and felt empty and lonely and full of self-doubt – and yes, full of shit. I look back on those years now and realise how damaging they were, because the gap between how I was feeling and what I was doing was immense. It's not just about making the edit, it's about making the edit healthily and authentically. And that takes a lot of work.

You'd be forgiven for thinking, given what I do for a living, that it's easy to make myself heard, and in some ways, like when I'm onstage or on social media, it is. But I am not blessed with the unwavering self-confidence of an ex-Etonian. I've spent most of my life sure I was an extrovert, not least because everyone told me I was an extrovert. I have been Myers-Briggsed (not a euphemism) on three separate occasions, and each time I came out as E for Extrovert. If you're not familiar with Myers-Briggs, then congratulations: you probably didn't have an office job in the nineties/noughties, and therefore avoided being personality-tested up the wazoo.

The Myers-Briggs Type Indicator is a psychometric personality types test which scores you according to four categories: introversion or extroversion, sensing or intuition, thinking or feeling, and judging or perceiving. You end up with a four-letter test result telling you which of the sixteen possible personality types you are, and each time I came out as ENTJ - Extrovert Intuitive Thinking Judging. Not the snappiest Tinder bio. However, I have relatively recently discovered that I am actually an extroverted introvert.

I always thought extroverts and introverts were at opposite ends of the scale, but it turns out that many people fall on the continuum between introversion and extroversion - we are ambiverts! Extroverted introverts or introverted extroverts, we flex to the situation, sometimes preferring an evening alone, sometimes to be the life of the party. I'm an extroverted introvert: we're shy, we're cocky, we're all over the place. Ambiverts are highly adaptable and flexible, which is odd, as generally I am rigid and inflexible (just look at my yoga poses).

Putting the effort into effortless

It takes a lot of effort to make anything look effortless. Making the edit involves stamina; it involves keeping on keeping on. If you watch a herd of giraffes rushing across a sweep of savanna, you'll be hard-pushed to spot the pregnant one. (That's if you're at home watching it on the telly; if you're there watching it live, there'll likely be other things to be thinking about.) The survival of the species depends upon the pregnant giraffes keeping up, which is no mean feat. By the last weeks of her nearly fifteen-month pregnancy, a female giraffe has gained hundreds of pounds – her foetus alone weighs up to 150 pounds. Each of mine weighed nearly ten pounds, and I'm still banging on about it nearly three decades later. And yet pregnant giraffes run as fast as non-pregnant ones in order to keep predators from targeting them as easy prey. As Ginger Rogers said: 'I did everything Fred did, backwards and in high heels.' Oh, and giraffes give birth standing up; the baby giraffe drops head-first on to the ground from a height of almost two metres. How about that for an entrance into the world?

Public speaking or death

I found boardroom life and business trips increasingly unbearable, but the bits I did like were the speeches, interviews and panels. That was very much my time to shine, but it hadn't always been that way. If you'd told me twenty years ago that I'd be making a living out of speaking in public, I would have bet my home that you were wrong. I was properly averse to giving any kind of presentation in rooms with more than a handful of people in them.

Jerry Seinfeld once said: 'According to most studies, people's number one fear is public speaking. Number two is death.

Death is number two. Does that sound right? This means to the average person, if you go to a funeral, you're better off in the casket than doing the eulogy.'

Apparently Martin Luther King Jr got a C+ in public speaking when he was at school. I'm not sure what's more surprising: his grade, or the fact that they taught public speaking at his school. At my school, we didn't even learn our times tables (but we did learn sex education from a BBC Schools video while our teacher said nothing and ate a Bakewell tart).

The biggest fear for a comedian or anyone doing a speech is dying onstage, and if you're doing your first stand-up gig at forty-five, you're already a bit closer to dying than most. I couldn't have done stand-up in my twenties, partly because I didn't have a clue what my voice was, and partly because of my conviction that I was incapable of public speaking. It's not just patriarchal society but also physiology that puts women at a disadvantage in terms of making ourselves heard. On average, women speak at a higher pitch than men, about an octave higher, and in human society we have assigned social characteristics to the pitches of voices. Studies have found, for example, that we are more likely to vote for political candidates with lower-pitched voices. There are stories of female broadcasters being taught to speak in a lower register. 'A woman without bass registers in her voice would find it very hard to get on in broadcasting unless she was exceptionally beautiful,' news anchor Jon Snow once said. Christ. I'm not exceptionally beautiful, but I do have a low voice, and I wonder if that has unwittingly helped me in the male-dominated circles I have inhabited since childhood. Not that my voice was particularly low in childhood; life was hard enough being overweight, bespectacled and ginger without sounding like Tom Jones.

Tom Read-Wilson – 'Celebrate your idiosyncrasies. Don't even think about augmenting them, just celebrate them, because if you celebrate them, other people will, and also people tend to fall in love with them. I mean [...] certainly for me, the people that I'm most attracted to, I'm attracted to those idiosyncrasies that, no doubt at some stage, they would have considered masking. And to me, they're always, always the most appealing parts.'

A recent study shows that deeper male voices in primates may have evolved as a way for males to drive off competitors in large groups that favoured polygyny – mating systems where some males have multiple mates.[5] Deeper male voices help fend off the competition without having to engage in fighting by making males *sound* bigger. Turns out one of my exes was a polygnist. He should have said. I just thought he was a cheating bastard.

Agency

Alex Bell, *QI* elf – 'Commit to the bit. I have a lot of passions and interests and I like to delve deep into things, and if I'm creating things I like to really go hard. And whether it's in my work life or my personal life, I never hold back. It's easy to think people won't be as into it as you, but actually people always appreciate it more than you think.'

Making the edit is not just about voice, it's about agency. No one likes to be talked over, misunderstood or ignored. I mentioned on page 27 that many of the comments I received in response to my 'what makes you feel invisible?' post related to medical situations. One woman posted about her GP diagnosing her with tension headaches after several visits during which she had expressed her concern about various symptoms that were becoming more and more pronounced.

She felt overlooked and belittled until she had her 'tension headache' (brain tumour) removed in emergency surgery a couple of months later. Many women shared experiences that they'd had while they were giving birth, like being called the wrong name, having their birth plans and wishes overruled or ignored, or being talked over 'like a piece of meat'. One woman said she had been in labour for the best part of forty-eight hours, 'naked, tired, scared', while the midwife talked over her to her (then) husband, who's an actor, about what shows he'd been in and whether he could help her daughter who was in drama club get on the telly. Apparently, the same midwife later told her that Katie Price had been in the week before and had 'pushed like a good 'un', and she could do with taking a leaf out of her book.

Then there were the medical professionals who had experienced invisibility themselves. One clinical nurse and cancer specialist said she attends a weekly multidisciplinary meeting where a group of specialists in the area she works in all meet and discuss patient cases (consultants, histopathologists, radiologists, surgeons), and that recently the consultant chairing the meeting in which she happened to be the only woman had said: 'Well, you've got seven expert opinions in the room.'

'Eight,' she pointed out.

Then there was the comment from a woman who called out an electrician because her hall light kept flashing on and off, and he asked her if she was sure she wasn't just blinking. I know that one's not medical. It's just too incredible not to share.

When to speak out

Members of any marginalised group get used to being talked over, undermined and having others take credit for our ideas.

Women of all ages get used to having our appearance commented on, being mistaken for someone without authority, and having our competence questioned. Microaggressions are comments or actions that reflect bias, and despite the 'micro' in their name, they are not subtle or small. Far from being micro, their impact is large and long-lasting. It's a fact that women face more microaggressions than men. We are twice as likely, for example, to be interrupted or to have our emotional state commented on. This is where self-shielding comes in, the antithesis to making the edit – adjusting the way we look or act in an effort to protect ourselves, to make it stop. We choose not to speak up in order to avoid seeming difficult or aggressive. The stress caused by self-shielding cuts deep: we burn out, we leave jobs, or both.

There was a survey in 2016 called 'Elephant in the Valley',[6] which looked at the challenges of being a woman in Silicon Valley. The survey set out to record the frequency of such phenomena as interview questions about marital status and family planning, unwanted sexual advances, or demeaning comments from male colleagues and clients. It aimed to 'take the temperature' of what women experience in tech. Of the women who responded to the survey:

> 84 per cent had been told they were too aggressive (with half hearing that on multiple occasions)
>
> 66 per cent had been excluded from key social/networking opportunities because of their gender
>
> 90 per cent had witnessed sexist behaviour at company offsites and/or industry conferences
>
> 88 per cent had experienced clients/colleagues address questions to male peers that should have been addressed to them – and of those who reported this kind of experience, 56 per cent said this happened on a monthly basis

75 per cent had been asked about family life, marital status and children in interviews

60 per cent reported unwanted sexual advances

Tech, like boardrooms and the comedy industry, sees women's agency and voices compromised. The movie business is another. Still. In 2019, just 28 per cent of speaking roles in Hollywood movies were for women, and there was a 50 per cent pass rate for the Bechdel test (where two named female characters talk to each other about something other than a man). We weren't chaining ourselves to railings and burning our bras for this bollocks still to be going on. The burden is not on women to fix these problems. It's incumbent upon all of us, regardless of gender, when we see something, to say something.

Edith Bowman – 'Don't wait on anybody else giving you the opportunity, just make your own.'

Mansplaining the gender pay gap

Not long ago, I wrote a social media post in which I said that if I had a pound for every time a man mansplained to me on a post where I mention mansplaining why it's not OK to say 'mansplaining' I'd single-handedly be able to close the gender pay gap. In response, I got a slew of mansplanations about the fact that there *is* no gender pay gap. And so, like a hair advert of old, here comes the science bit.

Employers with 250 or more workers are legally obliged to submit gender pay gap information annually. So it's not subjective; the statistics exist. The latest information tells us that women in the UK work for free for nearly two months of each year. According to TUC pay analysis, there was a gender pay difference of 14.3 per cent in 2024.[7] The national average property price is equivalent to 6.2 times the wage of a man and 7.3 times the pay of a woman. Women between the ages of fifty and fifty-nine have the largest pay disparity with men of the same age, at 19.7 per cent, and even in fields where women predominate, like education, there remains a large salary disparity of over 21 per cent. There are various myths about why women earn less – like the fact they work fewer hours – but none of them are true, if you look at like-for-like disparities.

The campaign group Pregnant Then Screwed (I'd never heard of them until I started researching this, and I'm a little bit in love with them now) drew my attention to a TUC study that revealed that in 2023, mothers made, on average, 24 per cent less per hour than fathers.[8] At the current rate, it will take until 2044 for the gender pay gap to close. Just 40 per cent of financial assets will be in women's hands by 2030. The gender pay gap is not a women's issue, but an economic issue, and society as a whole is paying the price.

It's not what you know . . .

Baroness Ayesha Hazarika – 'Be brave, be braver than you think you can be. Because the more brave you are, the more amazing things you achieve. And I think being brave can be simple things like asking for things and putting yourself out there. I think that for so many women, the penny drops when we're in our late thirties, early forties. The tragedy for women is this happens so much later than it does for our male counterparts. And just as we're starting to hit our stride and get brave, the menopause hits.'

Addressing the imbalance, whether in terms of pay, status, treatment or airtime, isn't about confrontation or putting yourself at risk. A good approach is to first take a beat in which to notice that something isn't OK; not colluding in or normalising something unacceptable, even internally, matters. A second step is to set about identifying allies. Having an advocate can make a big difference, and someone needs to speak up, whether or not that's you. If we do decide to say something, the received wisdom is that that may make us feel more empowered and in control, with the added benefit that it can also change other people's behaviours.

I look back at many of the times when I felt compromised yet stayed silent in boardrooms and business situations – and it still happens to me in comedy, broadcasting and keynote speaking. My would've/could've/should've self is always full of it the next day in the shower. But it can be almost impossible to take on a tricky situation on one's own. Nor should we be expected to.

We shouldn't have to be scared, but we should be willing to get a bit uncomfortable in order to make the edit. In my experience, if we're feeling a bit too comfortable, then something probably isn't working as well as it might. Making the edit involves retraining our primal brains not to walk away from discomfort, but to walk squarely towards it.

Crowd-pleasing and communication

Research tells us that a woman will wait until she has 100 per cent of the attributes for a job before she applies. That figure for a man is 60 per cent. It's similar when it comes to getting our voices heard; there is a temptation to think that we should wait until we have something 100 per cent worth saying. What makes us uncomfortable about saying things is a fear of looking stupid – or, worse yet, of not being liked. As a female comedian, when you get onstage, it's not just that you have to be funny (a prerequisite for all comedians, quite reasonably) but also that you have to be liked.

First impressions are important. What is easily overlooked is the fact that the content of what we say makes little difference in those first few seconds. Only 7 per cent of an immediate first impression is based on what we say; a whopping 93 per cent is based on non-verbal stuff and *how* we say it:

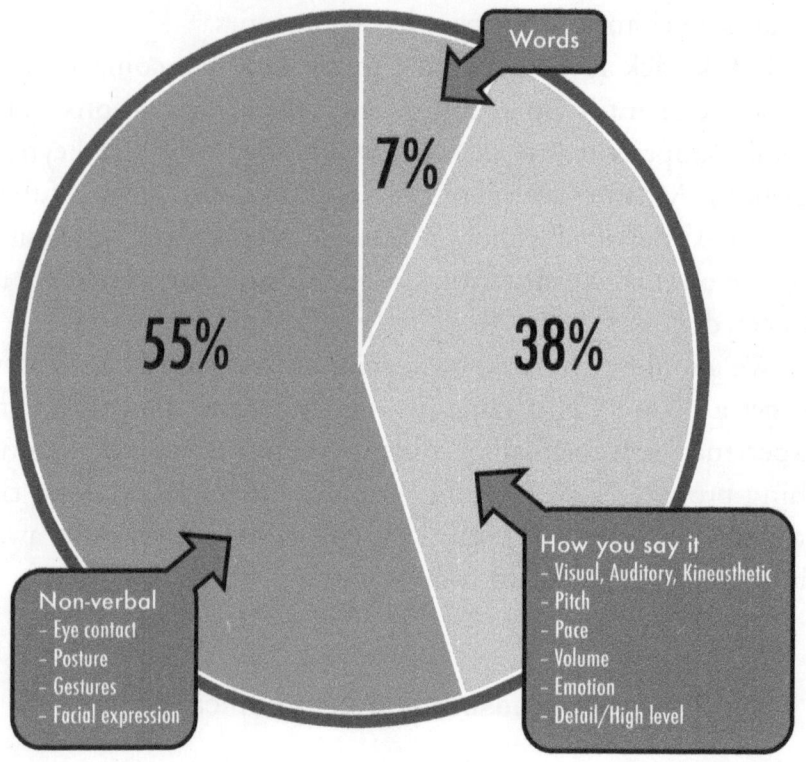

This balance swiftly changes over those first few minutes to a point where what we say becomes responsible for more than 50 per cent of the other person's impression of us. But that still leaves our words barely in the majority over non-verbal communication, like body language, gestures, tone and pace. And when did a marginal majority of just over 50 per cent ever cause a problem for anyone?

I've never been a fan of a pie chart, but this one could have saved me a few decades of pain in my long-standing battle with my fear of public speaking. In the early noughties, I nearly left my first board-level job at ITV when I was told I was going to have to present to more than a thousand people on the stage of a West End cinema. It was an all-company presentation with a famous news anchor hosting, and when I was told I was going to be a part of it, death wouldn't have seemed like such a bad alternative. I took a couple of days' holiday – not to go to Dignitas, but to put myself on a stealth presentation skills course. It didn't occur to me to tell anyone, let alone ask them to pay for it. Fast-forward a couple of decades, and I make a living out of words – sometimes written, more often spoken. So, what changed? It wasn't a miracle course, but there was a 'wow' moment for me, which was simply focusing less on *what* I was going to say and more on *how* I was going to say it. As Billy Connolly famously said: 'A good comedian is a funny person saying things, not a person saying funny things.'

When you get out of the 'what' and into the 'how', everything changes. Hopefully the words I say as a speaker or comedian resonate, but how I say them and the person the audience take me to be is what sticks. You need to work out what you're going to say, of course, but no one knows what you were *planning* to say apart from you. One reason why we think we're the only ones with our shit not together is that ours is the only inner monologue we can hear. We take others at face value, and whatever vibe they're giving off, we buy it. But what's easy to forget is that they're doing the same with us. 'The illusion of transparency' is the name psychologists give to the idea that our feelings are written all over our faces, but it turns out that's usually not the case. For most people, there is a disconnect between how we feel and how we are perceived. We can never fully grasp, much less control, how others see us – so why get into a right old flap trying?

We have all the freedom in the world when it comes to determining how we choose to communicate, and there have been trailblazing women at the forefront of communication innovation for decades. Dr Helen Fry told me about women in World War One knitting coded messages into jumpers and throwing them over the fence for waiting Allied forces to decipher. My knitting's so crap I'd have probably knitted, 'Hi, my name's Cally and I'm a spy,' and messed it up for everyone. To make the edit in modern-day scenarios, something more immediate than knitting our way out may be required.

Confessions of a public speaker

The benefit of having learned to present the hard way is that I know that presentation skills are not just for people giving presentations; they can help anyone make an impact and get their voice heard. Coming from a family of teachers, if there was one thing I was sure I was never going to do it was teach. Motivational speaking is much like teaching, only instead of kids who may or may not want to learn, you've got business executives who may or may not want to stay sober long enough to listen. Me finding my own voice onstage directly correlates with being better equipped to occupy my own space in everyday situations.

There are a few principles that apply to getting your message across in whatever scenario. The first is, keep it simple. Churchill said: 'Today I am giving a long speech because I didn't have time to prepare a short one.' When I worked for big corporations, I cannot tell you the amount of faff involved in speeches getting written and delivered. Teams of people would write and rewrite content; design teams would create slides. When I jumped off the corporate hamster wheel and did my first solo speaker gig, I thought perhaps there was a reason it had all been that complicated, a reason I had missed. Turns out, there was no reason. Nowadays I go by this: 'Say what you're going to say. Say it. Say what you said.' And if I use slides, they're images only; a visual accompaniment to keep it interesting. No pie charts! (Apart from the one on page 86. Sorry about that.)

That's not to say I don't prepare. I *really* prepare. It's only when I'm overprepared that I can forget about the speech and know I'll be OK. As Mark Twain said: 'It usually takes me more than three weeks to prepare a good impromptu speech.' I'm a big fan of an 'ad fib' – bits that seem off-the-cuff but are tried and tested, and as close as you can get to bullet-proof.

Then there's thinking about one's audience. It's easy to get so wrapped up in what we want to say that we forget that all that really matters is the message landing. It's very tempting to showboat our own knowledge, but what really matters is what the other party needs to hear. We need to mind the gap between our world and other people's worlds, because the gap will inevitably be bigger than we think.

Vulnerability and resilience

Perhaps most importantly of all, making the edit involves vulnerability, which is easier said than done when you're dead scared of falling off the stage or looking like a bit of a twat. Remember the wise words of Annie Lennox: 'It's understandable that we feel fear. Fear paralyses you – fear of flying, fear of the future, fear of leaving a rubbish marriage, fear of public speaking, or whatever it is.'

I hit upon the power of vulnerability in getting your voice heard by mistake. I'd been booked to speak at a conference back when I still had my boardroom job – there were going to be a couple of thousand people in the audience, and several of my team and colleagues would be there too. I'd had some bad news the night before and had spent the night crying into my pillow. I managed to get suited and booted the next morning, but I wasn't sure I was going to manage to style it out onstage. When I got up to speak, I found myself starting by telling the audience that while I might look the part, I wasn't feeling it, and that I wasn't sure I could get through an hour's speech without falling apart, but I'd do my best. I then did a perfectly good speech, wishing all the while I'd never said anything. Afterwards, I'd never had such a positive response, including from members of my team, many of whom I had known for years. Turns out vulnerability and authenticity onstage are inviting and compelling.

I was recently the closing speaker at a showcase and, as it happened, the only female speaker of the day. The other speakers had incredible stories, one and all – taking on the Taliban, climbing Everest, winning Olympic medals (not all the same bloke) – the overarching theme in each case being 'overcoming adversity in order to do great things'. *Look how great I am at what I do! You can be great too!* My approach is more, *I'm making it up as I go along! You can too! I've no idea what I'm doing half the time! If I can, anyone can!* And guess what? The audience gave a collective sigh of relief, lapping it up.

Talking of Olympians, I did an event with the Olympic gymnast Matt Whitlock a few months ago, and he was fantastic. There was a pommel horse onstage, and he did his thing on it before speaking (this is why I sometimes use PowerPoint, in lieu of a pommel horse). I'd been sitting next to him in the green room, and I'd noticed a Tupperware tub under his seat. I remember thinking how nice it was to learn that I had something in common with an Olympian, because I always bring a snack, too! It was gymnasts' chalk for his pommel-horsing, as it turned out. Not Parmesan.

Your way or the highway

Viv Groskop's book *I Laughed, I Cried*, about performing 100 gigs on 100 consecutive nights in the early 2010s, was something of a bible for me, helping me both in terms of getting into stand-up and also keeping doing it once I'd started. Viv is a public-speaking guru, author of *How to Own the Room: Women and the Art of Brilliant Speaking* and host of the *How to Own the Room* podcast. She and I talked about what she's learned from interviewing the likes of Hillary Clinton, Margaret Atwood, Professor Mary Beard and Julie Andrews. She told me:

> There's no way to be you that someone else can copy; you can only do that yourself. And that's not just an artistic thing that's important for stand-up [and] performance; [it] is true [in] any walk of life. And it's especially true if you're trying to be in a leadership role. Or if you're the first or the only – whether you're a woman or you're somebody who doesn't look like the sort of person who occupies that role – only you can do it like you. It's something that artists have to do all the time: to sort of have the guts to make it up as you go along, to try something new, to get it wrong. So it's exploring how you do that.

I asked her if there are practical tips she's picked up. She told me:

> How many slides is too many slides? Should you have slides at all? Does Hillary Clinton use note cards? Or does she use an auto cue? How does she deflect a question that she doesn't want to be asked? A million questions. People who really have done a lot of public speaking have certain go-tos that they've learned to rely on. And often those are pretty dependent on them as a person. So it might be that you're better when you're underprepared [but] other

people need to massively over prepare. Some people want to have cue cards, some people want to have nothing. Some people want to have it memorised. It's tempting to want to check in with the teacher: did I do this right? And the answer is, well, you're prepared for it if it feels right to you.

When to shut up

Making the edit is about knowing when and how to talk, and also when to be still and listen. Plato said: 'A wise man speaks because he has something to say, a fool speaks because he has to say something.' I reckon he'd be OK with us applying that to women too. Silence doesn't mean there's nothing to say or that a situation is awkward. People have different paces of processing and delivering information, and the breaks in conversation give us a chance to turn up and to listen – and that's listening to learn, rather than listening to respond.

One of the things people are most fearful of when it comes to public speaking is forgetting what they are going to say, imagining an anxiety-dream silence as they try to regain their thread. Actually, silence onstage is powerful. Speakers who can confidently hold silence in a room have instant gravitas. When you first start out in stand-up, you usually know exactly why you had a stinker of a gig – bad jokes, nerves, inability to get off script, often all three. As time goes on, it gets harder to pin down the reason. The best way to describe a gig not quite going right for me now is that it's like playing a record at the wrong speed, and I almost always put it down to a failure to 'turn up', to fully inhabit the moment and live in the room at the exclusion of all else. The difference between an OK gig and a good gig often lies in the first couple of seconds onstage;

whether I race over to the microphone and crack out a joke, eager to convince the audience I've got this, or instead take a moment to arrive, to look at the room, at the audience, to let them look at me, before the first word.

Women aren't funny

A cornucopia of misconceptions and assumptions exists about female communication, our voices sometimes judged before we have even said a word. Something that gets my dander up is the trope that women aren't funny. A few weeks ago, I'd got onstage at a gig and before I'd even said a word, a bloke shouted: 'It's a shame women aren't funny!'

So I asked him, 'Why do you think women aren't funny?'

And he said, 'Because you just do crap jokes about periods and stuff.'

And I said, 'I can't believe that you think I'm young enough to have periods.'

Ah, periods. I remember them. Bit of nostalgia comedy – don't mind if I do.

I love the saying: 'Be yourself, everyone else is taken.' If I think about invisibility and how it affected me as I performed my *Super Cally Fragile Lipstick* show in what was to become my annus horribilis (more on that soon), I wanted to disappear from my corporate working life entirely and never be seen again. But really the problem was more existential and central in that I had become invisible to myself. It sounds a bit yurt and joss sticks, but I'd lost my relationship with myself – and if there's one thing you need in order to make the edit, it's a sense of what's really going on with you. Nothing's funny about a glossy, look-how-great-I-am persona on a comedy stage. Comedy is all about the cracks in the mask. We studiously curate which cracks we do and don't reveal (not *those* kinds of cracks, grow up), but it does help to know one's own cracks to begin with.

Making the edit means taking responsibility for our lives, with the added bonus that by practising more agency, we have a greater impact on the lives of others. There's plenty that gets in the way of making the edit, without us getting in our own way too. We don't have to wait until we have the perfect thing to say in order to be part of the conversation, and we don't need to be too accommodating either. Higher-agency people will speak out or take action if they are 80 per cent sure. We don't need to over-deliberate before acting or speaking, and we can always reassess later if needed. Making the edit is about celebrating difference but being ourselves.

My daughter lives in Madrid. I'm back today from a trip over there to see her, and last night we watched flamenco dancing. The dancer was a woman in midlife, the central presence, sharing the stage intermittently with a young dance partner and three male band members who sat behind her. All eyes were on the female dancer, and the power was all hers. She made the edit with her feminist, voiceless declaration of strength, resilience and empowerment; of love and of struggle. I'm a shit dancer, as you'll see if ever I get to do *Strictly*, but comedy is my flamenco. It took trading years of sitting in edit suites in favour of becoming a clown before I learned how to make the edit, my way. Turns out, louder is not always better; it's all about being heard.

DO TRY THIS AT HOME

Diving into difficult conversations

One thing I was repeatedly asked to do in my executive coaching days was to help address and challenge work cultures where people – even those at the very top – were reluctant to give honest feedback to each other. The principles of having difficult conversations are really simple. Putting them into practice can be somewhat harder – but it's doable.

> Work out what it is you'd like to say, if you really could say whatever you like, and write it down.
>
> Now ask yourself, what's the closest version of this you can actually say? This is about diplomacy, not dilution. Hold yourself to account and keep to the core message.
>
> What's the simplest/clearest iteration of this? Write it down.
>
> When are you going to say it? Commit to a date, and make sure it's soon. Give yourself a difficult conversation deadline.
>
> Say it, avoiding phrases like 'I'm sorry it's taken me a while to come back to you' or 'I'm afraid I can't do that' (each time you use one, you can put a pound in the feminist jar and give it to charity), replacing them with things like 'Thanks for bearing with me' or 'That's not going to be possible for me'.

Don't unsay it. You speak. Then wait, while others respond.

And then listen – *really* listen, remembering to listen to learn before you listen to respond.

Calling out unacceptable bollocks

When it comes to calling people out for poor behaviour or unacceptable attitudes, you can try any of the below, whether you're speaking up on your own behalf or advocating for someone else:

> State the facts. If someone assumes you're not qualified, tell them your job title.
>
> Explain the impact of the behaviour, saying, 'This is how I feel,' rather than 'This is how you make me feel.' No one can argue with how you feel, because it's how you feel.
>
> Ask a question that pushes the other person to reflect on what happened and their thinking. Something like: 'What makes you say that?'
>
> In books, films and TV shows, when a character acknowledges the audience, it's known as breaking the fourth wall. You can do this in real life, by 'breaking character' and acknowledging that you're actually finding it hard to speak out. For example: 'I don't find conversations like this easy, but there's something I want to say . . .'
>
> Aim to be appropriately assertive, which is not the same as being confrontational or aggressive. Being

aggressive means ignoring the other party's needs, and being passive means ignoring your own needs. You're hitting the right spot when you're thinking about your own needs and the needs of others.

Appearing calm helps get a message across (which doesn't mean you need to be *feeling* calm). Take a beat to notice what's going on for you and how you're feeling. Noticing it and giving yourself permission to feel it might change the temperature for you.

Stress-busting

Most stress comes from things we can't control, things that will never happen, or both. So, visualise success. Do what professional athletes do (not the pommel-horsing bit) and spend some time beforehand picturing yourself presenting well, or the difficult conversation going to plan. If you get into the habit of challenging unhelpful thoughts, over time you can succeed in changing them into more positive ones. It's not a bad idea to believe in humanity in general, in my experience, and in your audience's goodwill. Most people want you to succeed, and they want to be interested and entertained. People who want to watch people screw up can fill their boots with reality TV and TikTok, leaving you free to say what you want to say, with a fair chance it will go your way.

LAST WORDS

My final presentation tip is to open and close with a bang. They say start with your second-best joke and end with your best joke, so I'm going to end this chapter with a banger from Joan Rivers, as told by Shazia Mirza:

> 'Women, stop getting an education. You want to educate yourself? You want to read books? Fuck all that. No man has ever put his hand up a woman's skirt looking for a library card.'

We've had an abundance of life advice that's apt for making the edit, from an abundance of incredible women. When Philippa Perry came on the podcast, she quoted Susan Jeffers:

> 'Accept yourself exactly where you are. You are good enough exactly how you are and where you are, and who you are is a loving and powerful human being, who is learning and growing every step of the way.'

And no one embodies getting out of your own way better than Bryony Gordon:

> 'Just do you, babe. Stop dismissing yourself. Stop dismissing your feelings. Stop dismissing your wants, your needs. Like, come on, babes!'

And, with that, it's a wrap.

4
THIS TOO SHALL PASS

LEANING INTO TRICKY EMOTIONS

'We need never be ashamed of our tears.'
Charles Dickens,
Great Expectations

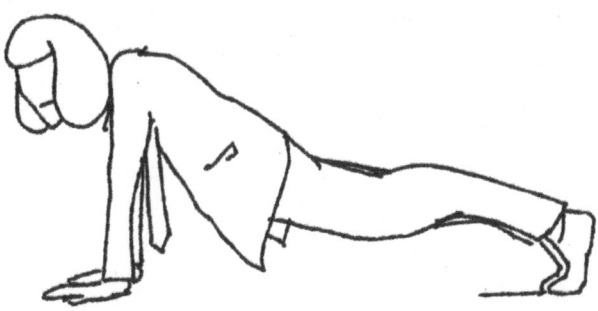

emotion

/ɪˈməʊʃn/

noun

a strong feeling (such as love, anger, joy, hate, or fear)
'he spoke with great emotion'
'the defendant showed/displayed no emotion when the verdict was read'

Source: https://www.britannica.com/dictionary/emotion

> The expression 'crocodile tears' comes from the mysterious tendency of crocodiles to release tears as they eat (one of the few occasions I tend *not* to cry). Elephants have been observed having the capacity to feel empathy and need time to process loss. Elephants are better than my last two boyfriends.

Leaning into sadness

I used to be a secret crier; now, it's more of a hobby. Here are some things that make me cry:

a sad song coming on at Pilates

old people looking happy together

old people looking unhappy alone

an old man I saw today with big ears

bagpipes

when my Sainsbury's Local moved the aisles around and I couldn't find the ice cream

The Repair Shop

my son sending me a picture of an animal he's looking after at work (even the not-cute ones)

hanging up the washing in my daughter's room since she's long left home

smells that remind me of things (despite brain fog mainly obscuring what they remind me of)

the news

when I see a bee, because there aren't enough bees

I don't just cry at the cry-y bits of telly and films; I cry at the people on *Gogglebox* watching the cry-y bits of telly and films. Happy crying, sad crying, ugly crying – I'm in. I also do pre-emptive crying: about my parents' mortality, my dog's mortality, my own mortality – anyone's mortality, really, apart from that of Trump, Weinstein, et al. Someone I met recently told me they cry because their partner is so incredible and they feel so grateful. I was torn between being happy for them and being sick in my mouth.

Western culture tends to be quite sadness-avoidant. We find it uncomfortable. God forbid when someone asks you how you are, you actually tell them. Anyone who's lost someone close will know that after the first flurry of support, it gets mentioned less and less until it recedes into let's-crack-on-and-not-mention-it obscurity. As Richard Coles, who lost his partner David when he was just forty-three, explains:

> The weird thing is that everybody wants you to be fine, because grief is embarrassing, and bereavement is awkward. And embarrassment is such a powerful motive in our interactions if you're an English person. So everybody wants you to be better. They sort of frame the question 'How you doing?' in such a way as to invite the response: 'Fine, thank you.' But it's not fine. If you were to see grief as sort of linear, [then] on Tuesday you'll be angry, on Wednesday you'll be accepting. It doesn't work that way. It's much more landscape than that. You walk around, and sometimes you're in a valley, and sometimes you're up a hill. You just accumulate experience of them not being alive.

I've not encountered as much death as most people my age. Each of my four grandparents lived to their late nineties, with my paternal grandfather making it to just shy of 100; my mum and dad are still going strong in their eighties. Losing my paternal grandmother – a single feminist eco-warrior born in 1910 (she admired Thatcher, though, so she wasn't perfect) – hit me hard. One of my earliest and most significant female role models, she'd travelled to New Zealand with her sister in the 1930s, decades before cheap flights and gap years were a thing; she'd taught herself to drive by reversing a tractor up and down a hill when she was a teenager, and continued to drive (cars, not farm vehicles) until her late eighties; and she made us recycle things in the seventies when no one was talking about recycling. At her funeral, my then seven-year-old daughter, having watched me cry so much I could barely finish the reading, said: 'If it's making everyone so sad to remember Great Grandma, why don't we just stop talking about her?'

Instead, I too settled for accumulating experience of her not being alive.

Cabin pressure

Having spent much of my adult life flying around the world as part of my job, I know that when we fly, we are more likely to cry – but why? The first reason is that we bring ourselves with us, which includes anything we are carrying, both emotionally and in terms of our (often measly) luggage allowance. Going back to Maslow's hierarchy of needs and its foundation tier of physiological needs (see page 50), it's not comforting to fly when our basic needs – food and drink, blankets and pillows – aren't always (or often, depending on the airline) provided for. Then there's the cabin pressure and the relative oxygen deficiency, which can make you feel weepy, sleepy or hormonal – three of menopause's seven dwarfs. Add all this together, and it's not surprising we sob at 36,000 feet. Even if we're not knocking back mini alcoholic beverages, we feel a bit weird because we're not in control; we're vulnerable. This explains why we enjoy terrible romcoms or cry at tourist board ads. As we cry, cortisol and adrenaline are released, which eases stress and helps us feel better. We laugh more easily miles high in the sky, too, which makes me wish I could perform stand-up to captive in-flight audiences – and I hope that some of you are reading this book whilst airborne.

At a time when my life was akin to George Clooney's in *Up in the Air*, I was mainly feeling like a mouse and acting like a lion. Even if my son wasn't a zookeeper, I'd know that wasn't right. I wish I'd known then a bit more about leaning into emotions like fear, anger, sadness and overwhelm, rather than trying at all costs to make the painful ones stop. I was a child when I first heard the saying 'Tears water our growth'. It was around the same time a boy in my class had had to go into hospital to have a genital growth removed, or so the year-six rumour mill would have it, so I thought it was really important *not* to cry; the last thing anyone wanted to do was to water their growth. In time, I discovered the saying was in fact referring to our inner growth as human beings. I love that line in *When Harry Met Sally*: 'Someone is staring at you in Personal Growth'. I'm not sure what Nora Ephron thought about crying on planes, but there is something special and intimate about it.

I've cried on planes loads. I cried the first time I left my baby behind to go on a work trip. I cried some more when my boobs started leaking and I couldn't get into the plane toilet with my breast pump because there was a MAN in there. I cried the first time I flew to New York after 9/11. I cried the time they offered me warm complimentary nuts on a flight to Singapore and they weren't warm (it wasn't about the nuts). I cried when they offered me a hot towel and it was too hot. I cried when I ended up next to a child eating chocolate buttons, back when we were all wearing white jeans. I've cried about illness, break-ups and make-ups, and I've cried watching *The Lion King* on the screen of the person sitting in front of me. And I've cried every time I hear the music on *The Office*.

I've cried. And I've cried. And I've cried.

I also cried when I realised I'd forgotten to bring my HRT patches on a hot holiday and it was very, very hot. The majority of the 3.4 million women aged between fifty and sixty-four in the UK will be experiencing symptoms of the menopause. I just had a perimenopause symptom checker come up on my feed, so here goes: hot flushes, cold flushes, insomnia, low libido, dry eyes, watery eyes, tinnitus, itchy skin, dry skin, burning mouth, sore mouth, gum disease, palpitations, reflux, wind, weight gain, hair loss, muscle loss, vulval soreness, urinary leakage and joint pains. If that was a dog, you'd put it down.

Real talk (active listening)

Planes also offer that most brilliant of things: the sideways conversation. There is an honesty and intimacy that comes when one finds oneself side by side with someone else, the pressure of eye contact removed. Eye contact is a significant aspect of non-verbal communication – not just among human animals, but non-human ones as well – and removing eye contact is significant too. Many species of animals perceive eye contact as a threat. Avoiding direct eye contact with unknown dogs can lessen your chance of being attacked, yet extended eye contact between dog and owner generates oodles of oxytocin, a fact to which I can attest. It's a contradictory old business, eye contact.

When I went hiking in Yosemite National Park, we were given a leaflet at the gate advising us how to handle the various wild animal encounters that might await us. We were to avoid direct eye contact if surprised by a bear – not a problem – but if we stumbled across a mountain lion (or, indeed, they upon us), we were to fight them. Bit more of a problem. Among primates, eye contact is especially aggressive. There was an incident in 2007 at Rotterdam Zoo where Bokito the gorilla escaped and injured a woman who visited him multiple times a week and stared at him every time, holding prolonged eye contact with him on each occasion. Visitors were later given special glasses that masked their gaze when looking at Bokito (guess they weighed up that expense against the cost of NO VISITORS EVER AGAIN). Cats, proud contrarians of the domestic pet world, use eye blinking rather than eye contact to indicate friendly intent, and will blink at humans they trust. We should, if we want to make or stay friends, apparently blink back. And cats don't meow at each other, just at humans – that's got nothing to do with eye contact, it's just something you should know.

Eye contact safely removed, sideways conversations are where the big stuff often happens. Think for a moment about travel conversations you've had, whether on planes, in cars or on trains. Sideways or low eye-contact conversations are not solely reserved for activities that are bad for the environment, incidentally – they can happen when you're walking, cycling or at the hairdresser too. In September 2015, hairdresser Tom Chapman founded the Lions Barber Collective, a group of international barbers raising awareness for suicide prevention, stemming from the fact that the barbershop is a great, safe place for men to talk. They now run training for hair professionals across the globe to help them 'Recognise, Ask, Listen and Help' those in their chairs.

My children were born before everyone had mobiles, and long before anyone had smartphones, so their early years weren't dominated by iPads. It wasn't that we weren't reliant on the telly and Walkmans and whatever the hell else we could lay our hands on – I'm not being smug – but the quality of our communication was enhanced by the lack of temptation to get lost in screens. By their teen years, technology had revved up (alongside their growing conviction that all parents are, in fact, arseholes), and communication became something more of a challenge. When your kids are brought up bilingually, it's even worse because there are two languages in which you're not communicating. That's where sideways conversations come in. Apparently that's why chairs in therapy rooms are often positioned at a slight angle. I just thought it was therapists messing with people like me, who like everything in straight lines because we need to be in control.

A lot of meaningful conversations happen in cars; especially in cars in the dark. I remember picking up my daughter from a friend's house one evening when she was about thirteen, and out of the blue she said: 'Mum, tell the truth. I want to know all the drugs you've taken. Don't lie.'

That's a big moment. Tempted as I was to do eighty in a thirty with the stereo turned up to ten just to avoid the conversation, instead we went there. I wonder if she'd have asked me the same question across the kitchen table – and, if she had, how differently the conversation would have played out. Luckily, when we moved from my opening statement into further questions, the first was: 'Have you done heroin?' and I was able, hand on heart, to say no.

Away from the privacy of your car and on to public transport, there's the possibility of intimate connections made during serendipitous encounters with strangers; not necessarily romantic ones. A few months ago, I lost a big bit of work that really mattered to me, so I headed out for a walk. I walked past a woman with a buggy and we ended up next to each other, waiting to cross the road. She said she really liked my coat. I really liked her coat, too, so we had a lovely stranger-to-stranger chat. Then I started crying because she was being so nice to me and I'm menopausal and I'd just lost that job. Then *she* started crying because she'd just had a baby. We both had green coats and screwed-up hormones. *Hakuna matata*. The circle of life. And of loss.

You may or may not know the names Jonny Benjamin and Neil Laybourn, but you'll likely know their story. Jonny and Neil met in 2008, when Neil approached Jonny, who was sitting on the edge of Waterloo Bridge, and asked if he was alright. Jonny was not alright; in fact, he was about to jump. The conversation that followed saved Jonny's life and changed both their lives forever, as they subsequently shared in the Channel 4 documentary *The Stranger on the Bridge*. Eye contact was not possible for the majority of their conversation that day on Waterloo Bridge, with Jonny sitting on the edge and Neil above and behind him. Jonny told me that part of what was most significant about how his life was saved that day was the fact that his conversation was with a complete stranger.

Life and loss

As a society, we experienced a collective living loss during the pandemic; loss of things we took for granted, like going out with friends, or walking in the park, or being able to turn a blind eye if people spat a bit when they talked. Pandemics aside, there are myriad things that can throw us into a grieving process: break-ups, job changes or endings, kids leaving home, ill health, what might have been. Whoosh; there goes my dream of being a Premier League football player. Shit, I'm older than Jesus was when he died. Sometimes, my sense of sadness comes from a pincer movement of a) not having enough years left and b) not having spent the ones I've had so far right, a nagging 'what the fuck have I been doing?' sort of a feeling.

And then, of course, there's actual loss, and the fear of it. Reading Emily Dean's *Everybody Died, So I Got a Dog* was part of the reason I got a dog, even before anybody had died. Now I can't bear the thought of Jeff ever dying, and sometimes (most days) I cry about that. Pre-emptive crying, like when I was holding my firstborn in my arms when he was ten days old and his dad came in to find me crying my heart out. 'What's the matter?' he asked.

'I don't want him to go to school,' I replied.

One in four of us will experience a mental-health problem at some point, and the NHS is not resourced to cope; the number of psychiatric beds in England fell from 67,000 in 1988 to just 18,000 in 2019.[9] At the time of writing (with the exception of the Covid-19 period, when many beds were closed due to infection control), the current numbers of mental health beds in England (17,836) are at their lowest level since data collection began in 2010/11.[10] Around 6,000 people die by suicide every year in the UK. That's seventeen every day, or one person every ninety minutes. On 5 July 2023, I hosted the homecoming event at the Brighton Dome for The Baton of Hope, the biggest suicide prevention and awareness initiative the UK had seen. Two fathers, Mike McCarthy and Steve Phillip, made contact following the suicides of their sons, Ross and Jordan, and together they created the event in which a baton was carried by people who had a connection to suicide, spanning twelve cities in twelve days, starting in Glasgow, and finishing at the Houses of Parliament in London. I'd heard the acronym HOPE with regards to mental health being used to mean: 'Help One Person Everyday', but that night I heard it talked about as something else: 'Hold On, Pain Ends'.

Neil Laybourn – 'Mental turmoil is a condition of the human spirit. Don't be hard on yourself about how it affects you on the day, or the week or the month that you're going through it. Everybody is going to have trials and tribulations to go through – it's part of your journey of being a human being on the planet. If you haven't had that yet, it's coming. If you've gone through it, well done, congratulations, you're still here. I think our story is a testament to that. The pain does end, and life will go on.'

I'm not a Buddhist, but . . .

In 2016, I ended up having intensive treatment in a psychiatric hospital, where I was torn between keeping myself alive and not bothering. I was lucky enough – very lucky – to find a couple of things that helped. The first was getting my HRT sorted. Ask any midlife woman you can find, and they'll vouch for the fact that whatever the opposite of being handed out like Smarties was, was what was going on with HRT at that time. When I went on Clive Anderson's *Seven Wonders* podcast, where you get to pick your own personal seven wonders, never mind Machu Picchu or the music of David Bowie, I was tempted to make my number one my HRT patch. In the end, it was my dog Jeff who topped the leader board, and when I told the kids, one of them asked: 'Which number were we?', at which point I remembered I clean forgot to mention them. Guess HRT can only go so far.

The hospital food was great, too – in a comforting, stodgy, old-fashioned school dinners kind of way – but even with an HRT patch the size of Australia on my arse, and a belly full of spotted dick, things were hard. That's where group therapy came in. As someone who had never belonged, suddenly, I belonged, and it changed *everything*. Having always felt the need to be 'on', I could be off and just see what came of doing nothing but being present and listening. It was in those groups that the concept of self-soothing and mindfulness came into play. There's a cycle in coaching of moving from awareness through acceptance and into change. People are often great on the awareness, but the reason things sometimes stubbornly refuse to change is that there's a big missing piece: acceptance.

Mindfulness may have originated from ancient Eastern and Buddhist philosophy and date back around 2,500 years, but it always seemed a bit like gimmicky new-age bollocks to me. In my thirties, the peak 'single mum who's overdoing it' years, someone more serene than me – a low bar back then – suggested I set my timer for just five minutes a day to do nothing and see what happened.

'I don't *have* five minutes a day!' I yelled, checking messages on my BlackBerry with one hand, while throwing Mini Cheddars at toddlers like seals with the other. They told me that if you don't have time to stop and breathe for five minutes a day, then you probably need to meditate for a full hour. I don't remember what I said in reply, but I remember what I thought. Suffice to say, I wasn't there yet.

Lots of things had put me off mindfulness, and the last thing I wanted was serenity. Supposedly serene people have often seemed to me to be the most irritated. I remember talking to a woman at yoga once about a miracles course that had changed her life, teaching her to let go, be more accepting and achieve inner peace. I asked if it was nearby and she said: 'No, it's really tricky to get to, and these other two women there know I need a lift and never offer me one, so I have to get the fucking bus home.' Eat, pray, livid.

And anyway, who's got time to meditate? I was all about the 'just keep moving and you won't feel the pain' way of living. But have you ever considered the idea that if you're driven, what are you driving out?

The thing that first made my workaholic mind willing to give mindfulness a whirl was when an instructor I met said that ten minutes of meditation can equate to one hour's sleep. Doing nothing thereby made it on to my to-do list, and I signed up for a meditation class at the local Buddhist temple. In for a penny, in for a lentil.

When I first used to meditate, it made me panic. And it

made me sad. I would mainly just cry. It was embarrassing, and worrying, and I looked like a panda. Then something weird started to happen. By letting the feelings in, they started to lose their power and, rather than overwhelming me, they just came and went. My friends noticed a positive change in me – so much so that one of them, Tash, decided to go to a mindfulness class at a Buddhist temple too. It had a profound effect on her. She hated it so much that, never mind never trying another mindfulness class, she's never visited that part of London again. We're still friends, me and Tash, we just don't mention fat wise men sitting cross-legged, not unless one of us is sleeping with one.

Mindfulness may not work for everyone, but it worked for me. The shitty, tricky stuff is a part of us, but it need not debilitate us. Often it's the anticipation of how bad something might be that far outweighs the thing itself, and mindfulness helped me get somewhere close to sitting with things in the present, rather than having my sights set on the past or future. I started to feel less depressed and a bit less stressed.

The woolly mammoth effect

Stress usually comes from things we can't control, things that may never happen, or both. The world has raced on since our cave-people days, but our endocrine systems have not. The term 'stress' was coined by the Hungarian-Canadian endocrinologist Hans Selye in 1936, who defined it as 'the non-specific response of the body to any demand for change'. Catchy. General adaptation syndrome (G.A.S.) is what Selye came to call the process by which the body confronts stress. My body sometimes confronts stress with gas, too, because I have IBS. (Of course I have IBS.) In Selye's G.A.S., the body passes through three stages of coping:

An alarm reaction in which the body prepares itself for 'fight or flight'.

A resistance to the stress being built because we can't sustain this condition of excitement.

A state of exhaustion if the duration of the stress is sufficiently long.

If you imagine our cave-people days, it was necessary to our survival that we responded to bursts of stress with a fight-or-flight response. The heart-in-your-mouth stuff actually isn't bad for us; it's chronic stress that leads to wear and tear and, if it keeps going, to burnout. People like me with addictive personalities are very drawn to the fight-or-flight chemicals offered by the pituitary and adrenal glands, preferring any number of highs and lows over flat and steady. Sensory overload holds a particular thrill. In my early twenties, I took up skydiving. At the time, I barely had money for bananas, let alone a hobby that cost close to three digits a pop. Luckily, in this country, a weekend's skydiving mainly involves sitting at a drop zone waiting for the weather to clear, so often all you're spending money on is Diet Coke and the pool table. The first time the British weather permits you to jump out of a plane, you experience sensory overload over a period of a few seconds. The more you do it, the shorter that period becomes, until, on the rare weekends when you get to do six, seven, eight jumps, it ends up feeling no more alien than stepping off a stair. The human brain can learn to normalise walking into nothing at 15,000 feet. Similarly, with stand-up, you tend not to remember much about your first few gigs due to sensory overload. Luckily, thanks to mates who were at my first gig, I'm reminded that all I've blanked is that I was a bit crap. Nowadays, it's more of a red flag if I don't feel any nerves before going onstage, as there's a need for some adrenaline. Stage fright is there for a reason; it's the performer's equivalent of being a cave person ready to square up to a woolly mammoth.

That is where the 'amygdala hijack' comes in, which changed a lot for me when I first heard about it – and now I can even spell it. The term was coined by Daniel Goleman in his 1990 book *Emotional Intelligence* to describe a specific fight-or-flight response to stress. Sports psychologist Steve Peters built on this concept in his book *The Chimp Paradox*. The amygdala is part of the limbic system within the brain; when you think amygdala, think stress hormones that prepare the body for fight or flight. The cerebral cortex evolved long after the limbic system and gave us logical reasoning. The amygdala works automatically, with the frontal lobes of the cortex allowing us to process our emotions for a more logical response. Goleman's hijack rests on the premise that the amygdala sometimes perceives a threat and triggers a fight-or-flight response that's out of proportion to the actual threat, and before the frontal lobes have a chance to get involved. Our capacity to be rational is therefore hijacked. An amygdala hijack can be useful – for example, it can stop us from walking out in front of a speeding vehicle before we have even registered a car is there. In other situations, however, it can be less helpful – like causing us to lose our shit at a pharmacist who is just doing their job (a story you are about to hear).

There is considerable power that comes from recognising and harnessing the hijack when it happens, and this is at the heart of how we can look to retrain our primal brains to negotiate and build a dialogue with stress and anxiety more generally. You can't overpower it – and in many situations you wouldn't want to, because it's also what makes you laugh uncontrollably and fall in love and experience intense pleasure, of whatever variety. But there are ways to learn to notice and work with, rather than against it, some of which I've included at the end of this chapter (see page 124).

And so: that pharmacy story.

I realised HRT was cutting through stuff, once I finally convinced a doctor to give me some, but I didn't know quite to what extent until there was a nationwide shortage, part Brexit supply chain (hurrah – blue passports *and* dry vaginas!), part Davina McCall et al. getting menopause on to the agenda to the point where GPs were finally more routinely prescribing the stuff. I kept going to my local pharmacy to collect my oestrogen prescription, and I kept getting told to come back in a couple of weeks. A couple of weeks? 'If this was diabetes or heart medication, you wouldn't be telling me to come back in two weeks!' I shouted one time, only for the diabetic man waiting in the queue behind me to ruin it all by saying actually, that is what sometimes happens. A woman with a heart condition summoned up some breath and concurred.

After two more goes of 'coming back in a couple of weeks', I lost it again: 'It's because it's women's medicine! If it was men's medicine or veterinary medicine, you'd be taking it seriously and it would be properly funded. Stop treating me like a dog!' There was no need for the diabetic man or the heart woman to ruin this second outburst; I'd ruined it all by myself. If I was a dog, I'd be getting the royal treatment, according to my own argument. My HRT-deprived stress and anxiety soared, not helped by the fact I was spending all my spare time at the pharmacy.

Hysteria

I have the luxury of a brilliant therapist, known between me and my friends as 'Yoda'. At the end of a recent session, I said: 'See you next week, Yoda!' I panicked and went on: 'Sorry, I don't know why I called you Yoda. You don't even look much like Yoda.' Until then, I daresay it had never occurred to her that she did. (Not as bad as a mate who ran, almost literally, into her therapist at a nude spa. Therapists shouldn't be allowed to go to nude spas, on the basis that there's even a small chance this might happen. There's not enough therapy in all the world to sort that one out, particularly when you've seen the undercarriage of the person giving you the therapy.)

Yoda takes no prisoners and is always challenging me to get into the deep stuff. The other day, she was telling me not to underestimate the powerful part of me that avoids getting into really tricky emotions. Then the fire alarm went off, and we couldn't finish the session. And I thought, 'Wow, I really am powerful.'

Our emotional responses are ingrained in us for a variety of deep-rooted reasons: familial, personal, societal. As a little girl growing up in the 1970s, I was told it wasn't nice to get angry. Meanwhile, little boys were being told it wasn't OK to cry. So girls repressed their anger and boys took out their upset in aggression. As adult women, we're sometimes told we're a bit naggy, a bit passive-aggressive. Luckily, we're fine with that. Absolutely *fine* with . . . that. Nothing's wrong. Why would anything be wrong?

I still reckon it would be good if men cried a bit more often, not just every four years at the Euros. Women, on the other hand, have form when it comes to getting hysterical. Through the mists of time, hysteria has been a wastepaper-basket diagnosis for women who reported anything that could not easily be explained another way. And this was going on long before the invention of wastepaper baskets. Plato's theory was that hysteria was caused by childlessness: a childless womb becoming distressed and moving throughout the body. I'm glad he died centuries before he could become a GP and give me a smear test.

'Wandering womb' (good name for a feminist festival) was widely adopted as a theory, and women continued to be diagnosed with female hysteria, based on a long list of symptoms including: headaches, forgetfulness, irritability, insomnia, writer's cramps, hot flashes, use of coarse language, hyper-promiscuity, mood swings, nausea, anxiety, drowsiness, loss of appetite, ageing, back pain, swollen feet and desire for clitoral stimulation.

Sounds a lot like my book club.

How to treat it? Why, clitoral massage of course! Doctors rubbed clitorises much and often during the late 1800s and early 1900s to treat female hysteria – which is annoying, as not all modern men have this skill. As literacy rates among women increased, doctors attributed higher rates of hysteria to the alleged dangerous behaviours of intellectual women, such as attending school and working outside the home. According to Havelock Ellis, author of *Psychology of Sex*, a study estimated that in 1913, 75 per cent of women suffered from female hysteria. If they were getting rubbings on prescription, I'm not surprised.

All good things come to an end, and the medical rubbing men couldn't always be bothered, paving the way for the invention of the earliest vibrators. In 1869, an American doctor named George Taylor patented one of the first medical vibrators. It was called 'The Manipulator' – my character on *The Chase*, if ever they ask me. This first vibro was large, heavy, expensive and coal-powered (I'm envisaging a Bernard Cribbins character powering it, like in *The Railway Children*), so it didn't widely catch on; it was more likely to catch fire. In the early 1880s, Mortimer Granville invented the first portable, battery-powered vibrator, weighing in at a mere 40 pounds. Never mind hiding it in your carry-on, that's excess baggage in the hold. How spoiled we are in the twenty-first century, with first AA batteries and now the rechargeable variety.

There was a day I had to bury a vibrator. I wasn't trying to grow a vibrator tree, although I wouldn't mind – no, my children had found it in my sock drawer while I was at work. I got an after-school text saying: 'We're trying to watch *Harry Potter* in your study and your vibrator keeps going off next door.' In panic, I enlisted a friend, who has a key for when she feeds the cat, to let herself in, disarm it and shroud it with a tissue. By the time I got home, any feelings I once had for it were gone. It was dead to me and I had to get rid of it, so I buried it in the garden like a family pet. Straight into the ground it went, like a failed North Korean missile test, laid to rest under a paving stone, between a dead hamster and two goldfish: my rabbit. I told the kids it had gone to live on a farm.

In 1952 the American Psychiatric Association's revisions of the *Diagnostic and Statistical Manual of Mental Disorders* finally removed hysteria as a medically recognised diagnosis for women. Now we can be as hysterical as we like without anyone rubbing our clitorises (unless we ask them to).

The power of play

Bo Burnham – 'Laughter is the best medicine, y'know, besides medicine.'

Did you know that bonobos can learn rock-paper-scissors? And that dolphins can giggle? I could have done with a front row of dolphins at my first gig. When I started out in stand-up, I was alright wielding a microphone in front of an audience, but too polished and uptight to be a comedian. What a couple of decades in boardrooms and being a single parent had knocked out of me was any sense of play. If your life seems too 'together' onstage, people get blinded by the armour, when what they've really come for is the chinks in the armour. No one goes to a comedy night to feel worse about their lives because the life of the person onstage is so infuriatingly perfect. I went through a phase of helping ex-Premier League footballers hone their after-dinner speaking skills, and a key aspect was getting them to express their vulnerability in a humorous way. Not that audiences don't want to hear about their winning goals for England and all the football stuff, but they really sit up in their seats if they get a peek behind the mask.

Play made an unlikely reappearance in my life – not through my becoming a comedian, but because the year I turned fifty, I signed up to do the Hoffman Process. The Hoffman Process is not therapy, but an immersive, experiential week aimed at undoing some of the damage done in childhood. A sort of reverse 'They fuck you up, your mum and dad.' It was founded in 1967 by Bob Hoffman, not a guru but a car salesman. It has been described as a 'life-changing detox that celebrities swear by' – those celebrities include Thandiwe Newton, Sienna Miller, Naomi Harris and Goldie. None of them were on my one, though there was a bloke there who claimed he'd once been Madonna's personal trainer. (I'm fairly confident that doesn't narrow things down enough to breach client confidentiality.)

People who've done the Hoffman – which isn't a cult, honest – don't tend to reveal much of what goes on, but here are a couple of headlines they've said it's OK for me to share:

> You're in there for seven days, with no contact with the outside world: no phone, no books, no social media.

> Periods of time are spent in silence.

> You share a room.

> There's a part where you beat the shit out of a beanbag with a baseball bat.

Of all those things, the bit that traumatised me the most before I went in was the thought of sharing a room. Whether it goes back to boarding school or whether I'm just a queen who likes my own space, the thought of sharing a small twin room with a stranger didn't thrill me. You have a couple of in-depth calls with the Hoffman team before you go in, and on one of them, they said that the thing you're most worried about before you start is often where the biggest change will happen. Sure enough, it did. My roommate, Averil, was one of the best things about the experience, and has been a precious friend ever since. I didn't choose her, she didn't choose me, but I couldn't have had a better person by my side on the Hoffman journey.

The process is not about analysis. You don't talk much about your back story; there is a journaling element, but that's more about expression. The aim is to let go of the negative, often parental patterns that are holding you back. One blissful aspect of the process is that you get to rediscover your sense of play – or, in my case, discover it for the first time. I won't go into the details, but it's a whole day of ditching adulthood and inhibitions, with surprise after surprise after surprise; it's magical. I realised that in my childhood, there hadn't been much play; playing the piano, yes, but sheer for-the-merry-hell-of-it arsing about, less so.

I've always been self-conscious, and at first my pretending to have fun onstage was just that – pretending. Ten years later, and it's finally in my bones. My minutes onstage are often the most fun on any given day; the long drives home from gigs in the wee small hours, fuelled by service-station pasties, less so. (When people ask my friend Paul McCaffrey what it's like being a comedian, he just says he's a driver, and does comedy in his breaks.) Long after the baseball-bashing blisters have subsided, rediscovering play has been unexpectedly revelatory for me. Laughter does everything from releasing endorphins to boosting the immune system to burning calories to making me wee. When we lose fun and laughter from our lives, we lose a lot.

At the start of the Covid-19 lockdown, after I had watched my work diary empty over a period of about forty-eight hours, I decided to get back into something I hadn't done for a while: coaching. I offered a hundred one-off, one-hour Zoom coaching sessions to people in creative industries who had also lost their work. Part altruism, part sod-all-else-to-do-ism, my hundred coachees over the period of the next few months were an eclectic bunch, with just two things in common:

They all thought everyone else was coping better than them.

They had all lost any sense of fun or play in their lives.

It's understandable that in lockdown, the first thing on people's minds wasn't how to have a massive laugh, although I actually got really into doing comedy gigs on Zoom (more so than my audiences, in many cases). It's not surprising that the second-deadliest pandemic the world has ever seen sucked the joy out of things, but it's all too easy in 'normal' adulthood to lose any sense of play. Yet play is less of a luxury item than we might think. It's a big part of our mental wellbeing, and it's also the playful side of our brain that unlocks creativity – and, with it, possibility. Finding a balance between the left brain (verbal, logical and analytical) and the right brain (visual, intuitive and creative) at best makes for a fulfilling life and at worst helps us avoid burning out with the sheer misery of it all. People tend to get pigeon-holed as being either left-brained or right-brained, but despite their opposing styles, the two halves of your brain are connected and work together. So actually, we're all on a spectrum of both. The executive function that had served me so well in boardrooms needed to make space for the giddy kipper that fuels my stand-up. Board member + giddy kipper = much less likely to have a breakdown.

Happy ending

A few years ago, a mental-health programme called *kulturvitaminer* (I won't patronise you by translating it) was launched in Denmark.[11] Targeted at unemployed people suffering from depression, it offered a crash course in culture. There were eight strands, including history, music, nature walks, trips to the theatre and singing (which is proven, when done in groups, to promote a sense of belonging and release dopamine).[12] According to the leader of the culture course in Aalborg, Mikael Odder Nielsen, if you are depressed to the point of being preoccupied with just getting through the day, culture is often the first thing to go. The aim of the programme was to reverse this. Restorative playlists were put together by music therapists, including 'boring' music intended to give your brain a break, which included stuff like Jack Johnson (don't suppose that's helped Jack's depression). The programme worked in partnership with the Aalborg Symphony Orchestra, and participants got to watch rehearsals and performances. There was even a strand where you got read aloud to for a couple of hours in the Aalborg library. Time to get me a Danish passport. Who knew Sandi Toksvig was such a catch? The link between mental health and culture is an increasingly important part of the Nordic welfare model. And best of all, it has no side effects.

John Lloyd – 'There are only five commandments, and they are: 1. No fear; 2. Be kind; 3. Don't worry about what anyone else thinks; 4. Do what you know to be right; and 5. Cheer up, for God's sake.'

We're only halfway through the book, so this is no time for a happy ending, but it's worth throwing in at this point that my fifties have been my happiest decade so far. This is largely linked, I think, to the fact that I've learned how to allow myself to be sad. I've always felt much better after a good cry, but more recently, I've felt better during one. It's not just me who's feeling chirpier in midlife; there is an increasing amount of research to support the fact that adulthood is marked by a U-shaped happiness curve. According to a study by economists David Blanchflower and Andrew Oswald, happiness declines from youth through to middle age, hitting a low at fifty and rising thereafter to peak at seventy-plus.[13] Jonathan Rauch's book *The Happiness Curve: Why Life Gets Better After 50* is based on this concept. I spent a lot of my first five decades setting my sights on being happy, which I increasingly think is a fool's errand, nice as it is when it happens. My fifty-something focus is more achievable: noticing. I notice what I'm feeling, let myself feel it and dare to express it, knowing it won't kill me.

Tears need a rebrand, whether on planes or elsewhere. Crying, after all, is just another form of nonverbal communication. Tears are not a shameful sign of weakness, but rather of courage, authenticity and wisdom. I don't always feel very wise, but I do know this: I prefer to swim with the tide of midlife tears, not against it. I no longer think of crying as something that has to be done secretly, into a pillow in private. I was just on the Eurostar back to King's Cross, in a full carriage, and I cried at a video of a puppy and small dappled piglet sharing a lettuce. Never has anything felt more right.

DO TRY THIS AT HOME

Unhijacking your amygdala: notice and name

It's no wonder an amygdala hijack feels extreme – a matter of life and death, even – given its origins. The below steps will give you a beat in which to recalibrate so you can respond, rather than react (thereby keeping your job/relationship/freedom). You don't need to do them all. Think of it like a pick 'n' mix, but without children's dirty fingers giving you a tummy bug.

Notice when you've been hijacked. How do you know? Pay attention to your mind and body – what's happening?

What specifically are you feeling? Anger, upset, panic? Name it.

Try the six-second rule. It takes the chemicals that are released during an amygdala hijack about six seconds to dissipate. Count six seconds in your head (more if the situation permits) before doing anything.

Breathe. Become aware of your breath and slow it down. This activates the parasympathetic nervous system: your 'rest-and-digest' response.

Be mindful. Look around you and notice things in your physical environment, outside of yourself.

Take a moment. If you are truly feeling out of control, excuse yourself from the situation you are in; a slightly awkward pause in proceedings is better than an unfettered outburst.

Don't look at me: sideways conversations

We all know about the power of looking at things from different angles, but how about just not looking at them at all? If there's a big conversation you're going to have, think about having it with eye contact removed (maybe don't go for this option if it's a marriage proposal). Think of any side-by-side stuff you can be doing – travelling, cooking, walking or whatever – and see what happens if you have the conversation then. You can relax a bit and listen to learn, the pressure of a locked-eyes response removed.

Cally's culture vitamins

The calming effect of classical music has been proven time and time again. It eases nerves, decreases your heart rate, lowers your cortisol level and increases blood to the brain. Recent studies have shown thirteen minutes to be the optimal listening time.[14] I'd send you a mix tape if I could, but failing that, here's a thirteen-minute-long classical music playlist, made for you with love:

> Jean Sibelius, Etude in A Minor, 13 Pieces, Op. 76, No. 2 (1 minute 10 seconds)
>
> George Frideric Handel, 'The Arrival of the Queen of Sheba' (3 minutes 10 seconds)
>
> Edvard Grieg, 'Arietta', Lyric Pieces, Book 1, Op. 12 (1 minute 23 seconds)
>
> John Pachelbel, Canon in D Major, P.37 (4 minutes 48 seconds)
>
> Carl Orff, 'Gassenhauer' (3 minutes 4 seconds)

LAST WORDS

When Lucy Porter came on the podcast, she shared a Barry Cryer joke:

> 'A woman's walking a dog in a graveyard, and she sees a man squatting down behind one of the gravestones. She calls out, "Morning!" and he says, "No, just doing a shit."'

It would be remiss in a chapter about crying not to include some life advice from Helen Russell, author of *How to be Sad*:

> 'Sadness is the message; it can tell us what's wrong, and even what to do about it, but we have to listen.'

Arthur Smith was feeling lyrical when I asked him for his life advice:

> 'This is a quote from T. S. Eliot, if you're feeling down: "Despair and disillusion, they are essential moments in the progress of the intellectual soul." And I'd also say, remember: you are no more and no less important than anyone else. And finally, I'd agree with Lothian Council, who say Tuesdays and Fridays are rubbish days.'

The last word goes to the Reverend Richard Coles, who quoted the old adage:

> 'This too shall pass.'

5
LESSONS FROM AN AUTISTIC ZOOKEEPER

BE MORE BONOBO

'Why fit in when you were born to stand out?'
Dr Seuss

Bonobo

/ˈbɒnəbəʊ/

noun

> a rare anthropoid ape (*Pan paniscus*) that has a more slender build and longer limbs than the related common chimpanzee (*P. troglodytes*) and that inhabits a small geographic region in equatorial Africa south of the Congo River
> called also *pygmy chimpanzee*

Source: https://www.merriam-webster.com/dictionary/bonobo

> A whopping 99 per cent of our human DNA is the same as that of our closest primate cousins: chimps and bonobo apes. We're just 1 per cent removed from a bonobo. I've dated people less human than a bonobo.

The good life

My son introduced me to bonobos, and indeed to many animals whose names I otherwise would not know, like the hellbender (a salamander), the sarcastic fringehead (not my family nickname, but a fish with a very big mouth) and the white-bellied go-away bird (a white-bellied bird that goes away). Forget the birds and the bees – it's thanks to him I know there is an actual thing called a penis snake. Google it. Actually, don't.

I've spent many hours, days and weeks travelling first around the UK, and later the world, chronicling primates with my son, marvelling at how he decodes human behaviour via the lexicon of the animal kingdom.

My relationship with the natural world predates my son by the best part of thirty years. My brother and I grew up in the grounds of first one school in Buckinghamshire, then another in Dorset. I was born at home in Bucks, in the little wooden bungalow where we lived. When I was a child, it felt big and airy. When I went back decades later, it had more of a portacabin vibe, but it's stood for over fifty years and its surroundings are still very beautiful. In the early 1970s, when *The Good Life* was all the rage and everyone wanted to look like Felicity Kendall in dungarees, my parents had hippy tendencies. We had a Volkswagen campervan, my mum built a kiln to make pottery, and we kept ducks and goats.

Growing up surrounded by animals was brilliant, and sometimes brutal. During the drought of 1976, the littlest duckling of a batch to hatch, Beaky (so-named because only his beak and his feet grew), fell into a crack in the soil and was pecked to death by his siblings. I learned early on: nature balances the books. Our goat Anna had a kid called Emily, who, when she was on my knee, would pull chunks of my hair into her mouth and suck. Childhood didn't get much better than that, for her or me. Anna died some years later, and one Sunday we sat down to a yummy roast lunch, which turned out to be . . . Anna. Well, part of Anna. Suffice to say, I became vegetarian as soon as I got a casting vote.

On a tree in the garden, we had a monkey swing: a round piece of wood with a rope through the middle, attached to a tree. When I was three, my mum bought me a pair of those knickers that are plain at the front, with frills at the back. I put them on, deciding that of course you'd want the pretty bit at the front, not the back, and off I went into the garden to have a go on the swing. These were the days before kids were being put in hard hats and high-vis to cross a flower bed, and were fairly free of adult supervision, so I was alone as the swing twisted around and around, pulling my frills ever further into the thread of the rope. I don't know how long I was there, swing and pants as one; it felt like two hours, but it was probably about ten minutes, before my dad came to cut me down. I survived, the pants did not, and we all learned something that day.

Goats, ducks and monkey swings: animals have always been in my blood. It is perhaps more surprising that they are also in the blood of my children, particularly my oldest child, brought up as he was in North London, surrounded by all of life in Kentish Town.

Becoming an MTV mum

I had not long relocated from Amsterdam to London for my dream job at MTV when I found out I was pregnant. Fair to say, it was not entirely planned. At the time, MTV Europe was a fledgling business that did not yet have a fully formed maternity policy, so their US maternity terms were applied. It was not a generous arrangement: twelve weeks of unpaid leave from the last day in the office. If your baby was a couple of weeks late, as mine was, and assuming you stopped work two weeks before your due date, that meant going back to work with a two-month-old. No shared parental leave, and no Mumsnet upon which to vent one's spleen.

There are not many things I regret (which is not to say I haven't made my share of mistakes), but going back to work with a two-month-old is one of them. It caused heartbreak of the highest order, and I feel a bit sick writing about it even now, twenty-eight years on. There were upsides to having an MTV baby – I loved my job, I lived near the office so his dad could bring him in to meet me after work, and I was able to take him with me on some of my work trips. By the time he was ten weeks old, he'd gone to the MTV Europe Music Awards in Rotterdam. I say *he'd* gone; I went to the awards, leaving baby plus daddy watching the whole thing on the hotel telly. Nothing rings life's changes like finding oneself in an awards venue toilet, others availing themselves of smooth surfaces for pick-me-up purposes, me changing my soaking breast pads, my body staging a dirty protest in its urgent need to be reunited with baby. My metallic nineties jumpsuit was ruined; my nostrils saved.

A couple of months later, he came with me to a convention in New Orleans. I was working long days, and we managed to get him registered as 'talent' so he could come into the convention centre with me. I have happy memories of that trip. My colleagues took him in like the little MTV mascot he was for that week. One day, his dad took him to New Orleans zoo, and we have a picture of him with his fuzzy ginger baby hair, watching the orangutans, and looking from behind much like a baby orangutan himself. Maybe that's where his whole fascination with primates started.

Animal lessons in feminism

Jake was six when *Finding Nemo* came out, just when we were starting to get a sense that his wiring might not be quite run of the mill. As the film finished, he pulled on my arm and whispered in my ear: 'Mum, none of it's true.' As we walked out, I explained the concept of cartoons and that none of it is strictly true (I saved breaking the news about Father Christmas until the next cinema trip). What he went on to explain, however, was that Nemo's mum and dad would never have been a couple and in love. The upshot was that clownfish have a hierarchal social structure with the largest, most aggressive female at the top, so they would never have been equal – let alone loving – partners. I looked into it afterwards and indeed this is the case, with every male serving the female throughout her reign, with the one who pleases her the most becoming her mate. Sounds like a utopia.

I took the kids to watch *Madagascar* when it first came out (we did do things other than go to the cinema sometimes) and this time my son, now eight, whispered: 'This is not a film for feminists.' I stuffed down some popcorn and tried not to overthink things.

Afterwards, he explained that DreamWorks had spun us a yarn about King Julian, who would never have been in charge – and not just because of his demonstrable lack of leadership skills. Female ring-tailed lemurs, I learned, are more involved in the leadership and peacekeeping of groups than males. The film had missed a chance to celebrate strong females, he told me. Just when I thought I was doing an OK job at parenting, he kicked his sister and called her a dick.

Fast-forward twenty years, and Jake is an autistic primate keeper (by that, I mean *he's* autistic, not that he's looking after gorillas with a gift for solving Rubik's cubes). It is not uncommon for autistic people to have intense, highly focused interests from a young age; these interests might change as time goes on, or they might be lifelong. Jake's love of animals was there from the get-go, at the heart of his happiness, his routine, his comfort – of him. There used to be a bison farm down in Dorset near where my parents live, and he loved to go there. I remember him telling me that you can learn a lot from bison, not least in terms of tough skin and female leadership. I loved that this had stood out to him. In a European bison group, the leader is always female, and family herds are made up of several mature females, a few males and young adults not ready to breed. The chief female bison will leave the herd to give birth, returning a few days later with her babies.

Once, when Jake was in his mid-teens, I had a go at him for not clearing up after himself, and the last thing I said before I raced out the door to a gig was that if there's one thing I wasn't going to do, it was spit a man out into the world who expected a woman to clear up after him. By the time I got to the gig, this text had arrived:

> *'I get that I drive you up the wall but one thing I refuse to accept is that my gender is anything to do with it. I get why women are so sick of men thinking we know better than you. I am a feminist, and you should know – you raised me to be one. Yes, I'm a man, but I am an advocate for women in power. So if you want to get cross at me for being a shit, go for it, but it has nothing to do with me being a man.'*

I was almost as proud as I was the time my thirteen-year-old daughter and I were window-shopping in Tiffany's, and an old woman walking by said to her: 'Maybe one day someone will buy you a ring like that.' My daughter looked a bit surprised and asked me: 'One day, if I want a ring like that, won't I buy it for myself?'

Matriarchy was what my kids knew, it was run of the mill round our place, but females take the lead in many species, not just human Beatons. Jake told me that amongst the most cognitively advanced mammals after humans – namely apes, elephants and cetaceans – matriarchal societies are normalised. In the case of chimpanzees, bonobos, elephants and dolphins, females – in many cases, older females – act as keepers of knowledge, passing down their skills through the generations. Other female-led animal species include most, but not all, lemur breeds, meerkats and the very emancipated red-necked phalarope. It's usually the male of the species that has razzmatazz plumage to attract a mate, but with red-necked phalaropes, it's the females. Once the female has wooed her dull white-and-grey partner (I've had partners like that), she leaves the nest and the eggs in his care and lets him get on with raising the babies, while she gets on with her independent life. Spotted hyenas are ahead of their time, too, living in matriarchal groups led by alpha females. Fun fact: female hyenas have a clitoris of up to eight inches. And because it's a female hyena, it actually is eight inches.

Opening our hearts and minds

My son is the sort of person I might have taken the piss out of a bit at school – in fact, I know I did – a bit different, a bit nerdy, dead clever. I am not proud of this. Standing by as a powerless parent during his many hard times at school, it was excruciating to realise that I had, at points during my childhood, made others feel like that (and they me, but that's no excuse). It took being his mum to learn to suspend my natural instinct to judge people who are not like me, and instead find a way to be open to the fact that learning often comes from unexpected places. Unless we get talking to people who are not like us, then we never get to know what we don't know.

Susie Dent – 'Embrace the geek. Really, don't ever be afraid of being a geek. It links into: don't be scared of what people think. Honestly, it's the coolest place to be. And love your dictionary.'

By the time I was part of senior management at Viacom, overseeing brands such as MTV, Nickelodeon and Comedy Central, it's fair to say I was pretty far removed from the core viewing demographic of sixteen- to thirty-four-year-olds (for some brands, younger than that). We put in place reverse mentoring, where newer, less experienced staff would help advise on content decisions, given their editorial instincts were in tune with what people their age wanted to watch. We knew it was working when we dropped the word 'reverse'. It was just mentoring. Why wouldn't someone my age have much to learn from someone decades younger? All mentoring is reciprocal, after all. I'm not crazy about people stereotyping me for my age, so why should it be OK to generalise about millennials or Gen Z, or indeed Generation Alpha after them? In case you're interested, this year marks the start of Generation Beta, which will encompass those born between 2025 and 2039. Whatever bracket we fall under, we should underestimate those in other brackets at our peril.

Albert Einstein – 'The important thing is not to stop questioning. Curiosity has its own reason for existence.'

There's a phenomenon in business whereby someone new comes in at the top and sees part of their remit being to ditch much of what the old regime did. Many books, blogs and articles have been written about the importance of your first

180 days in a job and how you can make best use of them. The Jentz and Murphy Technique, for example, involves asking stupid questions early. Contrary to what people told us when we were kids, there *is* such a thing as a stupid question, and more importantly, there's stupid timing of a question. Barry Jentz and Jerome Murphy, colleagues at Harvard Graduate School, hit upon an approach that rests on the premise of 'starting confused'. Asking the big, fundamental questions that challenge ideas, strategy and direction can be powerful at any stage in your career. The more basic questions, however, should be asked during that period of grace in which it's fine to ask almost anything. Their theory is: it's best to make the bloody most of it. The longer you put off asking a question, the harder it will be to ask, and they argue that in the first few weeks, you are totally in a safe zone when it comes to question-asking, so you should be getting out as many queries as you possibly can.

Actually, what happens much more often is that leaders come in keen to show assurance and decisiveness – and so, babies are thrown out with bath water. I love the idea of embracing confusion, openly not having all the answers; it brings with it a humility all too often lacking in fresh leadership – or any leadership, come to that.

It's hard to have the courage of your convictions when doing things differently unless you can somehow get to the point of also seeing and thinking about them differently. When I was studying to become a master practitioner in Neuro-Linguistic Programming, we learned an exercise called 'Perceptual Positions', the purpose of which is to engender curiosity about what's going on for others. I've outlined how to do it on page 141, but what it comes down to is looking at a given situation from three different viewpoints: your own, the other party's, and that of an outsider. Once other perspectives have been seen and worked through, they can never be unseen – and with distance and objectivity comes empathy.

Professor Matthew Williams, author of *The Science of Hate* – 'We must take the time to put ourselves in the shoes of others and show empathy. Viewing counter-stereotypical characters on TV and spending time with others who are different from us can teach us a little bit about what it's like to be somebody else. We should not have to rely on celebrities to make us feel empathy for those who are experiencing prejudice and discrimination on a regular basis. Restorative justice programmes used by criminal justice services bring victims and hate perpetrators together to encourage empathy. When we encounter representations of the plight of others in newspapers, online and on TV, we can make a habit of imagining ourselves as the protagonist in their story. Would I trade places with them, and if not, why not? What do we have in common? What must it have been like to endure their loss or pain or trauma? When we think hard enough about others, we begin to see ourselves in them, and them in us.'

It's easy to criticise and avoid difference; it's so much harder and richer to walk towards it with an open mind. Not that we haven't had our fair share of bumps in the road, but the sometimes black-and-white thinking of my neurodivergent son has undoubtedly helped me to better deal with the grey areas of life.

Up with the matriarchy

It's not like being a football or ballet mum, with a football or ballet mum social life. It can be a lonely life, being a bonobo ape mum. Not that I'd switch it. Our mum–son red-letter days have included time in the orbit of Margaret, the oldest bonobo known to exist – the oldest ape, indeed, known to exist. She was born in 1951, and we saw her together at Frankfurt Zoo not long before she died in 2022. Margaret was also the name of my paternal grandmother, and I don't think she'd mind me saying that what the pair of them had in common was that they were exceptional matriarchal role models. While chimps tend to be male-led, bonobos take their lead from females. It is not always the oldest female bonobo who's in charge, but the best suited (although that often means it's the oldest anyway). When the incumbent is no longer up to the leadership job, she doesn't get toppled aggressively, as usually happens with male chiefs; instead the next female in line simply becomes the de facto leader as the power of the matriarch emeritus naturally diminishes.

Bonobos are known for 'making love not war'. In the case of a conflict, they rub genitals (Rub Genitals, sounds like someone you'd go and see at Ronnie Scott's) to reduce tension; that's got to be easier than holding a referendum, surely. Imagine how efficiently skirmishes with Extinction Rebellion could be resolved – no riot gear, no force, no police horses; batons down, batons out. Female-to-female sex is common among bonobos, and is known as 'G-G rubbing'. I should know. I've witnessed G-G rubbing with my son, standing side by side in our anoraks, early in the morning before my first flat white of the day. 'I know you're a comedian,' my son said, 'but don't start.'

Male-to-male sex is also common among bonobos: the males sometimes hang from a tree, face-to-face, while penis fencing. How fun is that? It would certainly liven up the Olympics.

Counting sheep

There's no good time for a child's parents to separate. On the upside, my little one was so young that she doesn't remember much about it; then again, she doesn't have much of a memory of a household with both her parents in it, either. It hit my son harder. As the weeks went by, I was increasingly getting the feeling that my parenting of him in particular wasn't quite cutting it, and that I could use some help. And so, a few months after their dad had moved out, I got an appointment with an NHS child psychologist, Jayne (I'm wondering as I write this how much harder that would be now, twenty-five years of funding cuts on). Before we started talking, Jayne had put some toys on the floor for my son to play with, and as we talked, he built a pen and put all the little toy sheep in it. But the pen had a gap and all the sheep kept escaping. He kept shooing them back in, and then out they would run. Out of the mouths of babes: 'Put a fence up so the sheep are safe! I am the sheep!' In wanting to make life kind and easy for them – and for me – I had loosened the rules since their dad left, and there had been less strictness, less saying 'no'. Jayne didn't have much spelling out to do; her laying-out of toys had done the trick, and after that we got a bit more back to normal. I did less tiptoeing around, was less afraid to say things the kids might not want to hear, and we went back to clear boundaries. We didn't know my son was autistic back then, but the need for structure and clear rules and consequences made even more sense once we did.

My boy left home at nineteen to study for a foundation degree in animal management at an agricultural college – think Hogwarts with animals. The day I drove him there to drop him off, the weather was beautiful, the perfect English setting for empty-nest heartbreak. After settling him in, I drove off, and as soon as I was out of sight I stopped the car, tears streaming down my face. For a long while, I literally couldn't drive. The tears only lasted a couple of minutes, but a herd of sheep decided a good place for a lie-down was right in front of my Mini. The natural world afforded me ample time to contemplate my new situation, one without Jake in it, and it was quite the body blow.

That ovine intervention was almost ten years ago now, and I've got used to daily life without him – without either of my kids – in it. I still miss them both so much it hurts, but luckily they come back often. Jake was home for a few days last week, and one evening I had a bit of life overwhelm and a snivel. He was lovely, all six-foot-something of him, and I got a hug and was listened to.

'That's probably the worst half hour you've had in a while,' I said.

'Not really,' he replied. 'Yesterday, I had to give a mandrill an enema.'

I tweeted that afterwards, then realised later I probably should have mentioned he's a zookeeper.

Jake modelling getting uncomfortable on a daily basis as he navigated the neurotypical world encouraged me to take the leap from corporate to comedy. Through him, I've also learned to walk towards difference and discomfort. As a society, we still have a long way to go on the path towards diversity, in a depressingly large number of ways. It's only in the last couple of years that the number of female CEOs outweighs the number of CEOs called John in the UK, so there's work to do there – not least all changing our names to John. And there's work to do in not just accommodating, but truly valuing and celebrating neurodiversity. Anyone whose kid doesn't quite fit the mould knows that the in-crowd's loss is the world's gain. Different, not less.

DO TRY THIS AT HOME

Perceptual positions

They say there are at least two sides to every story, and this technique is about experiencing a situation in someone else's shoes, without having to walk a mile in their shoes first (my son has size-twelve feet; no way I'm walking anywhere in them). It goes like this:

Pick a specific scenario, like a situation with a boss, colleague, friend, partner or family member that's causing you consternation.

Sort out your physical space. The technique relies on moving to a different place in the room every time you change positions to become someone else. Often, you might just have three different chairs in a room. Set up your three separate spaces (known as 'spatial anchors' in NLP terms), and make sure you know which space you'll use for each viewpoint:

first position – you

second position – the other person

third position – objective outsider

Go to your first position, close your eyes, and think through the specific situation in your mind, as it happened, seeing it through your own eyes. Try to remember exactly what each person said, and how you felt. The more specific you can be, the better it will work.

Between viewpoints, it's good to take a quick break, even if it's just looking out the window for thirty seconds.

After your break, move to the second position and imagine the situation from the other person's perspective, looking at yourself through their eyes. Replay what each of you said, this time really trying to imagine their perspective and how they see you.

After another quick pause, move into the third position, the one of the objective outsider. Sometimes it's helpful at this point to picture yourself watching the scene from above, or looking in through a window from outside at what's happening. Ask yourself questions along these lines:

What's happening with these two people?

Are they being reasonable with each other?

Is there a power imbalance? If so, in what way? Why?

What else do you see?

What advice would you give them to help resolve things?

This technique is about getting a more lifelike picture of what happened, away from our own bias and emotions. It works even better if you have someone else there asking you what it's like in each of the chairs, but that's predicated upon a) whether you can find anyone, and b) how much of a tit you want to feel.

(Don't) talk to the hand

I asked Jake if there was anything I should include here in terms of how he does or does not like to be communicated with. The main point he shared was about people

(OK, me) finishing his sentences for him. In my defence, he is apt to communicate in a lot of detail, and because I'm not the biggest fan of detail, it can be tempting to cut him off before he's got to the end. In terms of us getting along, I would say learning to steer a course between his love of detail and my love of the big picture has been pretty pivotal.

'Big chunkers', like me, are all about the bigger picture, wanting to get to the point and ideally spend as little time as possible getting there. Speed over accuracy – yes please! This means we feel we've received more than enough information long before a 'small chunker' has finished giving it. You can spot big chunkers – we'll be the ones who start saying, 'Yep, yep, yep,' and shutting things down once we're getting bored, preferring generalisations over specifics. We sometimes prefer to keep information in our heads, rather than explaining it or writing it down. Not very helpful for any non-psychics we're communicating with.

Small chunkers like to get into the detail, preferring to give and receive every bit of information going. They might analyse information in a way that is exasperating for a big chunker, and they may ask lots of questions. Small chunkers often operate using lists to convey and store information. They may also be more present and 'in the moment', while big chunkers charge through, eager to get the next thing done. All these characteristics are generalisations, but you get the gist (if I was a small chunker, I'd explain it better).

What you can do is get to know your own style, and be willing to notice and work with the other person's. Once we've taken a beat to try to notice the big-chunk/

small-chunk disparity, common sense usually tells us how best to bridge the gap. When Jake was younger, I articulated to him the fact that I tend to think in bigger chunks, and that it would really help me if he could tell me the headline version of some of his longer stories. This would still be a lot more intricate than *my* idea of a headline version, but it got him thinking about what I might need to hear, as well as what he wanted to say. Likewise, I tried to adapt my style of glossing over details and racing through things in favour of making sure he had the information he needed in a calmer, more detailed format.

The biggest change for me was not in how I talked, but in how I listened – not least learning to resist the temptation to jump in and finish his sentences (that's still a work in progress, as he'd be the first to tell you). Trying to cut him off usually has the reverse effect, anyway, making him keener than ever to get his point across. Sometimes, just letting him step into the space of my silence as I say and do absolutely nothing is what is needed. (If you're a big chunker trying this with a small chunker at home, set an alarm for an hour and, if they're still going strong, go for a walk – they'll most likely still be going when you get back.)

Younger and wiser: reverse mentoring

People who unhelpfully tell parents of young kids that the teen years are the toughest are lying. It's not that teens don't have their moments, but I found having my kids and their friends around at that stage in their lives brilliantly eye-opening – and I really missed my sneak peeks into the world of their generation once they'd gone. Kids and teenagers teach us the value of being willing to be influenced by other generations, and interacting with them helps us to have an open and curious mind – the opposite of the 'all music is shit since the Beatles' mindset.

Reverse mentoring in companies tends to involve an older, more experienced (or maybe just more knackered) person being mentored by a younger, less senior and less experienced person. In one's own life, flipping the traditional idea of older and wiser on its head can be a revelation. Try taking the time to engage with the strangers of all demographics you encounter in daily life, as well as questioning your assumptions about people who are 'not like you', being willing and open to the fact that they might have something useful to say.

As a comedian, I'd be foolish not to take on the wisdom of the many outstanding comics half my age (or less) whom I meet, and we'd all be clowns not to apply that same ethos to life outside the circus.

LAST WORDS

The jokes in this chapter are aptly animal-themed, starting with *QI* elf Alex Bell:

'How do you get a duck to sing solo music? Put it in the microwave until it's Bill Withers.'

Rachel Fairburn's joke works better when spoken rather than written, but I reckon you'll cope:

'What are the three most common owls in the UK? The barn, the tawny, and the teat.'

Meanwhile, Charlie Higson picked this one when he came on the podcast:

'A bloke goes into a pet shop and says, "I'd like to buy a wasp, please."
 The shopkeeper says, "I'm sorry, we don't sell wasps."
 The bloke says, "Well, you've got one in the window."'

In terms of life advice, Taylor Glenn, a former psychotherapist and co-host of the *Drunk Women Solving Crime* podcast, said:

'Don't worry about what other people think of you – aim to be as comfortable in your own skin as you can be, and fuck everybody else. Not literally, I don't recommend fucking everybody.'

And when I interviewed him for the book, my son Jake offered this life advice:

'The sun will rise again tomorrow. Life might hurt and some things might be unpleasant, but the world keeps spinning and the sun will always rise.'

part two

part two

6
REINVENTION

WITH AGE COMES POWER

'Above all, be the heroine of your life, not the victim.'
Nora Ephron

reinvention
/ˌriːɪnˈvɛnʃn/
noun

noun: reinvention; plural noun: reinventions

The act of producing something new based on something that already exists, or the new thing that is produced

'fairy tales are templates whose re-inventions tell us about ourselves'

Source: *https://dictionary.cambridge.org/dictionary/english/reinvention#google_vignette*

What do female elephants, orcas and bonobos have in common with midlife women? With age comes power.

Elephants are matrilineal – basically, older females run the show. Males live separately and never serve as leaders (a sort of reverse Boris Johnson, if you will). Bliss.

So many fucks left to give

The word menopause comes from the Greek words *mens*, meaning 'month', and *pausis*, meaning 'pause'. (Of course men had to make sure they were in it too.) It marks the end of the period itself, and the beginning of a new period. At this time in life, our bodies are literally reinventing themselves – so like it or not, reinvention is part of the package. I was ready, or as ready as a person can be, for bodily reinvention when it came to no more bleeding, but some of the other stuff took me a bit by surprise. Like losing hair down there. How exasperating, after all those years of militantly safeguarding the bush when it had all but gone extinct in the wild, for mine to decide one day on a whim to tap out of the game. And worse yet, to start growing hair elsewhere. Chin hair, facial peach fuzz, and those weird new pubey bits by my ears. I've got sideburns like the underside of a labradoodle. I'm fast turning into a ginger Elvis Presley.

I'm glad we've left behind the coyness of referring to menopause as 'the change', but it does involve radical physiological and psychological change. Even though it is enforced change, it's my belief that midlife reinvention need not come with resignation, but instead with ambition. That's not to say whatever we choose to do needs to be perfect, or even successful, whatever success is. But even with our plantar fasciitis-suffering feet firmly on the ground, we've been kicking around long enough to have earned the right to have our eyes on the stars.

My reinvention has been everywhere from the stars to the sewers. One of my first-ever gigs was in a converted toilet, deep underground somewhere in East London. Thankfully, things have moved on, mostly for the better. But not always. Last night, I had the sort of gig where the word 'period' silences a room, at a golf club, and I don't even have them (periods or golf clubs). But for all the toilets and stag parties and long drives home in the early hours, *je ne regrette rien*. I don't have a boss! That's right. I don't have a boss! And I only have so many fucks left to give.

The idea of females becoming more powerful with age may be taking a while to catch on in human society, but powerful older females have always been a thing in the animal kingdom. While the vast majority of animal species are male-led, female-led groups are a significant minority. There is, of course, wisdom that comes with age, regardless of gender. Wild animals have less chance than we do of making it to old age, and when they do, it counts. Animals value their elders, and it's often the oldest animals who have the most influence within their social groups. Kira Cassidy is a research associate with the Yellowstone Wolf Project, and in analysing sixteen years of data, she found that a pack was more likely to win a fight if one of the pack members was very old. She discovered that when packs of equal size meet, the pack with the old wolf is two and a half times more likely to win, not due to strength, but due to wisdom, strategy and life experience. Elephants too revere their elders, and the death of an elder can send the remaining grieving herd into disarray, impacting on all aspects of their social hierarchy and survival, sometimes for years to come.

Taking the music out of MTV

You might have heard the saying that insanity is 'doing the same thing again and again and expecting different results'. I would go one step further and say that insanity is doing the same thing over and over again, *knowing* you'll get the same results, but doing it anyway. If what you're doing isn't working, try something different.

MTV launched in the US on 31 August 1981, and just over a decade later I started working for them in London. At the time of its launch, MTV was quite simply a music video jukebox, playing music videos 24/7, and it was – and, indeed, still is – one of the most recognisable and iconic brands in the world. The Coca-Cola bottle is sometimes cited as the epitome of an iconic brand: if you see a shard of glass from a Coca-Cola bottle in the gutter, even if it doesn't have any of the lettering on it, you'll know which bottle it came from. MTV was like that – slice it, dice it, splice it, it was a world-beating brand. The very first video played on MTV when it launched in 1981 was 'Video Killed the Radio Star' by The Buggles. In order to have enough content to avoid running the limited number of American music videos on heavy rotation, MTV had to look elsewhere, and soon UK artists and their videos started to feel the MTV effect too. MTV needed UK talent as much as UK talent needed them, giving smash hits across the pond to acts until then unknown in the States, like Duran Duran, George Michael and Kim Wilde.

In 1987, MTV arrived in the UK, and it grew throughout the nineties as satellite TV took on over here. But you can't stay at number one forever. Soon, more and more channels playing non-stop music videos emerged, and the idea of waiting for a TV station to show the video you wanted grew tired. MTV had to reinvent itself – and fast. It switched out some of its music for long-form content, and from its hastily reinvented schedule arose adult animation like *Beavis & Butt-Head*, arguably laying the groundwork for *South Park* and *The Simpsons* and all that came afterwards. It commissioned the first-ever reality shows – *The Real World*, then its spin-off *Road*

Rules – long before (and one might argue serving as the inspiration for) *Big Brother*. Years before shows like *Who Wants to Be a Millionaire?* and *The Weakest Link* lit a flame under the global TV format business, MTV was doing format deals around the world for these shows.

MTV successfully reinvented to the point where if you look at the current MTV logo, it no longer refers to 'music'. They may have kept the 'M', but they took the music out of music television – and it didn't just survive, it thrived. I still feel a pang of something between pride and nostalgia when I see a bit of MTV merchandise kicking about in a shop or on a young person. My daughter recently FaceTimed me from a club she was in in Madrid to show me MTV playing on a massive screen. That amazed me (not so much that MTV was playing, but that she would FaceTime me while on a night out with her mates).

MTV may have acted quickly, but this apparent speed was relative; the process of greenlighting and creating shows wasn't agile thirty years ago. Now, content creators are increasingly doing away with the gatekeepers, preferring audiences to vote with their clicks, not willing to wait for people in offices to decide whether what they're doing does or does not make the cut. TikTok has been around for nearly ten years, YouTube for twenty already. Social media platforms are far from new, and their short-form content has increasingly taken over from mainstream broadcast media. I get more opportunities from one viral Instagram reel than I do for appearing on *Live at the Apollo*. There's little point looking ruefully at the world and wishing it wasn't so. It just is.

Voltaire – 'Uncertainty is an uncomfortable position. But certainty is an absurd one.'

Life lessons from Gen Z

Brian Logan, the *Guardian*'s comedy critic, wrote an article last year headlined: 'Crowd work is the hottest thing in stand-up comedy – and not everybody is laughing'.[15] Loath as I am to criticise someone whose job it is to criticise me, it got my dander up. The upshot was that comedians increasingly lean on crowd work, both in their shows and via the use of clipped-up online content to sell their shows, and that this is a bad thing. I get it when it comes to the basic expectation an audience should have that a comic has sat down, or stood up, and written jokes, taking the time to craft a show. But the need to get content out online thick and fast is real. I sometimes chat to fellow comedians, usually but not always of around my age, who are dismissive of social media; they're often the ones who've been doing it long enough that their profile is high without it. They made it big when social media wasn't a thing, and they've brought their audience with them. For those of us newer to the game, social media is what gives us a profile, and without it most of us would struggle to make a career out of comedy. We didn't create this brave new world in which we're operating, but it would be foolhardy not to look at how we operate within it. There's no such thing as a 'young person's game'. (Well, I suppose youth volleyball is a young person's game.)

That doesn't mean we shouldn't worry about the impact of tech on our minds, wellbeing and posture, and of AI on our future. I got as far as lunchtime yesterday and realised the only conversation I'd had that day was with Siri, who had in turn not heard me, asked me to repeat the question, and then said no. I might as well get married. But embracing change need not be as daunting as we think. If, a couple of years ago, when I started building a profile on Instagram and TikTok, I had thought about how I wanted to implement a social media strategy and what my monthly reach should be, first of all I'd have lost the will to live, and secondly it would have felt overwhelming. I tried not to overthink it, just pointing the camera at my face and talking about whatever was happening that day. My videos aren't curated or beautifully lit; my hair and make-up are only done if my day already involves being somewhere that calls for hair and make-up (better yet, a day which calls for someone else to be doing it). I'm no Selena Gomez with her over 4 million followers, but it's a platform that I can use to get my authentic voice out there. No one can stop me and, trolls aside, I like it. Sometimes I'm even grateful to the trolls, for illustrating my points better than I ever can.

Rachel Parris – 'Don't be too fixed in your dreams. I think, have high horizons; do what you want to do and have high ambitions. But I would never have thought of half of the things that I've ended up doing by accident. And some of the things that happen by accident are the best things that happen. If you've got blinkers on, you miss a lot of what might be out there for you. So yeah, hold your dreams loosely.'

I'm not a patient person – mindfulness can only go so far – but I do subscribe to the belief that some of the best things come about in small increments. Stand-up will teach you that. There's simply no shortcut to putting in the stage time (with a couple of notable exceptions, like Sarah Millican and Kevin Bridges, who seemingly came out of the womb able to do stand-up, not that they don't put in the hard yards). It's about unwavering commitment and putting the hours in, just like going to the gym (says me, who hasn't set foot in a gym since 2005 and is unlikely to ever do so again unless there's a gig happening in one). Building a skill takes work, per Malcolm Gladwell's 10,000-hour rule, and old habits die hard. I was reminded of quite how hard when my kids came home for my birthday recently, and the unspoken rule of all families came into play: that everyone must revert to the mental age of fourteen as quickly as possible. They hadn't even unpacked their bags, and we were straight back to arguments about screen-time and curfews and weed. In the end, I just told them: 'I'm your mother. I'll do what I bloody like.'

Shit gets real

At the midlife intersection, the parallel roads of sexism and ageism disproportionately impact women. I heard some bloke called Chip talking to Oprah Winfrey about midlife reinvention from a man's perspective, or at least from a man called Chip's perspective.[16] He said that, based on research, the issue for men in their fifties is irrelevance, while for women, it's invisibility. That seems to imply that men are more bothered by a loss of what they mean to society, while the price women pay is connected to the loss of how good they look in society.

Irrelevance and invisibility are close bedfellows, but I wondered just how close. I put out something on social media (see? It's not just froth, it's a research tool) asking people to sum up their experience of midlife in three words. The most used words were:

1) hot (mainly as in 'hot flush', rather than the sexy kind of hot)

2) invisible

3) fucking (as an adjective, rather than the sexy kind)

It was mainly women who responded, and only one used the word 'irrelevant', writing: 'invisible, irrelevant and ignored'. Others implied both invisibility and irrelevance, with comments like: 'hot, overlooked, undervalued'.

Here's a selection of the other eloquent, beautiful and clever things that came back:

Experienced, unappreciated, strong.

Live, laugh, lobotomy.

Ignored, sore, free.

Do not trampoline.

Leave me alone.

Oh, my back.

Sexy as fuck.

Big massive pants.

What's this bollocks?

Thrush, tears, hirsute.

Constipated, diarrhea, whaaaaaatt?

Where's my phone?

Hot filterless goddess.

Constant bloody change.

Happy, funnier. fucked.

Dogs, sleep, chocolate.

I can't find . . .

Hell ya, motherf*cker.

Sandwich-generation stress.

Where's the loo?

The plot thickens.

The waist thickens.

White chin hair.

Love your gynaecologist.

Is this it?

Always plucking hairs.

It is complicated.

Fucking livid, mate.

Desperate, depressed, dismissed.

Done bloody bleeding.

Sweaty, teary fury.

Learning self-love.

So many creams.

Take no shit.

Good at life.

My turn now.

Ow, nope, YES!

I gotta pee.

Fierce, determined, loved.

Tearful, calm, mental.

Who said that?

It's my time.

My three words? Aren't women brilliant. Always on the lookout for little answers to the big questions. Invisibility: who are we? Irrelevance: why are we? And brain fog: where are we?

Reinvention at work

Globally, approximately 150 million jobs will shift to workers aged fifty-five and older by the end of the decade.[17] This study doesn't break down the millions of jobs by gender, but my guess is that over half will be being done by men – call it a hunch. Menopause is one of the key moments where we lose women in the workforce. A study in New Zealand revealed that one in twelve women resign during menopause, with 84 per cent of women reporting that it adversely affects their job.[18] Over here in the UK, 23 per cent of women have considered resigning due to menopause, and 14 per cent have.[19]

The best is yet to come

Built-in obsolescence involves deliberately designing something with a finite lifespan, so that in time it will become obsolete or non-functional. The point of planned obsolescence is that we have to buy the thing again (phones, cars, software). In tech terms, the ways to combat this are along the repair, replace or upcycle lines. But nature was doing this to women long before the big brains of Silicon Valley started doing it to phones. I prefer to think of us as 'pre-loved' rather than obsolete, with our best adventures still lying ahead.

Fair play to anyone who opts to 'downsize' at this stage in life, but there's always the possibility of 'upsizing' too, at whatever age or life phase. I've brought everything honed over decades as a TV executive with me to help me succeed as a speaker and comedian – mainly talking the talk and having good teeth. (I know I have good teeth because after one of my first gigs, someone came up to me excitedly and said, 'I loved your . . .' Me: 'Yes?' Her: 'Teeth.') You can take everything you've been before with you, too – the bits you want, anyway. We don't put in a shift of several decades on the planet only to jettison everything when we move on to the next thing; all experience is relevant. It may not always feel like it, but you are not your job, let alone your job title.

Do you have to be brave to reinvent yourself? What does it even mean to be 'brave'? I used to skydive, and people kept telling me that I was brave for doing it, because of how dangerous it was. Skydiving has a few things in common with comedy – you get an adrenaline rush, it's male-dominated and you spend more time driving around the country than doing the thing itself. And in each case, when it goes well, there's little better. Statistically, skydiving is safer than scuba-diving or rugby, and no more dangerous than driving – as long as you're not an arsehole about it. I was once, and only once.

On that occasion, my addictive personality had seen me staying up drinking until the early hours at the airbase. At seven o'clock the next morning, conditions were exactly right and up we went. I exited the plane in the wrong position, hit my hand on the wing strut, and my parachute malfunctioned. I would have failed a breathalyser test. Just as you wouldn't think it safe to drive three hours after stopping drinking, nor should you think it's a great idea to jump out of a plane. Reader, I survived. And to this day, I maintain that skydiving is a safe sport. It wasn't skydiving that nearly killed me, it was Absolut Vodka. That led to another reinvention, because very soon afterwards, I pretty much stopped drinking. I'm one of the few people who, when the doctor asks how much you drink and you reply with 'One to two units a week,' isn't lying (although they always look at me as if I am).

Betwixt and between

Menopause marks a liminal period where we inhabit the betwixt and between. At this midlife gateway, who we were – or at least who we *thought* we were – is no more. In my late forties, I began to grapple with the question: 'Who even am I?' Liminality (from the Latin *līmen*, meaning 'threshold'), describes the process of transitioning across boundaries and borders; literally the threshold separating one space from another. Liminal spaces are literally neither here nor there, their sole purpose being to provide places through which things move or transition. Car parks are liminal spaces. Pavements are liminal spaces. Train stations and airports are liminal spaces. Sunrise and sunset are liminal spaces. In keeping with the spirit of crying on planes, I have a strange – or perhaps not so strange – love of liminal spaces. Because we can't stay there and have to move through them, I feel free of the burden of having to know what the hell I'm doing, or even the need to be doing much at all. How can we fail at something in a place we're not even meant to be? Liminal spaces involve doors closing behind you as you face an uncertain next door, and it's funny discovering which doors are apt to open once others are closed.

Trying to see the road ahead isn't helped by actual brain fog. I looked up the meteorological definition of the difference between fog and mist, and apparently it comes down to visibility: if you can't see more than 100 metres ahead, it's fog. I've definitely got brain fog, not mist. I'm not talking about walking up the stairs and forgetting what I came up for. I'm talking ninja-level forgetfulness, like calling the kids by the dog's name, the dog by the cat's name and then forgetting I've got a cat. Like having to hang up on my daughter because I can't find my phone. Sometimes, I send myself emails of things I really mustn't forget, only to get an email notification and think: 'Ooh, an email. I wonder who that's from?' Yesterday, I spent a full thirty seconds after getting off the tube trying to remember why I'd gone to that station. There's a good chance I only reinvented in midlife to become a comic because I forgot I was meant to be in a work meeting, wandered into an open-mic gig by mistake, and it just snowballed.

But amidst the fuzz and the frizzles, a sort of clarity emerges, a bit like when you stop looking too hard at something and it starts to come into focus.

Wayne Hemmingway – 'Understand why you're doing something – make sure you've got your own purpose and that you love what you do. If you think about work just in terms of getting really good money doing it, you're less likely to earn really good money in the long run, because you probably won't enjoy it as much. But if you can do something because it really excites you and you want to get up in the morning, you're more likely to succeed. If I didn't like doing what I did, or what I do, all of this wouldn't have happened. It's been bloody good fun. I have no problem getting up at four in the morning because I wake up and I think: I want to do that . . . There's really interesting things to do, and to think, and to deliver.'

Your wise mind just got wiser

When I asked people to describe midlife in three words, one of the offerings that came in was: 'Now I understand.' Hard relate.

Don't bullshit yourself. There's a difference between inner and outer change, between seeming different and being different. You can con the world about the difference between the two – that's what social media's for – but best not con yourself. Reinvention is about turning up the volume on ourselves, not imitating someone else. With our bodies and relationships with those around us fast changing, the ground is seemingly less sure beneath our feet. Identity and purpose can feel elusive, but keeping them in our presbyopic sights will save us. In fact, it's only in midlife that I've started to have the faintest clue of who I am and why I'm doing what I'm doing: a phoenix in support pants, rising from the ashes of the boardroom.

It's no wonder my identity was shaky in the corporate world. Being talked over and marginalised in male-dominated rooms was largely water off a duck's back to me; looking back, I normalised things that shouldn't be normalised, and I didn't speak out when I should have. The nineties might have been a good time for property prices, but they were shit for providing safe spaces for women at work. When it was my turn to take on a senior management role, I was adamant I wouldn't be a self-seeking boss and would try to be an ally for people who might need one, spurred on by the lack of allyship that had at many times up to that point cost me dear. It was only towards the end of my boardroom years that I realised that people who focus on managing upwards are often the ones who get richly rewarded. I also noticed that the people who made themselves the trickiest to deal with were the least likely to be called out by an organisation, and were quite likely to be promoted out of trouble so that a different boss would have to take them on. It amazed me how many times people were willing to kick the can down the road rather than face having a difficult conversation or making a difficult decision.

It dawned on me – admittedly, quite late in the day – that by focusing on those around rather than those above me, there were only so many places I could go. My friend Charlotte, a fellow board-level media person back in the day and one of my closest friends, has a sandwich analogy about organisational psychology. I might not be getting it quite right, but it's along the lines of there being one thousand people and just one sandwich. Who's going to end up with it? And, most tellingly of all, who will be the person who makes sure they end up disingenuously *next* to the person with the sandwich? In that analogy, I was going very hungry.

I never meant to get into working in 'business' in the first place, let alone what was effectively just a very senior sales job. My career in sales started young and inauspiciously. At seventeen, the proud new owner of a driver's licence, I got a job driving an ice-cream van around the army barracks of Salisbury Plain. It was a commission-only job, and I lived for the days when an old lady would buy a Viennetta, because you didn't make much off a Milk Pop. Each van had a route it had to take, arriving at each place at a set time. After a few days of low sales, I realised the boss's daughter had the same route, with arrival times an hour or two before mine. I was picking up whatever dregs nepotism left behind (the perfect testbed for a career in showbiz). She had the Mr Whippy van with an automated chime, while my van was one-up on a moped and you had to wind the chimes like a carriage clock. Try ten-hour days with 'Just one Cornetto' as an ear worm, RSI in your chime fingers.

Another problem was toilets. There were no public toilets on my route, and as a solo seventeen-year-old, I wasn't keen on popping in to use pub toilets along the way. Nor was there much ground cover to be had, it being an army training plain. A few hours into my first day, in desperation, I turned my van off down a tank track for a quick wee, only to find that the tank terrain was not ice-cream-van-friendly. Soon my tiny van – more of a roller-skate than a roadworthy vehicle at the best of times – was on its side. This was long before mobile phones were a thing, and I couldn't do much but wait. A while later, a tank came along, two soldiers hopped out and, unfazed, they tipped my little van back upright. Body and ego bruised, stock melted; I didn't last a week.

Somewhat more successful was my time on Camden Market as a student (and there was a similar lack of available toilets there back in the day). I got a job helping out on a stall selling off 1920s and 1930s clothing on behalf of a movie stylist who needed to rotate her stock once filming finished. After a few weeks, I asked if I could run the stall for her, working on commission, rather than being paid a day rate. Within two weeks, I'd earned enough to buy a washing machine for our flatshare, and that job went on to pay me through the rest of uni, even allowing me to get a crappy car.

I've spent the past twenty-five years living just around the corner from Camden Market, because that's where MTV was when I started working there. All roads lead to Camden, it would seem. And to sales. Getting people to buy whatever I was selling was in my blood, looking back, but it still felt like an accident that I ended up in a revenue-generating role for a big corporation. I just wanted my MTV, and that's where it took me. And that's where I stayed, for years and years.

Soon after I finally jumped ship from my corporate day job, I went for lunch with a mate at our local pub. (Why not spend the day in the pub when you're not working for the first time in decades?) She had done the same thing and jacked in a good job a few years earlier, when she had not long turned forty. Over our Tuesday lunchtime Thai-curry-for-a-fiver, she said to me: 'Your wise mind just got wiser.' And I knew exactly what she meant.

Shaun Keaveny – 'When people used to say to me, always listen to your gut, I was like, what the fuck does that mean? I don't even have a gut instinct. I remember saying that for years. But yeah, you do. You do have a gut instinct, it's just that it's almost imperceptible sometimes. But when there's something very important about to happen, or something momentous that you're about to make a decision on, you'll know what I mean. You just tune in to your guts, and you see what they do. Because [so many] times, they've squirmed just before I've done something, and I've really regretted it afterwards.'

Side hustles

Long live the side hustle. When I started doing stand-up, I was gigging on the open-mic circuit by night, and senior vice president of a US studio by day. Then one day, it was time for the side hustle to become the main event.

The 'grandmother hypothesis' is the premise that orcas experience menopause so that females can stop spending energy on their kids and save it for bigger things, including the long-term survival of their grandchildren and their pod. They have uniquely excellent memories for routes and hunting grounds (I can't even remember where I left my keys; one time, I found them in the fridge). They move out of the day job of raising little orcas and into the hustle of leading, not following. I left my last corporate job at an age at which society generally suggests women should lightly pixelate and fade. Never have I been more visible. But it didn't happen overnight.

Change can be massive, the kind of Damascene moments that come about a few times in one's lifetime, the kind of moments my guests talk about on the podcast. Or it can be something equally powerful but much smaller in scale, an incremental change, the butterfly effect: chaos theory. This is the scientific theory of chaos, that the tiny perturbation of a butterfly flapping its wings will have a direct impact on the date, the course and the strength of a tornado many weeks hence.

It's important to think big, but it's good to start small. Charles Handy was ahead of his time when, in 2001, he wrote *The Elephant and the Flea*, about how individuals (the fleas) relate to multinational conglomerates (the elephants). Back then, most of us were only too happy to be all aboard with the elephants, until it became increasingly hard to ignore the actual elephant in the room – the fact that we were free to flee (and to flea). Perhaps the clever money is on those who, for whatever reason, are having itchy feet and a career rethink. The only thing we know for certain is that the future will be different, and as you contemplate whether the gig economy is for you, it needn't be all or nothing. It might be radical reinvention, but you could equally side-hustle your way into a different way of living your life, a tiny butterfly flapping its wings and causing a typhoon.

Al Murray – 'My office is also a music studio, and is usually swamped with drums and cymbals. I've played drums since I was a kid, and in 2015 I started my own company, the British Drum Company, in Stockport. We make drums for bands such as Iron Maiden and Manic Street Preachers. Bizarrely, the neighbours have only complained about the noise once in the whole time I've lived here. I had a bunch of my muso mates over, making a bit of a racket. Admittedly, it was three in the morning!'

Reinvention does not always come about by choice, and sometimes circumstance twists your arm. When I first left ITV in the early noughties, I set up a little creative consultancy, mainly – OK, entirely – because it was taking a while to find the right job and I needed some cash. I wrote a couple of pieces in the trade press about the launch of my own business in a desperate bid to get back on the map. People got in touch to congratulate me, word spread, and next thing I knew I had a couple of freelance gigs. It all worked out, and for a few years that's how I made my money, without a boss and able to get along to kids' school pick-ups and concerts and sports days and whatnot as a newly single parent. Similarly, perimenopausal hormonal upheaval, coupled with the fact that I was starting to get work *on* TV, making it increasingly hard to work *in* TV, led me to pull the plug on corporate life. Necessity, the mother of reinvention.

And then, of course, there's reluctant reinvention. I arrived at a venue to give a speech a while back and asked one of the events team if I could just take a look at my slides to make sure they'd come through OK. We had a look, and everything was tickety-boo, except for the fact the holding slide had me down as 'Carry Beaton'. I said my name was Cally, if they wouldn't mind changing it. The events person said he'd been told it was definitely Carry. I said, 'Ah, well, not to worry – but it's me, Cally, so it does need changing, please.' He then went to his inbox to show me an email he had been sent to prove it really was Carry, not Cally. Even I began to wonder. All those years I'd been getting it wrong. Thank goodness he was around to correct me. And the lifetime achievement award for mansplaining goes to . . .

Old dog, new tricks

One way to unlock creativity, play and possibility is to learn something new. The theory is that while your creative brain is busy with the task at hand, on an unconscious level you will be coming up with inventive solutions in unrelated areas. While you can't duck the hours spent at your computer or notebook, many writers will agree that it's the hours spent away from the page, having put in the groundwork, where the magic happens. (At least, that's my excuse for the record-breaking level of displacement activities in which I am proficient.) Learning new things opens your mind up to new possibilities and fresh ideas, and brings with it a bit of a thrill; a fresh sense of being awake at the wheel.

Back in my seventies boys'-school days, I was OK during the time I spent in structured lessons, but free time was harder, which is why I filled all social time between classes with the piano. The idea of 'free' time was – and still is, although to a thankfully lessening degree – terrifying. The piano saved me from myself and, after a chance conversation with Alistair McGowan at Brentford football stadium, I'm learning to play it again, after a hiatus of forty years.

In March 2023, Alistair and I were both on the bill of a charity fundraiser. After I'd been on, he wondered why our paths had never crossed before, and I explained it was because I'd only got into comedy in my forties. He then told me about his own midlife reinvention, becoming a classical pianist, and I said, 'That's funny, I used to play the piano and haven't touched it in the best part of four decades.' He pulled out of his pocket a leaflet for the inaugural Ludlow Piano Festival, of which he is joint artistic director, and pointed to the celebrity piano concert on the opening night, a couple of months hence. Would I like to perform? 'No, I bloody wouldn't,' I said. 'I cannot stress enough how much I HAVEN'T PLAYED THE PIANO FOR FORTY YEARS.' Would I like to come along and watch then? Yes, I said, I would.

Professor Anil Seth – 'Keep learning and stay curious.'

My dad turned eighty that year: my dad who had retired from teaching just over twenty years earlier in order to dedicate time to things he enjoyed, not least playing timpani and singing as a tenor in a choir. As part of his eightieth birthday celebrations, he came with me to Ludlow in May 2023 and together we watched the celebrity concert (proper celebrities, most of whom could properly play the piano – I was underqualified on several counts). After the concert, in the bar with the performers, musician dad by my side, I made the commitment to find a piano teacher and return the following May to perform. Two months later, I'd found a teacher, and ten months after that, I played in Ludlow, with my dad and brother in the audience. Each performer was interviewed briefly onstage before we played. I said I hoped this might go some way towards paying my parents back for all those piano lessons as a kid, and that while I couldn't guarantee a perfect performance – in fact, I could guarantee it would be imperfect – I could guarantee that I'd play with love, from the heart. I'll never forget that first moment when I took my seat at that beautiful piano, ready to inhabit the piece, just as my teacher had taught me. Then I boldly played those first magnificent notes of the prelude from Debussy's Suite Bergamasque. They were the wrong notes – but hey. They were *my* notes. I chipped my Shellac playing Debussy that night – don't know whether I'm a Jane Austen character or a Kardashian.

Seann Walsh – 'In the words of Kate Bush, "Don't give up." You apply that to your life. Hang on, this isn't what I want. Who's telling me I can't do that? I'm going to do it. Do not give up. Give it everything.'

My dad's just sent me his upcoming concert list, and from Rachmaninov to Haydn, at eighty-one, he's gigging up a storm. Like father like daughter, I hope. There's a lovely symmetry that now I am playing on a Steinway again, a lovely, handed-down-through-the-family piano that, instead of being on a podium in a private school, is in the heart of a family home – not my family home, but my piano teacher's. And how rewarding to know that if I keep on practising, by the time I'm sixty, I might be as good as I was when I was eleven. Turns out, you can teach an old(ish) dog new, or at least long-forgotten, tricks.

I'll decide

Spoiler alert: the human condition is terminal. No one's going to look back and say to themselves: 'I wish I'd stayed in that job/life I hated.' An uncertain future is better than the certainty of returning to a situation that makes you unhappy, day in, day out. Life is for living, not running away from, even the scary bits, and if you don't like change, strap in – because in my experience, the cycle of change is never more than about eighteen months, whether you're in the mood for it or not.

I work as hard now as I ever have, but never, even for the briefest moment, have I regretted no longer having a day job. And my new life is going OK, although this week I found out I had lost a job to Joan Collins, a sentence my twenty-something self would find unfathomable. Small disappointments like that aside, let no one say I'm not nailing my reinvention. Only last night at a gig, as I walked through the venue, I heard someone whisper to their friend, 'She's somebody,' to which her friend replied, 'She's nobody.' I wouldn't mind, but they'd literally just seen me onstage.

Alistair Brownlee – 'The times in my life that I feel like I've been happiest or most content are the times where I have been really focused on having one kind of goal. I think finding something that means something to you, and being focused on that and doing it as well as you possibly can, has ramifications for you as a person, and you live way beyond that thing on its own.'

This is not a story of success or perfection, but one of choice. My life. My story. My decision. Comedy wasn't my last reinvention. I've a few left in me, and I believe we all have. I must be the only person to be writing a book and learning a musical instrument *not* in lockdown (although I still can't bake banana bread for shit). Midlife women are not one-dimensional, professionally or personally, and we take it all with us when we throw the dice. Our bodies may decline, at whatever rate and to whatever degree, but our spirit need not. We're all out there still, doing incredible things. And no one is more surprised than us.

DO TRY THIS AT HOME

From side to main hustle: planning your escape route

The original 'wheel of life' goes back to the *bhavacakra* in Buddhism, representing the cycle of life, death and rebirth. The modern-day 'wheel of life' exercise helps bring unconscious knowledge to the surface – think of it as giving your wise mind an airing. Here it is with its standard eight categories (you can, of course, pick others; for example, if you're off romance, change it for travel):

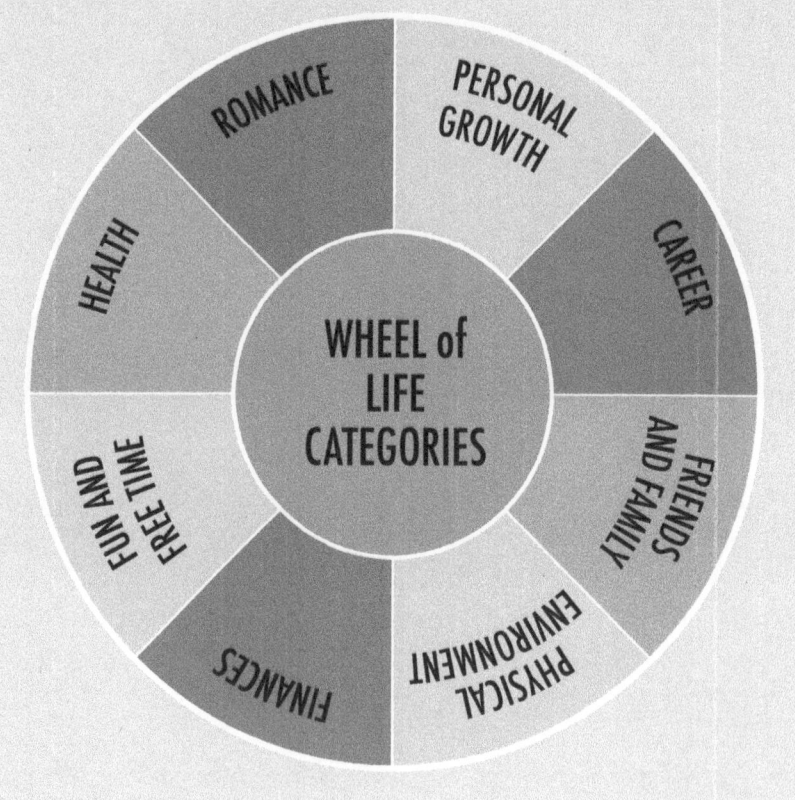

Simply rate each of the categories on a scale of one (least satisfied) to ten (most satisfied). The sweet spot isn't to have a full set of eights, nines and tens (although wouldn't that be nice?); rather, you're looking for balance. If you imagine drawing a line on each of the segments that corresponds with the rating you've given it, what you want is for the wheel to be round enough to keep on turning. No one wants a bumpy ride (definitely not after two ten-pound babies). Once you've rated each of the segments, have a look at it. Then ask yourself these questions:

How does it feel looking at it?

What stands out?

How much time do I spend in each of these areas?

How much time would I like to spend?

Are there any surprises?

Which things would I most like to change or improve?

What help and support might I need from other people?

What do I feel most energised about as I look at it?

The last step involves narrowing it down to whatever small steps you are going to commit to taking first. Which area(s) will you pick? What either excites you or needs addressing because it depresses you? Ideally, pick between one to three small actions you are committing to take; these might be across different categories, or they might relate to the same one or two. Write down, concisely but precisely, what the exact action is, and set a date by which you are going to have done it, making a note to check back in with yourself then. Oh, and various studies have shown that sharing with someone else a goal you have set yourself increases the chance of it happening, and arranging to check in with someone on how it's going radically increases the chances of it happening.

Remember: think big, start small.

Who cares what you think?

I do. And you should. Finding and maintaining your purpose in life is intrinsically linked to your values: the things that matter to you (and I mean really, really matter). A good way to identify your values – and these will change over time – is to do a brain dump for fifteen or twenty minutes, just scribbling down the words that come up when you ask yourself the question: 'What do I really care about?'

There are hundreds that might come up; here are twenty of mine:

love

kindness

independence

honesty

creativity

pleasure

purpose

laughter

competence

balance

    comfort

    music

    literature

    nature

    family

    trust

    peace

    opportunity

    excitement

    authenticity

Once you've written your own long list, walk away for a bit and do something else. When you come back, check first to see if there are any further words you would like to add. Now, the task is to narrow it down to your top fifteen, then ten, then five. Once you have your top five, take another breather. Now come back to it and write a few sentences about *why* each of those five things is important to you.

As well as revealing what's important to you, defining or redefining your values helps reinforce self-belief. Sometimes, when faced with a difficult decision, it can be helpful to hold up your choices to the light of your core values and see how it all stacks up. You'll know.

It's such a perfect day

Admittedly, the Lou Reed song was about heroin, but this is about a narcotic-free dopamine hit that hinges on letting your imagination, hopes and dreams run free – not just relating to a perfect day, but to a perfect life.

Pick a time frame – one year, eighteen months, or two years from now – and write out, in the present tense, how your life is. Get it down in as much descriptive detail as possible, in glorious Technicolor – every last tiny fact. Where are you? What sort of place are you living in? What's it like inside? And out? What do you do with your days? Who's with you? What can you see, hear, taste, smell? How do you feel? Keep writing until there's nothing more to write. Notice if you start to limit yourself as you're writing, replacing 'No, because . . .' thoughts with 'What if?' questions. It's for your eyes only – no one is going to mark it.

And that's it. You don't need to correct it, re-read it, or do anything further. Just keep it somewhere safe and see what happens.

Once you've created a compelling outcome, you may be surprised by how close to it you get. When I was thinking about leaving the corporate world, I wrote out how I would like my life to be – what I would do for work and for pleasure, where I would be doing it – all in minute detail. And it's wonderful how close to what I wrote back then my life is now – my working, family and social life, anyway. My dating life, on the other hand . . . But that's for another chapter. Or perhaps another book.

LAST WORDS

Kicking off the jokes, it's Angela Barnes, with a Rich Perry gag:

'I fell asleep on the bus and my head just kept nodding forward, and I kept hitting the dinging thing with my head [. . .] I didn't realise I was doing it. I just thought I was having a series of really good ideas.'

Sticking with the head theme, here's Kerry Godliman's pick:

'What do you call a nun with a washing machine on her head? Sister Matic.'

When it comes to life advice, Dr Kevin Dutton came on the podcast and shared this gem, attributed to Confucius:

'We have two lives, and the second begins when we realise we only have one.'

And someone who knows as much about hustle and change as anyone is Baroness Ayesha Hazarika:

'Put yourself out there and hustle for things. Ask for things. Go beyond your comfort zone. I think women, particularly in politics and in corporate life, get put in a box. You get put in a lane very, very early on, and you're allowed to do some things, but you're not allowed to traverse into something different. Expand beyond not just your comfort zone, but the comfort zone that other people see you in.'

7
SAY YES! BUT ALSO SAY NO!
MAKING GOOD DECISIONS

'Whether you think you can or you can't,
either way you are right.'
Henry Ford

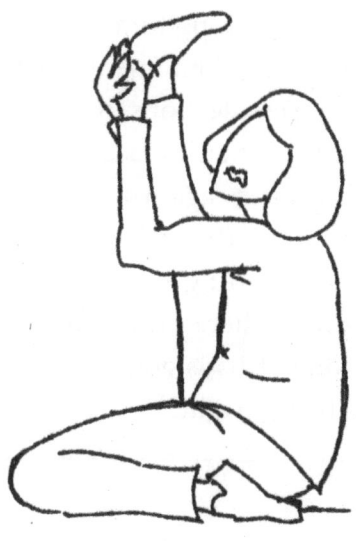

balance
/ˈbaləns/
noun
    physical equilibrium
    'he lost his balance and fell'
    equipoise between contrasting, opposing, or interacting elements
    'both parties were interviewed to provide balance in the report'

verb
    To bring into harmony or proportion
    'a balanced diet'

Source: https://www.merriam-webster.com/dictionary/balance

> It's only since the 1980s that female promiscuity within the animal kingdom has been studied, despite it being a phenomenon that is as old as time itself. Female lions mate up to a hundred times during mating season, with multiple partners, to protect against infanticide due to confused paternity. (Ironic that in a book about women whose breeding days are mainly behind us, there's a focus here on reproduction, but get on board. None of us is going to actually go and shag a male lion, alright?)

Hell yeah

A lioness mating multiple times is not a decision fuelled by feminism, or indeed hedonism, but rather by a fierce instinct to protect her offspring and the pride's lineage. It throws into doubt the sexual double standard often cited as coming from the animal kingdom that it is a matter of instinct for the male of the species to want to sleep around, whereas females by nature are passive and monogamous.

I'm all for saying yes, not necessarily to mating a hundred times – not since I've taken up the piano again, anyway – but to the concept of grabbing life by the throat. I loved Danny Wallace's book *Yes Man*, and the subsequent film rendition starring Jim Carrey. I had Danny on the podcast (still working towards Jim), and he exudes optimism and the power of saying yes. I'd like to posit, however, that if you're going to be a Yes (Wo)Man, you also need to know how to be a No Person. Last year, I said yes to everything, and some great things happened: work I've loved, friends I've made, and getting to write this book. And some not great things happened. I said yes to a boyfriend with a horrible form of cancer (he's fine now, so I can include this in a chapter opening full of levity); I said yes to shingles; and I said yes to taking a single-mum friend's seven-year-old to Legoland on what turned out to be the busiest day in Legoland's history.

We think of saying yes as being what it takes to make things happen, and of course there's merit in that, but for everything you say yes to, you're saying no to something else. I'm writing this while I've got Covid (for the sixth time – the *sixth* time!) which has meant cancelling all my non-home-based work for the week. I was feeling a bit sorry for myself about a big gig tomorrow night that was well paid and something I really wanted to be a part of. Then a lovely comedian pal sent me a care package. I posted it on Instagram, with Jeff photobombing in the background, thanking her for being a sweetheart. A TV commissioner saw the post, and now we've got a meeting in the diary to talk about the two of us co-hosting a show about dogs! Her dog is called Cheryl, by the way. Jeff and Cheryl. They should have their names up, not just in lights but on the windscreen of a Ford Fiesta. I didn't choose to say no to that gig, of course – Covid chose for me. But an enforced 'no' opened up an unexpectedly useful door to a possible 'yes', and it also got me questioning my long-held conviction that turning something down professionally would be a bad thing for my career, let alone that it might help it along.

Saying no does not come naturally to anyone born into a generation of women raised to put ourselves last; perhaps it's optimistic to think that that's not still the case for women and girls. It's good to be empathetic and to consider others, but sometimes it is also important to put our own needs first.

If a comedian talks about another comedian being a 'crowd-pleaser', it's usually a sniffy observation, but when I hear that phrase, I always think, 'Isn't that kind of the job description?' If being a crowd-pleaser is central to being a good comedian, then I was born to it. Forty-nine per cent of adults self-identified as people-pleasers in a 2022 YouGov poll, with women more likely to acknowledge they people-please, while simultaneously not liking to be seen as people-pleasers.[20] The difference between being considerate of others' needs and people-pleasing comes down to the fact that in the case of the latter, we risk negating our own needs and feelings altogether. We may not even know what it is we really want or think before saying yes to things, driven by an urgent wish not to offend or, god forbid, lose anyone. Sometimes it's helpful to take a beat, or even several hours, before saying yes to things that, in hindsight, might foster resentment, overwhelm or burnout. Those of us who are people-pleasers can build a new habit of checking in with ourselves before saying yes. Try asking yourself:

What do I really think/feel about this?

Would I like to be able to say no?

What's stopping me? What am I scared of?

When the answer to the second question is 'yes', the answer to the third question is often 'upsetting someone'. Regardless of what we say yes or no to, not everyone will like us! If being a comedian is good for one thing, it's proving that. Being on a lifelong quest never to upset anyone can be very upsetting indeed. It really comes down to just one question: how much will it really cost you to say yes when you don't want to? Because rest assured, it costs us dear.

The degree to which I've people-pleased in the past and, therefore, felt scared to say no shocks me a bit. One of the scenes I can hardly bear to play back in my mind is when I was having a tough evening conversation with my *Devil Wears Prada*-style then-boss over in the States, and as I struggled to cut off the long, unpleasant conversation, my firstborn took his first steps over to his dad. I saw it, but the soundtrack was a horrible work call. (To balance this out with a happier memory, when my second-born started crawling, her then-two-year-old brother said: 'Look. It creeps.' Aw.)

In corporate life, there were a few things I used to repeat a lot that caused my team to take the piss out of me; this is going to get a bit David Brent, so bear with, but here they are:

'Choose which hill to die on.'

'You can't boil the ocean.'

'Get out of the weeds.'

What a wanker. But here's the thing. I stand by them all – especially the last one. So, strap in.

Choose which hill to die on

'If it won't matter in five years, it doesn't matter.' I've heard that quote attributed to various people. I know Cher was told it by her mum when she was growing up. It's hard to remember to ask oneself which of the zillion things we're fretting about today will make an iota of difference in the long term. Things that really do matter, like writing a will – literally choosing which hill to die on – took me years, and the feeling of catharsis when I had finally got round to it was enormous; almost as enormous as the growing sense of guilt in the months and years leading up to getting it done. Something that stuck with me when I heard Bryony Gordon talking about her *Eat, Drink, Run* book was when she said that she rarely feels like going for a run, but never regrets having gone for one. I remember my running trainer saying to me that on days I didn't feel like running, I should just worry about getting my running kit on, then see about getting out of the house, then try walking a few steps, then perhaps running a few – next thing you know, you've gone for a run. Or you've gone for a cinnamon bun in your running kit.

Dr Kevin Dutton – 'I've looked at a lot of top sports people and people who have been successful, and what makes people really great and really successful is the ability to do what needs to be done when [they] don't feel like it. Everyone can do what needs to be done when they do feel like it, but what really separates out the great and the successful is the ability to do what needs to be done when you don't feel like it.'

Every day, we make hundreds of decisions, from the small to the big: What shall I wear? What groceries do I need? What time shall I leave for the meeting? Shall I say yes to that invitation? Shall I put a wash on? Should I stay in this relationship? Shall I book a holiday? Should I shave my legs? Shall I shave my face? We make decisions in various ways. We write lists, we follow our guts, we canvas friends, family and trusted colleagues, we watch random people online with little or no experience of the matter in hand because we like their vibe – and, somehow, thoughts turn to decisions, to actions. We weigh up advantages versus disadvantages to make a choice. There is a Buddhist theory that says that if you reach a crossroad in your decision-making, instead of thinking about whether it's right or wrong, you can ask yourself: 'Will this enlarge or diminish my life?' When I finally took the decision to leave my secure, salaried, ultimately soul-sucking job in favour of a largely unknown life as a comedian, asking myself this question was one of the things that helped me pull the plug on having a guaranteed income. Something else that gave me a nudge was a sense of foreboding as I sat in boardrooms that I was getting ever closer to saying what I was actually thinking. All roads led to a meeting point where leaving the safety blanket of that job was not so much a hill to die on as a mountain, rising inexorably out of the mist. My very own Callymanjaro.

Choosing which hill to die on involves flexible and creative thinking, and a willingness to see the inconvenient truths that may be staring us in the face, even if we'd just as soon not see them. It is a story of two parts – the first, working out what is important; the second, being able to say no to the things that aren't. Sometimes, the second is harder than the first. We spend so much time in reactive mode, responding to the multitudinous demands around us, that we lose the space and capacity to be proactive and reflective. Who's got time to breathe these days, or permission to think? Rumination is a dying art.

I've come to realise, in between panicking about it, that much of this book is getting written in my head while I'm on dog walks – not necessarily even the pretty dog walks in natural surroundings. Sometimes, it's the racing-down-Kentish-Town-high-street-to-get-to-something-I'm-running-late-for kind of dog walks. While my brain is busy with the task of walking the dog and getting wherever I'm going, my unconscious mind gets a wiggle on. Sometimes I'm aware of ideas coming in and dictate them into my phone; other times, I don't realise anything's happened until I next sit down to write. And there they are. Something similar happens for comedians onstage. Some ad hoc crowd work will lead into something once thought about and long forgotten, and out it comes, not fully formed, but the germ of something worth saying. So perhaps the first part of choosing which hill to die on is to go and walk up a hill. Or just go for a walk – as someone who spends a lot of time in the Netherlands, I know not everyone can just pop out and find a hill.

In his book *First Things First*, Stephen Covey, author of self-help classic *The 7 Habits of Highly Effective People*, looks at productivity and decision-making on the basis of 'first things'. He suggests we put the significance of the task over how pressing it is:

Zone 1 is for things like a writing deadline (eek), or a breakdown (car rather than mental, although that too).

Zone 2 is the most readily sidelined category, and also the most important: long-term planning, building relationships, time spent with people we love.

Zone 3 is all the tiny crappy bits that demand our attention for little or no benefit. These are things we should arguably not be doing at all, or at least seeing if we can spend minimal time on.

Zone 4 is the home of things that are neither significant nor pressing. I give you . . . TikTok! Covey differentiates between mindless scrolling (OK, he wrote it before TikTok existed, so let's call it time-wasting) and recreational activities that are restorative and therefore belong in Zone 2, like going to a concert or the theatre, or making a conscious decision to sit down and watch a good film.

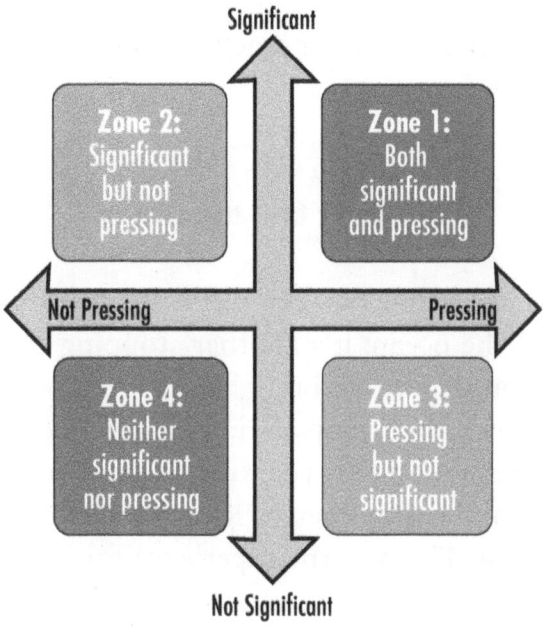

Covey's suggestion is simple in theory, if not in practice: that we make Zone 2 our hill to die on. Sadly, the workplace is rarely set up to encourage this approach. In *The 4-Hour Work Week*, entrepreneur Tim Ferriss looks at effectiveness versus efficiency in business. In his view, companies typically focus on how much work you get done – efficiency – because it's quantifiable, which doesn't necessarily relate to how well a company is doing. Large numbers of unimportant Zone 3 tasks can be ticked off without it having any impact on wider strategy and mid- to long-term success. We all have a personal version of this, like me cleaning the skirting boards, choosing which reel to pin on Instagram, putting my kitchen cloths on a hot wash and expecting my new tour show to write itself.

Chris Sutton – 'Don't just think about things; get out there and do them, whether it's physical exercise, phoning a friend you haven't talked to for a long time, a family member you haven't seen for a long time. Having a tribe with interaction is so important for everybody's mental health and wellbeing. Don't just think about things, get out there and actually do them, and your life will improve.'

You can't boil the ocean

Some days, I can barely boil the kettle. It's one thing realising we can't boil the ocean; it's another stopping trying. As one of a generation of women brought up to be people-pleasers, I grew up against a backdrop of: do well in school, dress nicely, don't gain weight, don't say the wrong thing; in short, be nice. And if you can't be nice, then at least only let the nice bits of yourself be seen. This was the experience for many of us who grew up in the seventies. I recently found myself close to a young couple in the park who were having a row. Well, one of them was screaming and shouting and levelling all sorts of unpleasant fury at the other, who in turn was doing everything in her power to pacify and ameliorate the situation. I saw so much of my younger self in her, trying to keep the peace and be perfect in order to be lovable; anything for him not to walk away. I wanted to call over to her: 'You're brilliant! Don't let his words in! Leave now! Come home with me and Jeff!' I had no idea of the full story between them, and hopefully it wasn't as one-sided as it seemed, but the phrase 'Don't set yourself on fire to keep others warm' came to mind. I hope she got home OK. And that someone's being kind to her.

One of the brilliant things about being fifty-six is pleasing myself, not at the cost of others' wellbeing, but there's definitely no more people-pleasing at the cost of my own. There are lots of reasons we don't like to say no. We're scared people won't like us, that 'no' isn't what the other person wants to hear, that saying it makes us not a nice person, that we'll lose people, or work, or opportunities, or there'll be a row, or we'll end up sad and alone. Saying no has, for most of my life, felt as if it will be catastrophic. Which is odd, when you consider the fact that it's more than reasonable to prioritise our own needs, set boundaries, disagree with people, walk away from unhealthy situations, stand up for ourselves, make mistakes and protect ourselves, our time and our space.

Abigail Burdess – 'The idea of all the promises you've made to the world, in your conscious brain, is quite full on. I'd have this project list of: get whatever sitcom made, get whatever book published, blah, blah, blah. And writing this list, I was like: Oh, I can't do those things. None of the projects which I have written down are actually within my power. The only thing which is within my power is to write the script, or write the book, and then to send it out. But I'm not a publisher, and I don't make TV. It was that moment of going, I don't have to hate myself as I write out another project list of things that I ought to achieve. Because I can't achieve any of these things. I am not omnipotent; I am limited. And what I should be trying to achieve for myself should be within my scope.'

Once you've decided what you can and can't do, what you are going to say no to, there's the small matter of saying no to it. Boundaries. Pesky boundaries. So hard to set, so invaluable once in place. It's like my son's sheep repeatedly escaping (the toy ones at the therapist's, not the real ones he looks after now); it wasn't impossible to fix the pen, it was more that I hadn't noticed the gap in the fence. It's hard to know when a boundary is appropriate, or when it's just us being square, not least when it comes to societal issues. Like manspreading on public transport. After posting an anonymous, faceless picture of a man on the tube, who couldn't have been taking up more space unless he'd put up an umbrella and a picnic table, I got a lot of mansplanations as to why men *have* to sit this way. Because they are taller. Really? I don't see the Dutch, the tallest nation in the world, taking out every other seat on public transport because everyone's sitting akimbo. Or because of their balls. Really? Then why aren't all men sitting like that all the time? What bollocks. My boundary is: 'Spread It. See It. Stop It.' In 2017, the Madrileños put a very clear boundary in place with signs like this all over the Madrid metro:

¡Muy bien, España!

Boundary-setting is a brilliant and hard-won skill, whether those are boundaries relating to other people, boundaries within society as a whole, or – perhaps hardest of all – boundaries within ourselves.

Get out of the weeds

Our brains are busier than ever before, and our to-do lists are longer. With the relentless information overload that is the backdrop to life in the twenty-first century, how do we know which of the unrelenting stimuli we can safely ignore? We end up so caught up in the micro we forget all about the macro, and at the end of the day, the macro is all that matters. There are so many excuses not to get on with the actual job at hand, an endless parade of displacement activities to delight and distract. As I sit in the garden writing this, the kid next door has been given a toy whistle. He is delighted; I am distracted. At least he's not on his iPad. Technology has a lot to answer for. On the one hand, it helps me sell books and tour tickets; on the other, it entices us to spend time on things that our rational brains would rarely elect to spend time on. We're not even being bombarded by a single technology; often, it's laptop plus phone plus TV, or whatever your devices of choice.

Multitasking increases the production of cortisol and adrenaline, and generates an addictive dopamine cycle, giving the brain a reward each time it loses focus and fuelling our incessant drive for external stimulation and validation. We answer the phone, send a WhatsApp, get caught up in photos of Michelle and Barack Obama's wedding anniversary, check emails, and all the good chemicals rush in.

Neuroscientists Peter Milner and James Olds placed electrodes in the brains of rats, in the specific bit of the brain responsible for dopamine production, the same bit that gets fired up when drinkers drink, or addicts shoot up, or any of us have orgasms – they referred to it as the 'pleasure centre'. When the rats pressed a lever, an electrical signal went to the pleasure centre, and they liked it so much that soon they did nothing else, including sleeping or getting food. They even preferred it to sex. As you'll have guessed when you saw the words 'electrodes' and 'rats' in the same sentence, it didn't end well. They kept pressing the lever until they died of exhaustion and hunger. Meanwhile, over in the human world, people have died from playing computer games continuously. This is serious stuff. We're quick-fix addicts! And like all good addictions, none of it does anything to help us feel good in the long run.

Back in my early boardroom days, a brilliant coach I worked with told me not to do the easiest thing first each day, but the hardest. I don't mean a run or a trip to the gym – not that those aren't good ways to start one's day. I mean starting with the hardest thing on your to-do list, resisting the huge temptation to do little things you know you can do, before starting on big things you're not so sure about. There's nothing like the feeling of it being 10am and knowing you've already done something you were dreading (or knowing you've got a clean pair of pants on and brushed your teeth, if you've traded a day job for a night job). Whether you're a morning, an afternoon or a night person, it makes sense that leaving the more comforting admin or online browsing tasks until later in the day is a good way to go. That same coach, who had sat on the boards of some of the biggest companies in the world, and in retirement went on to work on projects from prison reform to world-class opera programming, also told me that when he was in his most stressful corporate position in London, he would sometimes leave the office and spend half an hour looking at a portrait in the National Portrait Gallery.

'What if you didn't have half an hour to spare?' I asked.

'Then I'd go for an hour,' he replied.

Oliver Burkeman – 'The average human lifespan is absurdly, terrifyingly, insultingly short.'

Carving out space for the big stuff means not being afraid to switch off the small stuff. I muted notifications on all my apps, including WhatsApp, years ago, as well as disabling the invidious blue ticks, so that I'm less at the beck and call of devices. The people at whose beck and call you have always been don't typically like it when you elect to make yourself less available. My kids expect to be able to get me at the end of the phone any time, day or night. *What do you mean you're busy doing something else? What could you possibly be doing apart from being our mum?* (They don't literally say that, but it's out there.) We've colluded in a world where we're always on, and the impact is brutal.

One of the biggest pressures in my former life was that my roles were international, meaning I had teams positioned around the globe. It didn't matter what time of the day or night, someone, somewhere would be awake and emailing. I'd wake up to emails, have lunch to emails, go to bed to emails. Just a couple of decades ago, we could let a landline on our desk go unanswered during a meeting or send it to voicemail: 24/7 reachability wasn't a thing. Working for a big US company, evening calls were completely normal. These were the pre-Zoom days, and during the routine late-night conference calls, I would make jokes like, 'It's a good job you can't see me, haven't washed my pyjamas in a week,' to subtly, or not so subtly, get across the message that it was night-time for me. No one cared. When it came to the round-the-clock emails, I knew that if there was a crisis of some sort, I had to be aware of it, but I also knew that if I became someone who was known for responding at all hours of the day and night, that would become what was expected. So I would stealth-check my emails – having a look to make sure there was nothing that couldn't wait until the morning, but not replying or letting anyone know I was even looking. I must be the only idiot in the history of office jobs who was hiding how hard they were working behind the illusion of not working in the evenings. This is going back a while, and there is hope that things are changing. Someone sent me a work email quite late last night with this footer:

> I support flexible working and I'm sending this email now because it suits the hours I'm working today. Please do not feel obliged to reply straight away, as I understand that you will reply during the hours you work.

Hallelujah.

Dr Grace Lordan – 'I think for big decisions, people will end up making the final push with their emotions. Usually, when you ask somebody about choosing a partner or choosing a house, choosing a job, they will have had some kind of agonising time. People stay stuck for years; they go forward and back, forward, back, forward, back. But usually, the actual push to move is something that's emotional, or a gut feeling, or something that the person can't actually quite describe. Ultimately, it's pushing themselves into that risk, and you need a strong emotion to do that.'

Carrot or stick

Immersed in American work culture, I was often struck by how industriousness was prioritised over pleasure, and achievements over happiness. It was seen as a badge of honour if a woman went back to work soon after having a baby. I'm still haunted by a conversation I had with a New York colleague who had returned to work when her baby was just three weeks old, because she had recently been promoted and there was a big convention coming up. It's not that it shouldn't be anyone's free choice to go back to work when and how they want, but the fact that it was so lauded within the business that depressed me. To say it depresses me that companies like Amazon, at the time of writing, are timing toilet breaks and questioning warehouse staff if they stop working for more than a few minutes is an understatement. The idea that having your period or a stomach upset could lead to you being questioned and potentially penalised couldn't be less motivating. My daughter had a job like that for a few months (not at Amazon), where every minute of her day was logged and accounted for, and I watched from afar as her mental health took a tumble. Mine would have taken a tumble too. There is a big disparity between our societal belief that we are supporting mental health more than we used to and the ways in which people are actually being asked to live and work.

Here it comes, I'm going to say it: we should do away with the five-day work week. The standard office work week should be four days, for the same pay. Cally for PM. You can keep people at their desks, but you can't make them work with diligence and motivation, and you certainly can't make them not want to quit the minute they get another offer. I've always been more for carrot than stick, partly because I'm not a fan of confrontation, but moreover because I'm not a fan of unhappiness. Long before flexible working was a thing over in the UK, MTV used to give us 'summer Fridays', where we could either leave at lunchtime every Friday or take every other Friday off, from May to August. Productivity in my department went up, not down, partly because people felt loyal to a company who would do that for them, and partly because all the other shit that we have to get done as part of life – dental appointments, calls to utility companies or the bank, spending money we don't have with a company who times their staff's toilet breaks – could be done more easily during that time off.

A quick note on working from home – personally, I am not the biggest fan. Sure, it means there are more hours in the day in which you can be productive, but that doesn't mean you will be. The time 'off' talking to colleagues and friends before or after a face-to-face meeting was often the shot in the arm I needed to get stuff done. As an introverted extrovert, I find it hard to knuckle down unless I have had some external motivation and human connection. The light and shade of any given day is what stops it being grey. During lockdown, when working from home became not just the norm but the necessity, I loved the idea of the fake commute. Essentially, this means that during the time when you would normally be walking or driving to work, or reading a book or listening to a podcast on the bus or train, you use that same time to walk somewhere and change environments; to shift states. A reset.

Why looking at a wall is important

Kirsty Wark – 'Something I haven't always followed is, just take a beat. Don't jump in. Don't follow your first instinct. Just take a beat and have a think. As a famous interrupter, just take a beat and think, what's the other side of this? Have I got this wrong? I just think.'

Decision-making is intrinsically linked to productivity. I'm sick of books and influencers telling me how to stretch my time so I can do even more than I do already. One of the few bits of life advice I've been given by a podcast guest with which I didn't agree was that we should adapt and do whatever it takes to need less sleep, thereby giving ourselves the maximum possible number of hours in the day. As an eight-hours-a-night gal, this filled me with horror. I love my bed, I love that my cat curls up right next to me in my bed, and I love my books and my journals and my private time. Just me. The last thing I want is to spend less time there. I have no plans to learn to live with less sleep, but I'm working hard on giving myself permission to do less of pretty much everything else.

Zoe Lyons – 'We keep thinking, if I can just get there or if I can just do this, when I've done that, everything will be fine. It's meant to be now, isn't it? That's the bit that matters. I've got more into just sitting in the moment and being mindful. Next time you catch me staring off into space just flicking the fluff out of a knife, be respectful of my mindfulness.'

In 2017, John Cleese did a lecture on 'Creativity in Management' (the full thing is on YouTube), the premise of which was that creativity isn't about talent, but rather about a way of operating. He links creativity to a childlike state of play that we either inhabit or we don't, and we have little control over when that mood will take us. He talks about his work with Dr Robin Skynner, comparing the ways in which psychologically healthy families and successful businesses function. It comes down to people functioning in two modes, open and closed, and creativity not being possible in closed mode. You need to be in open mode to come up with something, and in closed mode to finish it.

A lot of John Cleese's advice hinges around creating a) time and b) space in which to achieve an 'open' state. His idea of space is less a hippy concept, more a disciplined regime whereby you assign a precise time at which you will switch off from the rest of the world, and a precise time at which you will re-engage. He suggests ninety minutes, since it will take the first half hour or so to settle, and then you will still have an hour left in which to create.

The longer you stick with a problem, the better and more creative your solution will be. Something many comedians do when we're working up new material – ideally not on a night when the *Live at the Apollo* scouts are in – is to commit to keeping going with an idea, even when all signs from the audience, verbal and non-verbal, tell us: 'This is crap; I hope you didn't leave your job for *this*.' Rather than backing out at the first sign of tumbleweed, we decide to catch it with a net. The only way out of new material that's not landing is through it, and that path is what – sometimes, not always – leads to what goes on to become the good stuff. It's enormously tempting to reverse into tried-and-tested material and get the crowd back on side, and indeed that may be advisable if it's a Friday-night crowd who'd just as soon not watch one's creative process unfurl, but this is one occasion when, if it's not working it's good to keep going, pushing through the pain barrier to a breakthrough. And the big upside is that once you've dared to do that live onstage, it's a damn sight easier to give it a go with words on a page, or a self-taped audition – anything where we can decide when, how and if the world will see it.

The bit I like the most, though, is that John Cleese talks about the fact that having put in the time where we proactively ponder and sit with whatever creative endeavour we're engaged in, the 'doing nothing' bit is equally valuable – like me writing chunks of this book subliminally while on dog walks. All of this is possible, and indeed probable, but it is contingent upon having put the hours in first.

John Cleese – 'This is the extraordinary thing about creativity; if you just keep your mind resting against the subject in a friendly but persistent way, sooner or later you will get a reward from your unconscious, probably in the shower later. Or at breakfast the next morning. But suddenly you are rewarded: out of the blue, a new thought mysteriously appears.'

It's all about finding a balance between the times when we are productive and the times when we consciously are not. I like to think of it as being mindfully a bit shit. You don't get fit enough to run a marathon unless you take the rest days as seriously as the training days. When I was having regular sports massages in the run-up to and after the London

Marathon, I was told that the biggest injuries come not from over-training on training days, but from not having enough days in between. I was also told it's normal to fart during a sports massage.

Stop faffing and get on with it

Oliver Burkeman – 'What do you think a really good friend would advise that you did? Jordan Peterson has a version of this in his book *12 Rules for Life*, which is to treat yourself as somebody you're responsible for helping. Trying to internalise some friend, or even a sort of ideal parent, who wants the best for you but understands that that isn't always going to be easy, is a really good perspective to try to adopt.'

I'm world class at spending more time thinking about and putting off a thing than doing the thing itself. I can spend six months putting off a bit of financial planning or admin that, when I come to do it, takes a couple of hours. Each quarterly VAT return, I repeat the pattern of leaving it until the last minute, feeling awful about it, apologising to my bookkeeper for not having done it and finally getting down to it. Then, when I finally do it, I quite enjoy snuggling into the mindful mindlessness of sorting through the receipts and the bits and the bobbins.

Writing this book has brought me hard up against my considerable talent for displacement activities. A friend who is a writer told me that Elizabeth Gilbert (she of *Eat, Pray, Love* fame) similarly struggles to write, or rather to sit down to write, and that she gets around it by telling herself that her only job is to get herself in front of her laptop. It's less about the capacity to write, more about the willingness to write:

letting go of expectations of quality or quantity in favour of simply turning up. Turning up can mean being present in the moment, or it can mean turning up – and thereby standing up – for yourself, which is what it felt like when I finally made my corporate career leap.

Waste time wisely

It is ingrained in us that we ought to be being productive 24/7, but one day the game's going to be up for all of us, and what will we have done with our brief time here? If the history of the universe was condensed to one year, and we live to be, say, seventy-five, that equates to 0.17 seconds of that year. Or, in other words, the average human lifetime is less than the blink of a universal eye. It could not matter more that we decide what to say no to so we can say yes to the right stuff. Or, to put it another way, for everything we say yes to, there's something else we're turning down. There's a cabbage white butterfly flying round the garden as I write this, lucky thing, not grappling with the concept of finitude. Although I do wonder if, with its three-week lifespan, it's asking itself why the hell it ended up in Kentish Town.

Matt Forde – '[My surgeon said], "We treat people who've lived for decades. Decades." And I said: "So if [the cancer] comes back, it's not necessarily a death sentence?" And he said: "No more than life is." I think that is one of the most incredible things I've ever heard.'

There are 'wrong' decisions, but it's hard to know if there are ever right ones because we'll never know what would have happened if we'd taken the other path. Even if missing that train that night and meeting that person and deciding to see them again has led to a happy relationship and kids, who's to say who or what might have come along if things had played out differently? Confession time: there can be wrong decisions . . . like turning down the rights to represent *South Park* when it first came out in 1997 (I didn't think people would 'get it' – my bad, let's call it baby brain) and spending the next couple of years trying to get them back. (We did get them back.) Even knowing that I'll likely wake up in a cold sweat about that particular showbiz snafu every now and again until I don't wake up anymore, I still believe procrastination is a greater enemy than making a wrong decision. So: say yes. Say no. But say something.

My final David Brentism is my belief in the merits of 'yes, if' rather than 'no, because' thinking. There are multiple valid reasons as to why we sometimes feel we're banging our heads against a brick wall and that nothing we're doing is working, but we may as well elect to control the controllables rather than endlessly sweating the stuff we simply cannot change or influence. And people with a positive outlook are a third less likely to have a heart attack than people with a negative one! Yeeay! Schooling ourselves in 'yes, if' thinking is about optimism over pessimism; it's less about saying yes to everything, more about deciding what to say yes to.

For the longest time, I lived in the grip of FOMO, always believing anyone doing whatever I wasn't doing was having a better time than me. With menopause, it's not so much I want to be still having periods or be able to get pregnant, more that I would have liked it to be my choice; like a wedding you don't want to go to, but you want to be invited so it's your decision to say no. These days, though, it's less FOMO, more JOMO – the joy of missing out. I'm still out and about as much as the next person – onstage, offstage, on-air, off-air, on-HRT, off-my-head – but when I decide I want to be *in*, I'm fine with that. More than fine. For Micky Flanagan's 'Going out out', I give you: 'Staying in in'.

Unless I do nothing every now and then, it seems, I'm incapable of doing something. 'She was really good at doing nothing' isn't something you hear much at funerals. Maybe it's time to change that.

DO TRY THIS AT HOME

The Eisenhower Principle – urgent vs important

Stephen Covey's 'first things' (page 190) is closely based on its forerunner, the Eisenhower Matrix, which is said to be how President Eisenhower organised himself. It's a quadrant of urgent vs important, which, like Covey's, splits tasks into zones:

	Urgent	**Not Urgent**
Important	**DO** Do it right away Examples • Finishing a client project • Submitting a draft article • Responding to some emails • Picking up your sick kid from school	**SCHEDULE** Schedule a time to do it later Examples • Strategic planning • Professional development • Networking • Excercise
Not Important	 **DELEGATE** Who is the best person for the task? Examples • Uploading blog posts • Scheduling • Responding to some emails • Meal prep	 **DELETE** Remove unnecessary tasks Examples • Social media • Watching TV • Video games • Eating junk food

Moving from being reactive to proactive, and ensuring you're focusing on important tasks, not just urgent ones (and only doing urgent ones if they're also important), is a game-changer — it's the simplest route to being productive. (This from someone whose toilet has never been cleaner, and whose dog never better walked than the times when I'm on a deadline.)

Baby steps: the 10 per cent shift

The 80/20 rule (the Pareto principle) states that approximately 80 per cent of outcomes come from 20 per cent of causes. It is used in business to assess effort versus return: things like 80 per cent of revenue coming from 20 per cent of clients, or 20 per cent of staff doing 80 per cent of the work. In everyday life, it's applied to everything from 20 per cent of footballers scoring 80 per cent of the goals to 20 per cent of people causing 80 per cent of the hassle in your life. But there's a 90/10 rule I like to live by, too. It goes like this. A complete overhaul of how and/or where we work and live and who we spend time with is daunting; a 10 per cent shift is not. Look at how you can make a 10 per cent shift in everything from meetings in your diary, to social engagements, exercise, staying in more (or less), or how you approach difficult conversations — anything you're grappling with. There has to be at least a 10 per cent chance you'll be glad you did.

Self-coaching: throw yourself off the hamster wheel

When I used to work as a coach, my coachees would almost always, in their final session, say how much they would miss having time set aside every couple of weeks to reflect on what was going on in their lives. An easy solution is to make an appointment with yourself for a self-coaching session, ringfencing it in your diary as much as if an actual coach was expecting to see you. It needn't be long – even fifteen minutes will do, though thirty minutes to an hour is better yet. Take yourself somewhere away from your desk or your kitchen, or wherever you normally find yourself swamped with your to-do list. Turn off devices, use a pen and paper, and simply ask yourself how things are going. What's bothering you? What's important to you? What are you doing that you wish you weren't doing? And what do you wish you had more time for? A mini inventory of where you're at and what's going on. Spend the last few minutes writing down three actions you're going to take or decisions you're going to make. Ideally, make it a weekly practice, trying to do it at the same time each week. Make an appointment with yourself to help yourself.

LAST WORDS

This chapter's jokes have in common that they are short, sweet and animal-themed:

> 'Two cows are in a field. One cow says to the other: "Have you heard about that mad cow disease that's going around?" And the other cow replies: "Yeah, it makes me so glad I'm a zebra."' – Toni Tone

> 'What's the difference between a dachshund and a street trader? A street trader bawls out his wares on the pavement.' – Reverend Richard Coles

And here are two bits of life advice pertinent to saying yes, but also saying no. The first from Jason Byrne:

> 'Never say yes unless you have permission to say no.'

The second, from Miriam Margolyes:

> 'I won't fuck anyone without a PhD.'

8
PERFECTIONISM

YOU LEARN MORE FROM A BAD GIG THAN A GOOD GIG

'A perfectionist walks into a bar. He says to the bartender,
"Leave it. I'll make the drink myself."'
Anonymous

perfect
adjective
/ˈpəːfɪkt/
    Having no mistakes or flaws
    'a perfect diamond'
    Completely correct or accurate
    'she spoke perfect English'
verb
/pəˈfɛkt/
    To make (something good) perfect or better
    'scientists are still perfecting the treatment'

Source: https://www.britannica.com/dictionary/perfect

> Baby mammals learn by literally falling over and standing back up until they get the hang of it. Every day's a late Saturday night at the Comedy Store for them. By playing and learning from mistakes, primates learn about cause-and-effect and how to manage sophisticated relationships and complicated tasks. It's the same with young humans. We don't look at a baby taking their first steps and take the piss out of them for falling over. We urge them on, help them up, film them for social media, and watch them try again. And again. And again. If they cared about failure, they'd never get up off their nappied bottoms in the first place. At a certain point, though, falling over becomes something about which we're not quite so sympathetic.

Bad gigs

There are many and varied ways to make a living, especially if you don't expect everything to be perfect straight out of the gates, and as a stand-up you soon discover that you learn a lot more from a bad gig than you do from a good gig. If a comic tells you they've never had a bad gig, they're lying. At the tail-end of the pandemic, when every person and every place was trying to find a workaround to get comedy back on its feet, we did outdoor gigs (fun), gigs with socially distanced tables six feet apart (not fun), and drive-in gigs. That's right. Comedy for people in cars. There's no worse heckle than when someone turns on their engine and sods off. We did gigs in farms, tents and back gardens; I once did one in a chocolate café in a craft village. I loved that one. As I walked out after I'd done my set, there was a sweet little garden centre with all the plants left outside overnight. I toyed with nabbing a tray. Time was I'd have been there for free drugs and beer; now all I want's a hydrangea.

You know when you've had a bad gig, and you know when the audience knows you've had a bad gig. Top of the chart of things you don't want to hear after doing stand-up is: 'Did you enjoy that?' I suppose every profession has its equivalent. At my first foray back into classical piano, there was a wonderful show manager – an erudite woman in her seventies who had, during her career, worked with some of the biggest and the best in classical music. After I'd done my turn, she said, 'Thank you for being such a good sport.'

There is more failure going on around us than success; people just don't tend to advertise it. I regularly turn up backstage before a gig, and another act will say how great it is to see things going so well for me. Often (mostly), it doesn't feel like that at all. I might have spent half the day slumped on the sofa, wondering how I'm going to transform myself to being all sparkly and 'on' onstage. Yet here I am, sparkly and on. I see it in others too, acts whom I really admire; they are, by any standard, doing great, yet when you talk to them, all they're thinking about are the gigs they haven't got, mining for evidence that they aren't good enough.

Michael Jordan – 'I've missed more than 9,000 shots in my career. I've lost almost 300 games, 26 times I've been trusted to take the game's winning shot and missed. I've failed over and over and over again in my life. And that is why I succeed.'

Michael Jordan is open about his failures, but he doesn't define himself by them. Tempting as it is to let the things that go wrong define us, we are not our mistakes. It's quite black and white when it's a matter of missing a winning shot, but most of us can afford to be less binary about what constitutes success or failure. Failure is inevitable, so we might as well strap in for the ride.

Bryony Gordon posted on Instagram about us getting a total of eighty summers (if we're lucky), and there we are worrying about how we look on the beach, or feeling guilty that we haven't kept on top of our emails. It's a wistful moment when we realise to what extent a fear of failure holds us back from really living the short lives we have. I used to say I didn't like dancing. I realise now that what I didn't like was the fear of not being very good at dancing, or of looking stupid; that I would 'fail' on the dancefloor. My daughter and I happened upon some jive dancing in a Paris square one Sunday morning when we were over there celebrating her birthday, and we stood and watched as people of every demographic jived like they were living their last day (some of them old enough that it might have been). A couple of months later, I was walking through an Amsterdam park and came across another group of people dancing – people of all ages, shapes and sizes, doing whatever the hell they wanted in plain view of whoever walked by. They looked so free and lacking in inhibition, and I wondered what it took for some of them to get there; they can't all always have been like that. (Don't be misled by the fact it was in Amsterdam; I'm fairly sure no substances were involved.) There was no way I was going to join in that day – unlike Jeff the dog, who was very keen and had to be put on a lead and distracted with treats – but nowadays I like dancing. I'm still not sure I'd be getting any tens on *Strictly*, but I like it.

Keep on keeping on

Roman poet Horace said: 'Once a word has been allowed to escape, it cannot be recalled' – and that was before social media. One of the liberating things about stand-up is that failure – unignorable, visceral failure – is frequent, and as a comic you're never meant to blame the room (that actual room or the people in it). In theory, even if the stage is poorly lit in the middle of a working bar with only two people in the audience, one of whom is pissed and both of whom hate female comics, that's no reason for a bad gig. Watching the Netflix series *Baby Reindeer* was unsettling enough, and it was only exacerbated by the fact that Richard Gadd's stand-up experiences are queasily realistic. When you're starting out, it's easy to self-critique and know exactly what made it a bad gig – material that didn't land, poor mic technique, something you said at the start that alienated the room, being physically tense or visibly nervous, speaking too quickly, not pausing enough, trying too hard, not trying hard enough, thinking rather than being. With all those variables, it's a wonder we ever get any good. The paradox is that as you get more experienced, it gets harder to tell what's not working. Over time, it's rare even at the bad gigs not to get at least a few laughs, and you sometimes have enough in the toolkit to get a room back onside.

Harriet Kemsley – 'One thing I've learned with dyspraxia is I've got very good at failing and falling over and making mistakes. It's very embarrassing a lot of the time, but you get really good at making mistakes. I think it's a really helpful thing, especially with stand-up when it's not always going to go well and sometimes it's going to be painful, but you just have to keep doing it and to get through it. One of my biggest strengths is the ability to just keep going, even when I'm absolutely doing terribly.'

Comedy is alchemical, involving a seemingly magical combination of things, with a slim chance of being able to rely on any guaranteed formula beforehand. One sign it's not working is when you find yourself disassociated, as if you're watching yourself onstage, or worse yet, remembering halfway through a set that you forgot to buy toilet roll. When that happens, it helps to notice how your body is feeling, to get out of your head and back into the room. If you're thinking ahead to what material comes next, that's a red flag, too; nothing like mentally rehearsing the next bit to screw up the here and now. When things aren't going your way, it's tempting to avoid making eye contact with the audience, let alone talking to them. Your instinct is screaming at you not to dive into the crowd (metaphorically – I'm not Iggy Pop), but when it's going a bit tits up, interacting with a live audience and slowing your delivery right down really helps. It feels as counterintuitive as turning the steering wheel in the direction of the spin when your car is skidding in snow rather than away from it – and the results aren't guaranteed in that case, either – but your chances are as good as they're going to get.

After a gig, I make notes – what didn't work, what did, new bits to add in, bits never to do again. You should make a point of seeing any comedian you like doing new-material nights as there's a good chance you'll get to see some material simultaneously making its debut and farewell performances. Shit jokes for one night only. The jokes that don't work are obvious, which doesn't always add up to abandoning them; in fact, as I explained on page 202, sometimes pushing further and further through the tumbleweed of a new idea is the only way to mine for what's eventually going to work. After an Edinburgh run of twenty-five-plus shows, ask any comic how they'd rate themselves for each day across the month, and they will tell you that it varied massively across those dates – from the soaringly successful to the soul-suckingly subdued, often with little rhyme or reason. Same venue, same lighting, same words, same music, but a different outcome; sometimes, radically different. Trying to work out what went wrong is like trying to check your reflection in a misted-up bathroom mirror, not easily discernible and therefore not easy to correct; the more you overthink it, the worse it gets. I do know that the more you keep on keeping on, being willing to get up there time and time again, the more likely you are to succeed. You have to square up to the real possibility of failure every time you perform – a masterclass in dusting yourself down and cracking on, as summed up by Millican's Law:

Sarah Millican – 'If you have a hard gig, quiet, a death, a struggle, whatever, you can only be mad and frustrated and gutted until 11am the next day. Then you must draw a line under it and forget about it.'

How many perfectionists does it take to change a light bulb?

One. And we'll do it as soon as we notice the bulb has gone, even if we're in the middle of a movie, or a dinner party, or sex (yes, older perfectionists can still have sex with the lights on). And if we don't have a replacement bulb available because we've forgotten to replace the last one we used, we'll be kicking ourselves all night instead of enjoying the dinner, or the movie, or the now-in-the-dark sex. A perfectionist is someone who wants to go from point A to point A*, and there is immense pain and loss that accompanies the quest to be perfect. Sylvia Plath referred in her diaries to perfectionism as a 'demon', and it contributed to her suicide at the age of thirty. She was always critical of herself and riddled with self-doubt, despite her academic and literary achievements. She wasn't just a genius – everyone fancied her! But no amount of external praise or accolades or attention could counter the demon within, because she lacked love for herself.

Robin Ince – 'One of my favourite things in the whole world is Patti Smith singing "A Hard Rain's A-Gonna Fall" at the Nobel Prize for Bob Dylan, getting the line wrong twice, and stopping and saying, "I'm sorry, I'm very nervous." And that, to me, is far more beautiful than anyone who goes, "But it's not perfect." I remember getting annoyed one year at Glastonbury [when] people watched Kris Kristofferson and said he didn't seem very well, why hasn't he quit? And you go, Kris Kristofferson is eighty-five years old. Kris Kristofferson is Kris Kristofferson. If you want to hear Kris Kristofferson singing the songs perfectly, they've been placed on vinyl and CD, and on some kind of cloud. If you want to see someone who carries with them an incredible history, whose voice may not be perfect anymore, but is still standing before you, that's a different story to having a perfect voice.'

I'm a procrastinator and a perfectionist. Someday, I'm going to be perfect.

I didn't write that joke, but I would have if I'd got round to it. I like to be overprepared. I also like leaving everything to the last minute. Actually, I *hate* leaving everything to the last minute, but that's the way it seems to pan out. If I have a new-material gig tonight, a couple of hours beforehand I'll get my head in the game and make myself write something new – always at the last minute. During lockdown, some comics used their downtime to create or to write or to establish themselves as YouTube sensations. Not me. Without a deadline, I'm nothing.

I've wanted more than anything to write this book, and I've been talking about it for years. One tends to have to knock out an alright book proposal in order to get a publishing deal, unless one is Prince Harry or Kylie Jenner. Knowing that proposal was what stood between me and getting a publisher on board, somehow I managed it, but each time it was only when my literary agent or a potential publisher gave me notes that I was able to shift from procrastination to action.

I got my book deal in January last year. I was with my children on a New Year's wildlife chronicling expedition, and my boy and I were out at dawn, watching a beautiful line of elephants walking against a sunrise backdrop, trunks and tails interlocking, with a baby elephant at the end of the line to make it full Disney. At that moment my phone went (it was on vibrate, I'm not a monster), and it was my agent calling to tell me I had a publisher, I had an advance and I had a deadline. When we got back to our chalet, we told my daughter, and she said: 'Does that mean you've actually got to write a book?'

'Shit,' I thought. 'It does.'

All the ambition and passion in the world didn't get me off the starting blocks until my editor sent over chapter deadlines. It was then that I realised I would have to write a chapter every three weeks, at around 8,000 words per chapter. So the first 8,000 words I wrote were 'FUCK!' 8,000 times. To quote Douglas Adams: 'I love deadlines. I like the whooshing sound they make as they fly by.' That's one of the reasons performing works so well for me – a deadline, and an audience.

It's not a fear of writing (apparently called 'graphophobia', which led me to wonder what a fear of graphs is, and it's 'xenographphobia' – I just looked all this up, not that I'm wasting time or anything), but a fear of not being able to write something good enough; ideally, something perfect. Brené Brown talks about replacing perfectionism with 'healthy striving [towards] mastery'. I really like this; it allows for ambition, bravery and discomfort, with the bar still aspirationally high; but it also allows for the inevitable fears and failures along the way. We are giving ourselves permission to try, try and try again, without the pressure always to succeed.

My inner critic is the harshest troll. American novelist Anne Lamott says:

> 'Perfectionism is the voice of the oppressor, the enemy of the people. It will keep you cramped and insane your whole life, and it is the main obstacle between you and a shitty first draft. I think perfectionism is based on the obsessive belief that if you run carefully enough, hitting each stepping stone just right, you won't have to die. The truth is that you will die anyway and that a lot of people who aren't even looking at their feet are going to do a whole lot better than you, and have a lot more fun while they're doing it.'

My thirst for perfection has long been insatiable, and it's kept me parched and set me up to fail. World-class business guru, famous stand-up, flawless parent, prodigal pianist, literary genius . . . is that too much to ask?

Yes. It is.

Pity the workaholic

I had a look at the Workaholics Anonymous website to see if I qualify. God knows I should – I've put the work in. Out of the twenty yes/no questions,[21] I said yes to sixteen. At the end, the website said: 'If you answered "yes" to three or more of these questions, you may be a workaholic.' Right. Here are some of the questions I said yes to:

> Are you more drawn to your work or activity than close relationships, rest, etc.?
>
> Are there times when you are motivated and push through tasks when you don't even want to and other times when you procrastinate and avoid them when you would prefer to get things done?
>
> Do you take on extra work because you are concerned that things won't otherwise get done?
>
> Are you afraid that if you don't work hard all the time, you will lose your job or be a failure?
>
> Do you fear success, failure, criticism, burnout, financial insecurity, or not having enough time?
>
> Have your long hours caused injury to your health or relationships?
>
> Do you feel agitated when you are idle and/or hopeless that you'll ever find balance?
>
> Do you feel like a slave to your email, texts, or other technology?

I said yes to all of that. Not exactly the stuff dating profiles are made of. Reading it back, it strikes me that I'd be the person you'd least want to go away with for a weekend or get stuck on a train next to. Perfectionism and workaholism are close bedfellows, and have in common their link to success. Life rewards you, and employers are big cheerleaders for workaholics. But it's no joke. The career highs get offset by increasing lows. Shiny milestones start to lose their sheen, until things seem altogether less dazzling and perfect. In the worst-case scenario, things start to feel dangerous, because workaholism, like alcoholism or anything else, is a real addiction.

Bryony Gordon – 'We live in a culture where overeating is seen as [a] kind of moral failure, in the same way that addiction, most addictions, are seen as moral failures.'

In twelve-step programmes, whether for substance addictions or behavioural addictions and compulsions, they talk about 'Progress not perfection': letting go of the end goal of a perfect recovery, and focusing on the smaller achievements along the way, one day at a time. I am a recovering perfectionist, putting significant effort into celebrating the times I drop the ball or am plain mediocre. (Luckily, there's no certificate for recovering from perfectionism or I'd be getting all competitive and overdoing it and wanting an A*.) Oliver Burkeman describes perfectionism as 'leaning unhappily into the future'. What really holds us back from trying something new is almost always the fear of not being good enough, a fear of failure.

The Workaholics Anonymous question about feeling hopeless about ever being able to achieve balance was the one that made me the saddest. How can I be nudging ever closer to sixty without having sorted this stuff out? For a high achiever, I haven't always done so well at this. But at fifty-six, I see my patterns – and once you know something, you can't unknow it.

Roxanne Pink – 'The pattern is the problem, and also the solution. Very often in our lives, there will be patterns, relationship patterns, work patterns, patterns [in] how we speak to ourselves [. . .] For me, [it was that] every time I went out and got drunk, something bad would happen. Or every time I'm in a relationship, it ends after a year. Pattern is the problem. There's some kind of problem there that you might need help with. [It's about] not shy[ing] away from looking back analytically at your own life and going, "Are there any repeating patterns here that I might need help with?"'

Ignorance is bliss

I used to run training courses in my industry in everything from negotiation to presentation, and when it came to introductions, people would generally have a strong awareness of their shortcomings. They would often say that they couldn't speak in front of groups (having just spoken in front of a group), and that they'd get so nervous they would visibly blush and/or shake (having just spoken without visibly blushing and/or shaking). We are usually painfully aware of the things we find challenging, and keen to change the bits we don't like, but the reason it's hard to leap from awareness to change is that there's a bit inbetween:

Awareness > **Acceptance** > Change

Acceptance is the bitterest pill to swallow, yet without it we get stuck. My inner critic has always been pretty vocal and it's led to a lot of self-deprecation, which is not the most fun quality to be around, not least because no one cares about us and what we're doing as much as we do. The reason we think we're shaking when we do public speaking but no one else notices is partly because we aren't shaking as much as we think we are, and partly because most people are thinking about when the next break is and whether there'll be a queue for the loo (if you identify as female, the answer is yes, there will be). We've usually bashed ourselves into submission before anyone else has a chance to.

Helen Lederer – 'Don't give up. Don't let them make you give up. Just stay with it.'

Sometimes, as we start to get better at something, we think we're getting worse. When I first took up the piano again, I was cock-a-hoop if ever I got the notes right. My teacher said playing the right notes was like having a blank canvas and a set of paints; the painting only emerges when you start to *do* something with them. Playing the right ones is still pretty important, as I proved with my impromptu Debussy rearrangement in Ludlow, but the more I play, the better I get, and the more aware I become of the things I know I still cannot do. These are the four stages of competence:

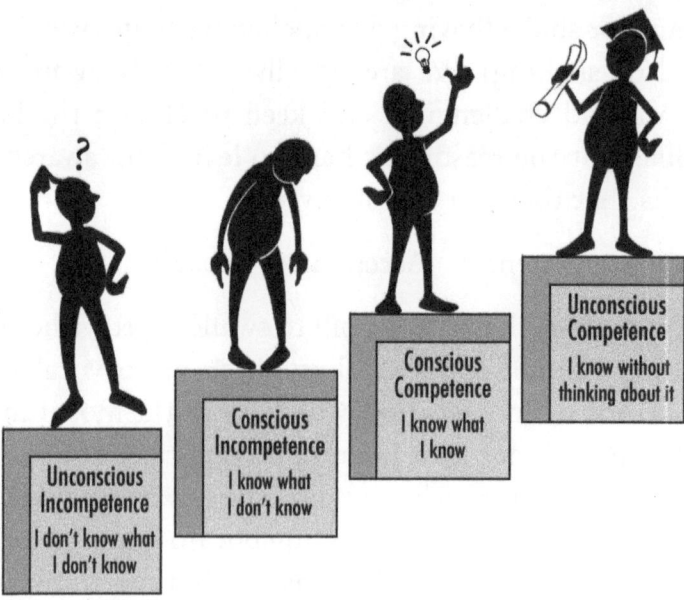

There's a freedom in the first, not knowing what we don't know, and it's all too easy to get stuck in the second, negative self-talk on a loop. I had some swagger when I started out in comedy, a kind of blind confidence that I look back on with awe, envy and a bit of cringe. I was used to holding the attention of a room, and anyway, it's possible to style it out when you're surrounded by other open-mic acts. As you start to move up the comedy echelons and find yourself surrounded by better and better acts, however, only the rhino-skinned could remain unaware of how much they can't yet do. You learn from the more experienced and talented acts around you and start to get better, but it's clunky and takes effort and practice. What you're heading towards, if you're lucky, is a flow state when you're onstage, and on the occasions that happens, I don't believe *Trainspotting*'s Renton ever experienced more of a high. All that effort – and all those late nights and lonely service-station sandwiches – pay off for those twenty minutes onstage when everything pours effortlessly out of you. It's the 'conscious incompetence' bit that we conflate with failure, and that's when it's tempting to give up, when actually that's the very stepping stone towards failing better, and ultimately becoming OK at the thing we're trying to master.

Scott Bennett – 'Even now, I still would love to know if it's going to work out. And I remember going to the therapist and she said, "Scott, no one's going to tell you that this is not going to fail. No one's going to tell you that this is going to work out. But that's the unknown and you have to be comfortable with the unknown."'

A comedian's best work often comes when we're not editing ourselves, in spontaneous moments of crowd work and unplanned riffs. It's the unknown that makes us the best we can be, yet it's also what holds us back.

Reverend Kate Bottley – 'It's called [having] faith, it's not called [being] sure. I'm prepared to be wrong. This could all be nonsense, but that's OK. I'm willing to take a risk.'

Fail better

Ellie Robinson told me her life-changing moment was not winning gold at the 2016 Olympics in Rio at the age of fifteen, but being beaten for the first time in 2019 at the World Para Swimming Championships:

> 'It just stripped that fear of failure away from me completely. In my head, the worst had happened. I had nothing to lose, and I felt quite free and liberated just to be able to try. There wasn't this big cloud of consequence looming over me, like, what if you fail? What if you do badly? I was able to just give 100 per cent without any severe consequence or pressure. It completely changed my mindset.'

Acceptance is the opposite of perfectionism. I recently worked with someone around my age whose brilliantly relaxed attitude to what she was doing, and doing really well, struck me. I only worked with her for one day, and as we talked, it became clear that she was always getting stuck into new things – painting, drumming, poetry, computer coding – without any goal or quality threshold; they were just things she wanted to try. I realised if ever I've tried my hand at anything, it's because I wanted to become great at it. I asked her about her ethos, and she said that it came from something her mum used to say when she was growing up: 'If a job's worth doing, it's worth doing badly.' They should offer her mum on prescription.

Henry van Dyke – 'Use what talents you possess; the woods would be very silent if no birds sang there except those that sang best.'

Hugh Jackman's 85 per cent rule hit the headlines when he first talked about it, based on his principle of relaxing and performing better when running at 85 per cent capacity. I suspect that when you're a middle-aged white man so handsome you should have your face carved into Mount Rushmore, it's easier to keep that extra 15 per cent in the tank and still set the world alight, but he's got a point. Given the fact that life inevitably features failure, maybe it's time to redefine success. The time in my career that is the most successful on paper is the same time that I became a single parent to two small children, and the things were undoubtedly linked. I spent most of my boardroom years scared of not maintaining a level of perfectionism that was impossible. Then, when I became a comedian, I had to unlearn my bullet-proof, glossy habits, because the funny is in the messy bits, not what's gone right. There are comics like Jimmy Carr who are incredibly slick and polished, and you don't get much of a peek behind the curtain, but they're the outliers. For the rest of us, it's about standing onstage, metaphorically flipping our skirts up and saying, 'Look at my bum.' If I actually do that, all the audience would see are the adhesive shadows of HRT patches left behind on my behind; a menopausal Mondrian.

Samuel Beckett once wrote, 'Ever tried. Ever failed. No matter. Try again. Fail again. Fail better.' I have it emblazoned on my home office wall. As humans, we are so scared of failure that on a primal level it can feel fatal, but unless you're base-jumping or eating Japanese blowfish, that is rarely the case. Even in the animal kingdom, where a bad decision could well kill you, failure is still an integral part of development. Sometimes, we help the animals along, like when we put stickers of birds on glass windows so that real birds don't fly into them. I've always thought it would be better to use stickers of something birds are scared of, like humans.

Deborah Meaden – 'We have to get things wrong to get things right. I would not be the person I am today if all of my businesses had been a huge success. I wouldn't have the resilience. I wouldn't know how to pick myself up. I don't like getting things wrong, and when I do I beat myself up for about thirty seconds but then I let it go. I don't carry it around like a sack.'

My kids' primary school headteacher used to refer to something as 'a good mistake'. I'll tell you something that wasn't a good mistake – when I overheard her saying how shit my cakes were at the summer fair. I didn't even make the cakes. I bought them at whatever local shop I decided the other parents were least likely to go to, bashed them up a bit and put them in Tupperware. They weren't even *my* shit cakes. So there.

I made my own not-good mistake when I recorded my interview with Alistair Brownlee, widely regarded as one of the best male triathletes the world has ever seen. We were recording remotely, me in London, him in Miami, ahead of a massive international race that weekend and, as we were saying our goodbyes, I said: 'Break a leg tomorrow!'

Alistair Brownlee – 'You can do all the preparation, that's 95 per cent of it, in terms of the getting your kit ready, knowing the course and all those things. But there's still a couple of per cent chance that your legs just don't work well that day. So you do want to think beforehand, "I need to make sure I have good legs today." Sometimes you do just have bad days and you can make the most of those bad days. Some of the proudest performances I've had are when I've started, dived in, and thought, "I just feel crap today," and managed to find a way to still race well. There are a couple of types of pain in endurance sport. There is the type of pain where it's good. That sounds a bit oxymoronic, but there's good pain, you know, it's painful, but you know it's painful because you're going really fast, and the race is going well. A positivity to it. Then there's pain where you know the race isn't going well and you just have to really dig deep, and it's really tough. I've been in race situations where all I'm doing is looking at a spot on someone's bike in front of me – or if we're running, on their shoulder – and just focusing on that and thinking, "Right, there's nothing else in the world that matters right now, the only thing that matters is that I don't get any further away from that point on them." I'm just completely hyper-focusing in on that. And just taking the pain out of it.'

We dine out on others' failures and disasters, yet are defensive about our own. I was given the advice in comedy quite early to run my own race. It's mad-making enough competing with the brutally high standards we set ourselves, let alone with everyone else. Ed Byrne is a Munro bagger, someone who aims to climb Scotland's 282 Munros (mountains over 3,000 feet). He told me it's not always as tranquil as you might think, when you're haring round the Highlands in search of your next summit, having set off later than planned, got stuck behind a caravan, then spent the whole climb worrying about getting down in time and taking the right route. He told me people rarely want to hear about the conquests; it's all about the fails.

Ed Byrne – 'People always ask you, "What was your most difficult experience in the mountains?" It's the same as the questions I always get asked about stand-up comedy: "Have you ever been onstage and something has gone wrong?" and, "What do you do if you are being heckled?" People always want to know about the hard stuff!'

On the subject of heckles, I don't mind a rowdy crowd. Dispatching a heckler reassures the crowd you know what you're doing so they can sit back and relax. God knows, they've paid for a babysitter to be there. It also unites the room, you plus audience vs heckler, because the room is almost always Team Comedian, not Team Heckler, wanting you to come up with the right put-down. What you don't want from a crowd is apathy. Give me a heckle rather than a yawn any day. My best heckle was at the Hastings Fringe. As with many of the smaller fringe festivals, every possible bit of space is repurposed to become a venue, and I was performing on a makeshift outdoor stage just off the high street with public benches and a few scattered deck chairs. There were a handful of people who had come for me, and many more who had come because it was a sunny day and they needed somewhere to eat their ice creams. A group of teenagers appeared on the walkway above and started sending down paper planes with messages on them. (Right? Gen Z using pen and paper. Never assume.) I started reading them out, until one which read: 'Don't give up!', shortly followed by another: 'Your day job.'

Celebrate the wins

Whenever I'm given feedback, there might be twenty positives, but it's the one negative that will haunt me. Businesses are always running sessions on how to give feedback, but I wonder if learning how to receive it wouldn't be more valuable. I could still quote pretty much verbatim every harsh sentence ever written about me by a critic. People say you shouldn't read reviews but even when your own willpower holds out, everyone you run into mentions them. Our negativity bias leads us to dwell on the bad, not the good, sometimes for decades. I remember being in the sixth-form library, a massive echoey room with big reading tables all around the edges and shelves of books in the middle, and I walked across the silent room to get a book, squatted down to get it off the bottom shelf and did a fart so percussive it should have won the sixth-form music prize. Forty years on, I can still feel it. And smell it. It's more likely I'll be taking that to my grave rather than any of the testimonials on my website about being able to knock out a decent speech. Damian 'Damo' Clark created this cartoon depicting a comic's view of their audience:

I make a mental note not to focus on the haters and to look elsewhere, even if one of them is right in front of me, oozing 'bugger off' vibes. I used to be drawn to them like a moth to a flame, not just looking at them but trying to convert them, deciding I hadn't succeeded until they found me funny or at least liked me. Now, I try to remember they don't represent the whole audience, and I aim to go where the ground is soft. (And if they do represent the whole audience, I aim to go home.)

Toni Tone – 'Amazing things emerge from loving who you are. When people get to a place of loving who they are as a person and what they see in the mirror, loving the way they think about life, they can show up for themselves and they recognise the value they bring into the world. It is such a powerful seed. Everything starts from loving who you are. That's not to say you need to be perfect, because I definitely am not perfect. I mess up all the time. Nobody is. But [try] having that grace and compassion for yourself and knowing that even when you mess up, you can try again. And that your mistakes don't define you.'

There was someone in the front row of a charity gig I did on Sunday with a T-shirt that said: 'Care and compassion are no longer in fashion.' It gave me plenty of material, but it's true that in our increasingly polarised society, it's hard to show compassion for others, let alone self-compassion. In Alcoholics Anonymous, you sometimes hear alcoholics described as 'egomaniacs with an inferiority complex'.[22] I reckon that sums up many comedians, too. To be a comic, you need to be enough of a cocky show-off to want to get up there night after night and have everyone look at you, while simultaneously being so riddled with insecurity you don't think you deserve to be there. A comic's stage time is a mini-break from the lunacy of it all.

Sally-Anne Hayward – 'I saw my agent at the time after a terrible gig. She was this woman who, as we walked down the street after a gig where I'd been terrible, would go, "Well, that was fucking shit, wasn't it?" And she said to me, "Did you take the money?" And I said, "Yeah." And she went, "You shouldn't take the money," and I went, "Oh, should I go and give it back?" And she went, "Too late now, you look mad."'

Compassion is not in everyone's wheelhouse. We can't guarantee the world will send compassion our way, but we can get into the habit of going kindly with ourselves.

Let it go

Philip Glass – 'If you don't know what to do, there's actually a chance of doing something new.'

You're never as bad as your worst gig, or as good as your best. I still get racked with fear about doing things wrong – even little things. Recently, when trying to log in to an online account, instead of the usual robot-snuffling squares with traffic lights or bicycles, I was asked to 'click on the entity that has a brain'. There were squares with doughnuts and snowmen – or perhaps snowpeople, I didn't look closely, so panicked was I about the test – and a goat. I was relieved there was no square with a menopausal woman in it, because honestly, I wouldn't be sure. My fear of failure extended to me thinking I'd fail a test to prove I'm not a robot, even though I'm fairly sure I'm not a robot.

Johnnie Walker – 'My [namaste motherf*cking moment] comes from a TV show called *Kung Fu*, starring David Carradine, when he was playing this monk in America. He and another guy have been accused of stealing horses, which is an offence that you could be hung for. So they're in this car, being taken into town to face trial the next day, possibly to be hanged, probably to be hanged. And David Carradine, as Kung Fu, is in the back of the car playing his flute, not a care in the world. And the guy said to him, "How on earth can you be so calm, sitting there playing your flute? We're going to be hung tomorrow." And he just turned around and said, "No amount of worrying ever changed tomorrow."'

There is no success without failure. It's easy to drive yourself into an early grave with anxiety and comparison and insecurity. The entertainment industry is a fickle lover, reeling you in by whispering sweet nothings in your ear, then dropping you like a hot coal. The extent of my ambition and my relationship with failure have changed with the passing of time, and they are changing still. It's partly having been round the block enough times to know that professional and personal failures may hurt like hell, but they rarely cost you everything. And it's partly about having reached a point in life where I have fewer fucks to give.

The perfectionism paradox guarantees we'll never achieve our self-set lofty goals, thereby setting in motion a lifelong cycle of failure. I love the Michelangelo quote: 'The greatest danger for most of us is not that our aim is too high and we miss it, but that it is too low and we reach it.' Brilliant, isn't it, that level of wisdom, and from a Teenage Mutant Ninja Turtle. I take those words to mean that we should be jumping in and taking risks, rather than focusing on how well we do once we've taken them. There's a difference between something you haven't achieved making you unhappy and that thing making you happy should you achieve it. When lockdown hit, I lost what at the time felt like a dream job, TV work that would have raised my profile considerably and involved being on the road every week for the foreseeable. Looking back, I wonder if any of that would have felt good – the travel, or the being more of a face and name. Some of the things that make me happiest are the things where you can't succeed or fail, like sitting under a tree reading a book or swimming with Jeff in a river or wandering around naked now the kids have moved out (at home, not around the neighbourhood). It turns out, perfectionism is for losers.

I learned a new Dutch word recently: *lanterfanten*. There's no literal English translation, in much the same way we don't have an equivalent for the Scandinavian *hygge*. The closest I can get is 'lollygagging', but that has negative connotations, and *lanterfanten* doesn't. When you *lanterfanten*, you delight in doing sod-all, in doing whatever takes your fancy in the moment, with a fuck you to your to-do list. When I spend a bit of time *lanterfanten*-ing and letting go, the things I was worrying about failing at in the first place start to flow. It's almost as if when you let go of having to be perfect, things get better. Funny, that.

DO TRY THIS AT HOME

Fail better: succeeding at failure

Learning to celebrate failures and link them to success involves a paradigm shift in our core beliefs, which have often been held since childhood. Use this technique to help you take a baby step in the right direction:

Write down your definition of success.

Now write about your relationship with it. Can you/have you ever achieved it? How did it/does it feel? How about when you don't succeed? Where does your need to succeed come from? Write down as much as you can of what comes to mind when you think of the word 'success'.

Finally, write about how you would like to redefine success. What would you like it to mean to you? How would you like to live your life in relationship to it?

You can do the same exercise replacing the word 'success' with 'failure'.

Wading through treacle: the only way out of it is through it

One of the reasons we go to such lengths to avoid failure is that we can't bear the feelings that accompany it. It's a reasonable instinct not to want to dwell on difficult emotions, let alone swim about in them and get to know them. It's so tempting to look back at what's happened or forward to what might be next, to think that if we're not feeling good, we need to put that right as soon as possible and move on. Sitting with tricky feelings is irksome but, ironically enough, not being able to augments their power. This is all about letting go of the wish to control and change things, and instead allowing yourself to experience them. So, next time you're feeling crappy, try this:

Write down what it is you're feeling. Notice it. Name it.

Now expand on it. How is it feeling in your body? In your mind? What's the inner dialogue accompanying it? Is it part of a pattern? What aspect of what you're feeling is about someone or something else? Do you have any control over that? What part of it sits with you?

What would you say if you were parenting a child who was feeling what you're feeling now?

Set a timer for ten minutes, and use that time to try to surrender to your feeling(s), letting them wash over you. If you feel like crying, cry. If you're angry, be furious. If you're comparing yourself with others, let the resentment rage. If you're impatient, notice what it's like to wait.

When the timer finishes, spend a minute or two just noticing your breath and your body, letting your thoughts go by like clouds in the sky. Notice what it's like to be in your body rather than your thoughts, the world still turning even with those unwanted feelings.

It's good to get into the habit of doing exactly the same thing with 'good' feelings too: spend a few minutes swimming about in them, savouring every last drop.

Letting go of perfectionism: swimming in compliments

It's not necessary to write down criticisms or trolling to hold on to them – they're sticky enough – but the nice stuff has a habit of floating off into the ether. It's not very British to accept a compliment, let alone write one down, so the first step when someone throws you some praise is not to counter or dilute or make a joke about it. Instead, say thank you, and bank it. (And if it's in reference to an item of clothing, *don't* say 'Oh, it's old' or tell them that it wasn't expensive.) Then, write down the compliment. This is to restore rather than inflate the ego; it's not a one-stop road to narcissism. I have a Notes document on my iPhone where I write nice things that are said about me. I've called it: 'Not a total twat'. I'm working up to calling it: 'Not a twat at all'. If I ever evolve sufficiently to call it 'I am enough', I'll think I am a twat after all, and be back to square one.

LAST WORDS

When Dr Benji Waterhouse came on the podcast, he picked this Barry Cryer joke:

> 'A man is at his wife's funeral, and he asks the vicar, "What's the Wi Fi password?" The vicar says, "We're burying your wife." And the man says, "Is that lower case?"'

We get regular life advice on the podcast about not giving up, but Shazia Mirza's advice had a twist:

> 'The point at which you're about to give up is probably the point at which you're going to break through, you're going to make it. Because that is the lowest point, where you think, "I'm going to give up, this is it." That's probably the point at which things are going to change, you're going to break through. So just keep going a bit longer.'

Hannah George's advice came from the ritual she and Taylor Glenn have before their live shows of *Drunk Women Solving Crime*.

> 'Before we go onstage at a live show, we will always say to each other, just have fun with it. Whatever you're doing, just have fun with it at the end of the day, because what else is there?'

And when Jonny Benjamin came on with Neil Laybourn (see page 108), he shared this:

> 'It's a Japanese proverb: fall down seven times, stand up eight.'

part three

LET'S GET PERSONAL

part three

9
GLOW THE FUCK UP

GROWING OLDER, BOLDER AND MORE BEAUTIFUL

'You know why I feel older? I went to buy sexy underwear and they automatically gift-wrapped it.'
Joan Rivers

glow
/gləʊ/
verb
    To shine brightly and steadily, especially without a flame:
    'embers glowed in the furnace'
noun
    Brilliance or warmth of colour, especially redness
    A warm feeling, as of pleasure or well-being

Source: https://www.thefreedictionary.com/glow

Female topi antelopes have rampant sex drives (think hen parties in Amsterdam) and during mating season, they pursue the males (also hen parties in Amsterdam). They are only ready to mate for one day a year (less so hen parties in Amsterdam), and will fight to break apart mating couples to reproduce with their desired partners (back to hen parties in Amsterdam). Like a topi antelope *Love Island*! They're not sitting about playing it cool and waiting for a nice male antelope to swipe right; they're playing by the rules they've written.

Debunking the beauty myth

Blanket octopuses don't play by the rules, either – or, at least not by our rules. They make very odd couples. The females are big, iridescent and powerful, the males unremarkable little walnuts. If only the same were true of humans, Andrew Tate would be so tiny you could put him on a keyring and throw him into the ocean. Mating is not an intimate affair for octopuses. The teeny-weeny male has something a bit like those plastic things people use to throw balls for dogs, only loads smaller; he detaches this, full of sperm, and gives it to the female, who keeps it safe in a body-temperature cavity until she needs it. When she ovulates, with 100,000-plus eggs, she spreads the sperm over the eggs herself, DIY-ing her way into motherhood, all six gorgeous, sassy feet of her.

I'm five foot six and a half, I'd be lucky to produce one egg, let alone 100,000, and I've never thought of myself as hot, but I am aware that whatever hot is, I'm closer to it now than I was when I was the age where you're meant to be hot. In my twenties, I was not conventionally attractive; I had low self-esteem, I masked depression with extroversion, I was overweight and a stranger to myself. In my thirties, I had little kids and a big job, and was busy splitting up with my kids' dad. In my mid-forties, career burnout and perimenopausal collapse dimmed my light somewhat. Only in my late forties did I start to see myself more clearly – and that's when other people started to see me more clearly too.

I'm not a fan of assumptions, and right up there with the worst of them is the assumption that women lose our value and appeal as we get older. Why should there be a clock ticking on our attractiveness and agency? Make way, Kamala Harris; at sixty, her time came (and then devastatingly went). Jodie Foster described turning sixty as 'one of the best days of my life', and Bernadine Evaristo was sixty when she won the Booker Prize (she also happened to be the first woman of colour to receive it). Philippa Perry became the *Observer Magazine*'s agony aunt at sixty-three, and her book *The Book You Wish Your Parents Had Read (and Your Children Will Be Glad That You Did)* is in the top 100 bestselling books of the past fifty years. She told me that one of the things that propelled her to write it was that she was sick of getting invitations addressed to Grayson Perry 'plus one'. She said: 'My name is not "plus one", so I thought, "Well, I'd better do something." And then I started to get "Philippa Perry plus one". And I've got to say, that's good.'

I was twenty-one when I first read Naomi Wolf's *The Beauty Myth* and came across the concept of women only being sexually attractive during our fertile years. It hadn't occurred to me until then that a woman's attractiveness had a shelf life. Twenty years after the book came out, Instagram was launched, and a new type of beauty myth was born. It was from my daughter that I first heard the term 'glow-up', meaning a positive change in someone's appearance, confidence or overall wellbeing. My glow-up isn't about nothing wobbling in a bikini, or indeed a structured tankini. It's about celebrating the bumps and the lumps, the risks and the piss, and the fact that in my sixth decade, I have grown up enough to stand behind the person I am. I'm so glad an eighty-one-year-old told forty-five-year-old me I was still young. I'm aware that in the blink of an eye, I'll be looking back at this time in my life and realising how young fifty-six was.

Flawed feminism

I'm at an age where I still look alright in sexy lingerie but need reading glasses to put it on (and someone who can locate their reading glasses to take it off). There's a theory about the freeing moment when you get to an age where you don't care how you look. That moment has yet to come. I do care. I am a flawed feminist. On one of my son's first visits home from university, he said: 'You're not going to like this, but there's a leader board of mums people fancy in the kitchen.'

'Oh,' I said. 'Which number am I?'

'You're number two,' he said.

'You're right,' I said. 'I don't like it.'

Deborah Frances-White told me the origin story of her podcast *The Guilty Feminist*. She'd always been a feminist, even when she was a Jehovah's Witness – not a popular stance among Armageddon-fearing, no-sex-before-marriage, blood-transfusion deniers. In the mid-2010s, she looked around her at what others were doing, things like Bridget Christie's *A Bic for Her*, Chimamanda Ngozi Adichie's *We Should All Be Feminists*, Laura Bates's *Everyday Sexism* and Caitlin Moran's *How to be a Woman*. She wanted to be a part of the feminist revival, but didn't feel good enough. She explains:

> And then Bridget Christie said: 'Deborah, you will never find your audience until you say the thing you're too scared to say. I was doing all this comedy, trying to please the industry, and I thought, "I'm going to scare my last few fans away by talking about feminism because that's what I really feel angry about." So that's what I did. That's when I found my audience. When I said what I really felt, suddenly I had this huge audience.'
>
> And I thought, 'What I want to say is, "I'm a feminist. But one time I went on a women's rights march, popped

into a department store to use the loo, got distracted trying out face cream and when I came out, the march was gone."'

I had her words ringing in my ears – 'Say the thing you're frightened to say, that's when you'll find your true audience.' I thought, 'Fuck it, I've got nothing to lose. Even if 100 people love this podcast, that's 100 people I'm speaking to. If it's 2,000 then you've got an audience of 2,000 every week. In a theatre, you'd think, wow, this is fantastic; that's the Palladium sold out.' And so I said it, I admitted it. I'm a feminist, but I sometimes fantasise about being sexually dominated by the famous fictitious misogynist Don Draper, and [I] truly believe that if I met him, I could make him whole and heal his pain. And when I said that, the audience roared with laughter. And you know what? Overnight, that podcast was a hit.

The Guilty Feminist takes on the big stuff but it's playful. It's fun. It's about the paradox of how we feel on the inside vs how we choose to look and live on the outside: a celebration of our inner conflicts, guilty secrets and imperfections. I feel as angry at the injustices and inequality women face daily as anyone, but that doesn't make me a perfect feminist. Personally, I have no intention of growing old gracefully. I don't mean growing old disgracefully, like a novelty apron slogan, more that I'm still working on my appearance. It's each person's choice what they do to their own face and body – lotions, potions, injections, or anything else. I exfoliate, wear night retainers, tint my eyebrows, layer on make-up onstage and assist my hair in remaining ginger, none of which gets in the way of me advocating for myself and other women, or disrupts my feminism. Not even my serious Shellac habit. I bloody love Shellac, no matter how much my nails protest. I was filling up my car this week and the man at the till said: 'Shellac?' I started to explain that it wasn't actual Shellac, but a gel manicure from a different brand, and he said: 'No. Shell *app*. Have you got the Shell app?'

A celebration of soft white underbellies

I am one of the millions of menopausal women whose tummies look a bit like that of someone in early pregnancy. I've always had a tummy, and I've been told I was pregnant many times over many years, far more than the eighteen months when I actually was (that's two babies – I'm not an Asian elephant). I had an osteopath argue with me once when I told him I wasn't pregnant. He told me he saw hundreds of bodies every year, and he knew a pregnant woman when he saw one. Hard to assert yourself when you're in your pants, you've put your back out and someone's just falsely accused you of being pregnant. Another time, I was buying clothes for my two-year-old daughter, and as I was paying, the cashier looked at my tummy and asked when my next baby was due. I said I wasn't planning on another baby. She whispered, away from my daughter, 'Oh, doesn't she know yet?' Doesn't *she* know? I didn't even know.

Why do people think they have the right to comment on pregnant bodies – or, indeed, any bodies? I've belatedly realised how much of the anti-curves culture I've internalised since childhood, and how, when I'm in the company of slim or petite women, I've always felt 'less than', like I've done something wrong because of my body shape. That's decades of wasted energy on something utterly natural. Our bellies reflect the shapes of our wombs, of our digestive systems and of the years we have lived. Mine not being flat has held me back from wearing a bikini, from dancing like no one's watching, from letting lovers kiss my belly. Only now do I realise that if anyone is lucky enough to get anywhere near kissing our soft white underbellies – or, indeed, any other bits of us – they should be grateful to be there. We have nothing, absolutely nothing, to apologise for.

Iyanla Vanzant – 'Comparison is an act of violence against the self.'

I was in Amsterdam with my daughter recently, and she decided to go for a swim (in clean water – think the River Ij, not a beer-cruise canal). I hadn't brought a swimsuit – we were in Amsterdam, not Ibiza – but my daughter goes nowhere without swimwear. Forty-plus years after puberty had started me on the track of hating on my body, something shifted that sunny day by the Dutch water's edge. After a quick mental inventory of my massive knickers and half-decent bra, I thought, 'Stuff it, no one cares.' I stripped, and I jumped. My daughter, in a proper bikini and tanned from living in Spain, jumped in beside me, and never have I felt more beautiful.

It's time to celebrate our soft white underbellies – literal and metaphorical – because God knows, they're hard won.

Glowing up is not about the physical, it's the whole package: a phrase forever tainted by the number of times I've heard women weighed up and, if deemed intelligent, funny and sexy enough, anointed 'the whole package'. I saw a recent tweet – still calling them tweets – from someone asking why, if a woman is fit and attractive, with a great job, is she single? (It wasn't directed at me.) Maybe, just maybe, there simply aren't many available people who are her equivalent. Maybe she's too fabulous for the people she's meeting, and she doesn't need or want to settle. Maybe she's just happy single. Maybe she's worked out who she is and what matters to her. Much of my life – around four decades, to be precise – has been defined by dating and body image, and I've had enough. There are so many things that really matter – whether or not I'm single is not one of them.

Valuables left at own risk

I'd like to think I've always had an evolved values system, but it's got more fine-tuned with age. Priorities tend to become increasingly clear over time, and things that don't align with them become harder to ignore. Having a better handle on who we are links to a better understanding of what we want, and to being less afraid to do something about it.

Miriam Margolyes – 'The job of an artist is to show the gap between what could be and what is. That's the job, that's what we have to do. It is a moral duty. I was taught by F. R. and Q. D. Leavis when I was at Cambridge, and they were the great moralists. They believed that English literature is not just for entertainment, but also to teach us how to live, and to live seriously and well. And I believe that.'

Living according to our principles becomes less and less negotiable as life goes on. I'm lucky to have some financial security after the boardroom years. I still need to earn a living, but if I say no to a job on the basis that it's funded by, say, the tobacco or porn industries, I'll still be able to put food on the table (and have enough left over for a few cigs). Nowadays, I consider the job before I consider the money, and what determines whether it's a yes or a no comes from a wish to devote time to things that matter, are fulfilling or are of some help to someone – or at the very least not detrimental. Five and a half decades in, and I've discovered there's nothing more valuable than values; I can even hand them down without the kids getting screwed on inheritance tax.

Angela Barnes – 'Whatever you're doing, just be someone that people want to work with. I've worked in so many places where there are people who just seem to want to make the work day difficult for no reason – that sort of passive-aggression they bring into the office [. . .] just to antagonise, and then wondering why they don't get picked for certain things. I think no one is so good at their job that the people who are also just trying to do their job will put up with shitty behaviour. For every job in comedy, there's a queue of 150 people behind you that could do the job as well as you. So just don't be a dick to people.'

Acts of microfeminism

The term 'microfeminism' had been around for a while when it gathered some zeitgeist steam. This was thanks in no small part to a woman called Ashley Chaney, who, one Sunday evening in March 2023, did a TikTok video from bed about what was on her mind before heading into work on Monday morning. The text accompanying the video read 'Girl's girl, corporate edition', and it went like this:

> 'My favourite form of microfeminism is when I send an email, let's say to a CEO, and you have to copy their assistant for scheduling purposes; if the assistant is a female, I will always, in the "email to" line, enter their address before the CEO's.'

Watched by millions, it sparked a global conversation about microfeminism, and the superb comments that accompanied it included:

Women involved in childcare calling the dad first if a kid was sick.

People asking, if someone mentions a lawyer, doctor, tradesperson, politician, firefighter or police officer, 'What did *she* say/do?'

A child spontaneously referring to the Easter bunny as 'she'.

A sports journalist only mentioning gender if referring to men's sport.

One comment came from a woman who'd once been going through passport control with her family. When the officer handed back the passports to her husband with the words 'Here you go, boss,' she grabbed them and said, 'Wrong boss.' Her kids still talk about it.

Two of my personal favourite micro acts of defiance include not getting out of the way if a man is taking up the pavement, and claiming the armrest on planes and trains (I believe you already know my thoughts on manspreading). Maybe we should all be more clownfish, where females set the pace. What my then six-year-old son did not tell me when we'd finished watching *Finding Nemo* (see page 132) is the sex-change bit. Male clownfish can become females if the female disappears or dies, and when two males are paired, they get into a scrap and the winner becomes female. That would give a whole new spin to male WWE tournaments.

I've had a (soft white under-) belly full of moulding myself to suit the patriarchal bias of society. I was recently trying to renew my home insurance – I say 'trying', because I'm not great at admin and couldn't locate my subsidence paperwork; at least it wasn't my GP asking for it – and for security, they asked my mum's maiden name. I have a proposal, and it's not even a leap year. Let's retire that question. I don't mind whether people get married or don't get married; I don't care whether they take their partner's name, or their partner takes theirs, or whether they go for a mum/dad surname mash-up like in Spain. My problem starts with the word 'maiden', implying doing something for the first time, like a maiden voyage: the innocent wife handing her virginity to her husband on her wedding day. And it continues because it's predicated on the fact that people have a mother who a) is or was married, and b) changed her name. If that security question remains a prerequisite, my kids won't be able to access their bank accounts, let alone insure the homes they'll never be able to buy. And anyway, it's not a maiden name, it's a birth name. My favourite alternative question is a memorable date; this is free from social stereotypes, and I'm guessing for most of us a reminder of a happy thing (unless anyone's putting down the date their partner left them for someone younger at work – which in my case would be too obvious, it being my birthday, more about this on page 276). My memorable date is the loveliest thing. I would tell you what, but God forbid you hack into my finances and manage to insure my house.

Seize the day

Judi Dench has the words 'Carpe Diem' tattooed on her wrist, an eighty-first birthday gift from her daughter. One of the things said by people who caution against tattoos is: 'Imagine how it will look when you're old.' Hard to level that at us older birds getting inked. Seize the day and let go of the outcome, because the moment is *now*.

The various states human beings inhabit during our limited life spans can be broken down as follows:

thinking

doing

feeling

being

I'm good at the first (as long as it's got 'over' in front of it), obsessed with the second and increasingly attuned to the third. But the fourth? I've always been crap at it – but I'm working to change that.

Colin Murphy – 'There's a great song by Seasick Steve: "I Started Out with Nothin and I Still Got Most of It Left". I wish I'd had that in my head when I was twenty-three, twenty-four, twenty-five. I was always running away and my life was at a really quick pace up until about forty, when I realised most of it's bullshit. [If] I went back again, I would just slow down and look around me. I would soak it all in. Five minutes of every hour you're awake, stop.'

During my twenties, thirties and forties, I conflated 'being' with 'being lazy'. The prospect of downing tools and surrendering control still fills me with awe. Most of us control freaks have become so because it's a strategy that's served us well during our early years, but it's funny how survival strategies from childhood can become hindrances in adulthood. Tracy Edwards quoted the Serenity Prayer as her life advice on my podcast: 'God, grant me the serenity to accept the things I cannot change, the courage to change the things I can, and the wisdom to know the difference.'

It's a great sentiment, isn't it, if you can get over the small matter of the word 'God'. A friend in Alcoholics Anonymous told me that for him, along with some of his fellow atheists, it's taken as an acronym for 'Group of Drunks'. I'm happy to take the principle of the Serenity Prayer in a spiritual rather than religious vein. After all, like David Bowie said: 'Religion is for people who fear hell, spirituality is for people who have already been there.'

Learning to let go does not come naturally to me, and I'm trying not to fixate on achieving it, as that would seem to somewhat defeat the object. There's ego involved in trying to control everything, the implication being that if we don't, it will all fall apart; not to mention it's a fool's errand, because we quite simply can't control everything. I've always overprepared, overworked and overcompensated, and it's exhausting. I've run out of overzealous steam. The weird thing is, that not only does letting go make one's existence infinitely more tolerable, it also has the unexpected benefit of often improving the outcomes. My podcast interviews are at their best when I haven't overdone the research; if I know every last thing about the guest, it's hard to have a spontaneous, interested conversation. I'm on the nursery slopes of letting go.

Not that there haven't been times when I've really let loose – like the time I was flying to New York for work. I'd eaten something in the lounge at Heathrow (I've reinvented my way out of having access to airport lounges) that, about eight hours later, turned out to have given me food poisoning. The lights dimmed for landing in the Big Apple, the 'fasten your seatbelt' signs came on, and my innards revved up. I pressed the call button and told the cabin crew I urgently needed to use the bathroom. They said I couldn't. I said I was pretty sure I was going to go to the toilet, either in the toilet or in my seat. An impasse ensued until, with a level of surrender the Buddha himself would be proud of, I let go. Boy, did I let go. The plane landed, the seatbelt signs were turned off, and I went into the toilet – about twenty-five minutes too late. I was so weak I could barely get off the toilet, let alone the aircraft. I was taken off by wheelchair – that's in a wheelchair, covered in shit, at once too visible and not visible enough. The woman pushing the wheelchair didn't acknowledge me, the immigration officer barely looked at me (it's worth shitting yourself and ending up in a wheelchair if you're crossing the border with spurious intent, although if I'd had drugs up my bottom they'd have long been a goner) and I couldn't get a taxi. I was irrelevant, written off. Not many benefits to that kind of letting go, but at least now when I ask myself 'What's the worst that can happen?', I know the answer.

Anna Akana – 'You're going to die. Everyone you know is going to die. Everyone you hate is going to die. [. . .] Some of us don't make it to old age; age is a privilege. So keep that in mind when you're working a job that you hate, when you're trying to decide if you want to leave your marriage, if you are wrestling with whether or not you want to have kids because that's what society told you to do versus that's not really a sacrifice you want to make. You're going to die. So live your life in accordance with that principle and let yourself try things; let yourself be bad. Everyone is so afraid of being bad. You need to be bad for so long, in order to be good. You might as well start now.'

Second chances

In many areas of life, the bigger the number, the better the thing. The iPhone started out a plain old iPhone, then it became an iPhone 3. Then it became an iPhone 3G and no one wanted an iPhone 3. Then the good people of Silicon Valley kept working their way systematically through the numbers until, after the iPhone 8, they skipped 9 for no reason and made it the iPhone X – that was before Elon Musk had ruined the letter X. Then there was the Pro, and no one wanted the X, and now we've got as far as 16. Progress. Just look at WD40.

In my twenties, I had no idea what WD40 was; now I think there's nothing it can't solve. OK, it can't make my dog live forever but my money's on it for everything else from squeaky doors to vaginal dryness. (Don't try it for vaginal dryness. I'm a comedian, not a doctor.) Nobody knows what WD40 stands for – and who cares? – but we do know if faced with a choice between WD40 and WD39, we'd choose 40.

I'm Cally version 56: a bit better than Cally version 55, and significantly more evolved than Cally the original.

I ran the London Marathon the same year I did my first stand-up gig, in 2014. One of the things I love about running – apart from the fact that you don't have to pay for gym membership and circumnavigate the grunty free-weights men – is that you are reliant on nothing but your mind and body to get you around. Every time I find a run tough, I'm aware the day will come when I'm no longer able to run. There's a saying about runners: 'What are you running away from?' Everything. I never tire of overtaking younger male runners. I ran a half marathon for charity with a group of colleagues the year I turned fifty. As we waited in the starting area, a young guy who I knew a bit from work said how great it was I was doing it, and gave me some running tips. Well-intentioned as it was, never once did he ask how serious a runner I was or if I wanted his advice. He set off like a greyhound out the traps, shouting good luck through the trail of dust behind him. I paced myself as I had in my training runs, and he didn't even notice when, around the halfway mark, I overtook him. I finished sixteen minutes ahead of him across a distance of 13.1 miles (not that I was counting or can still remember it six years on or anything).

Why is it that in the animal kingdom, female elders are respected and revered, while over here in the human kingdom we have turned the natural and normal process of ageing into a problem that needs to be fixed? There's mounting pressure to do away with the 'anti-ageing' description on beauty products, because why should we be anti the process of ageing? Ageing's been good to me. My second act brought me second chances aplenty – running, comedy, dating, ditching the day job, the kids ditching me – and my third act's bringing me plenty more – dog, piano, podcast, happy singledom, writing a book, and the chance to wave goodbye to perimenopause, along with its lightning fanny. (If you don't know what lightning fanny is, lucky you. It's shooting pelvic pain that sometimes accompanies perimenopause. Lightning Fanny – sounds like an unsung hero of World War Two, who gave their life valiantly for their country flying planes over Germany, and only after their death did we learn that they were a woman.)

One day before too long, I'll be waving goodbye to menopause, too, and for now it's not all bad. As I sit writing this on a chilly February day, with energy bills never higher, it's hard not to feel a bit smug. Never has a hot flush been more welcome. If fuel bills get any worse, they'll be paying women like me to sit in pub gardens.

Doris Lessing – 'Whatever you're meant to do, do it now. The conditions are always impossible.'

Eggless and fancy-free

I am nearly fifteen years older now than Shirley Valentine. The character was forty-two; Pauline Collins was forty-eight when she played her in the film. In another fifteen years, I'll be in my seventies, and hopefully still up for a trip to Greece to shag Tom Conti (he'll be ninety-seven, so we'll go easy). When *The Golden Girls* started, Blanche was fifty-three, Dorothy fifty-four and Rose fifty-five. I am older than all the Golden Girls (separately, not together), and I love an early dinner.

Today is the youngest you will ever be. Fifty-six feels exciting to me and the liberation that comes from no longer being fertile is real. I'm free of the sense that I must do certain things by the time I'm sixty, in contrast with how I felt as I approached each of my other milestone birthdays. Great things have happened post-fifty, and there's no reason to suppose they won't post-sixty and beyond, too, so fingers crossed I make it that far, eggless and fancy-free. With fertility dwindling, or likely dwindled, I'm getting back to a more childlike sense of play, and I'm grown up enough not to worry too much about acting like a grown-up. Life is good. (Of course, sometimes acting like a grown-up is unavoidable. By eighty-thirty this morning, I'd been up a ladder to clean out a blocked hopper. That's peak adulting, like when you bleed your radiators or work out what an ISA is.)

There are always going to be some challenging moments with growing older, like when you hit the new age bracket on forms: fifty-five to dead. Some new flats have just been built near my house with a sign outside that reads: 'Elegant living for the over fifty-fives.' I reject elegant living; makes me want to check into a hotel just so I can throw a telly out the window (obviously, I'll bend at the knees before I pick it up).

When I reference my age onstage, there'll often be someone afterwards who'll say something along the lines of: 'You don't look your age.' And I've realised that I do that to other people too. It hit me after a recent event where there were a few such interactions backstage that, by way of a compliment, it's a bit like saying: 'You've lost weight; you look great.' Fantastic, thanks. How would I be looking if I hadn't lost the weight? You know how little kids are so celebratory of their age? I'm three and three-quarters! Well, I'm fifty-six and a half, and when I grow up, I want to be an astronaut. Or a firefighter. Or half the person my kids have grown up to be. As long as we're alive, let's begin to live.

DO TRY THIS AT HOME

When I grow up, I want to be . . .

One of my favourite *Curb Your Enthusiasm* episodes is the one where Albert Brooks decides he should have a living funeral, because, he says: 'In the last three years, I've been to five real funerals. The idea that people get together and friends get together and say wonderful things should be done to a person who can hear it. It's just a different way of thinking about it. I can't stand that all this praise is going to somebody in a box.'

Now it's been set up as an idea with comedic merit, I'm inviting you to write your own eulogy. How do you want to be remembered? What would you want people to say about you? What would you *not* want them to say about you? Write as imperfectly or as beautifully as you like – no one else is going to be reading it (unless perhaps you too decide to have a living funeral).

Now read it back. What words stand out? Why do they matter? And how do they translate to your life now? Choose two or three of them and, for each, think of a small, simple action to get you a bit closer to the 'you' in your eulogy. Forget New Year's resolutions, these are New Eulogy's resolutions.

Microfeminism: strong women, strong world

Rather than grandiose actions, microfeminism is about small, intentional gestures. Decide on your personal preferred acts of microfeminism and commit to doing them every day, in some way. They could be things like:

Putting a woman's name first, like writing 'Dear Madam/Sir' or 'Mrs and Mr' on correspondence, or saying 'Wife and husband'.

Saying hello first to women who are present in meetings or groups.

Avoiding saying things like 'you guys' or 'that takes balls'.

Calling out a man if he takes credit for a woman's idea.

And if you want to be really feisty, you could insist that you know the correct spelling of YOUR OWN NAME and also that you are NOT PREGNANT.

Let it go, let it go, let it go

Across the divide from perfectionism is peace. It's tempting to think we're not good enough, that we haven't done enough, unless we wring something out of every minute of the day. That's where *lanterfanter*-ing comes in. Put down the whip you're cracking and pick up anything that makes you feel good. My *lanterfant* things include: flowers, hot drinks, baths, walks, the dog sitting on my feet, watching things, reading things and taking naps on a working day. Amidst all these acts of self-love, remember the best *lanterfanters* spend chunks of time doing absolutely namaste motherf*cking sod-all. Who knew that the more loosely you hold things, the stronger they become?

LAST WORDS

Following in the footsteps of Shazia Mirza (see page 98), Stephen Bailey also picked a Joan Rivers joke:

> 'Vaginas drop. One day you wake up and you're like, why am I wearing a bunny slipper?'

Kicking off the life advice for this chapter is Sir Grayson Perry:

> 'Turn up on time, put in the hours, and don't be the asshole; because all human happiness hinges on good relationships, particularly at work. And if there's one skill that we need that will probably get you through any other situation it is . . . can you just get on with people and be nice to have around and fun? Because everything else falls into place.'

Sally Phillips's life advice was more of a real-time observation, but no less valuable:

> 'Sorry, my phone's going off. Put your phone on silent when you're doing a podcast. That would be a reasonable piece of advice.'

And finally, this from Krishnan Guru-Murthy:

> 'Dream big, aim for the stars. Someone's got to do it, it may as well be you.'

10
HERE ENDETH THE MANIFESTO
EMPTY NEST AND BEYOND

'I am standing dead centre, still and balanced, living kids on one side, living parents on the other . . . don't move a muscle, I think. But I will, of course. You have to.'
Catherine Newman, *Sandwich*

empty
/ˈɛm(p)ti/
adjective
    Not containing any things or people
    Not sincere or without any real meaning
    Without purpose or interest
verb
    To remove everything from inside something
    'I emptied the closet'

Source: https://dictionary.cambridge.org/dictionary/english/empty

---

It's ironic that the term 'empty nest' comes from the animal kingdom and yet there is little to say that non-human animals experience this life phase in the way that we do. While animal offspring grow up and become independent, they don't often 'leave home'. No uni drop-offs or trips to IKEA for them. They continue to live in their multi-generational societies, their roles evolving within their original group. Sometimes, males have to separate once they reach adolescence due to rivalry with other adult males, but females rarely leave. Even when it comes to the chimpanzee and the bonobo, our closest relatives in terms of genetics, the differences are still vast. The human brain starts out the same size as the chimpanzee brain at birth, but grows during the lifespan of a human to become three times the size. Childhood is much longer for humans, with offspring remaining with their parents for longer because of the time it takes for the larger, more complex human brain to fully develop. Studies suggest that the human brain is not fully developed until the ages of twenty-five to thirty; my focus group (people I've dated) tells me that's optimistic.

Touching the void

Whether or not kids have been a part of your life, this feels like the right place to end the book. So far, my manifesto has seen us declining society's offer to become invisible, committing to finding and using our voices, electing to take up space and demand our seat at the table, and learning to lean into messy emotions. We've had life lessons from feminist animals and an autistic zookeeper, kicked the tyres of reinvention, said yes to saying no, no to saying yes, and given ourselves permission to fail. We've worked out how to grow up and glow up, and we've discovered a newfound sense of play. So now what?

There is a void that comes with this life phase – a sense of loss and grieving for what came before, and an emptiness as we look ahead at what might, or might not, come next; a liminal period of betwixt and between, discombobulating at best, debilitating at worst. If I'm lucky, I might have thirty summers left. Each May, swifts make the long journey to our part of North London, and when the kids were younger, we would all cram into a hammock on our roof terrace at sunset and lie together watching them screech across the sky. I always feel wistful when I see the last of them until they return the next year.

'Gung-ho joy-bringers, spring-harbingers, you drifting, gliding sleep-on-the-wingers.'
Robert MacFarlane and Jackie Morris, *The Lost Spells*

But this life phase is also the jumping-off point for whatever comes next. The Chinese word for crisis is *Wei Ji* (危机),

Wei meaning 'danger' and *Ji* 'opportunity', because in ancient Chinese philosophy, opportunities and crises are intrinsically linked. And so it is for women in midlife – the crises are undeniable, but the change we seek in response to the change foisted upon us need not be without reward, joy and ambition. In my case, offspring have jumped ship, along with the last of my eggs, and for the first time in my adult life, I'm mindfully and happily single; I'm touching the void.

One of my best ever moments was when I found myself unexpectedly pregnant in my twenties. Less of a surprising moment, but just as happy a one, was discovering I was pregnant with my second baby a couple of years later. I have my kids to thank for many things, like teaching me the meaning of unconditional love and giving me a deeper understanding of the natural world – and for the fact that when I sneeze, I wee. I've been in an empty nest for a few years – well, not quite empty, I have my nest mates Jeff (dog) and Crystal (cat) – like a pair of Brexiteers, propping up the bar with Farage in a country pub. You give your kids roots and you give them wings, and mine have flown far, to Devon and Spain (they could have at least flown in the same direction). I had brunch with some girlfriends at the weekend, most of whose kids still live at home, and it really helped. I was reminded just how much kids annoy the shit out of you when you see them every day.

For a couple of decades, you could have been forgiven for thinking I had it all – big job, lovely home, two kids – but it didn't always feel like that at the time. It doesn't matter if you've wowed corporate America with some fancy presentation earlier that day – if, two hours after getting off the plane, you haven't successfully fashioned a Tudor costume out of egg boxes, jetlag and cotton wool, you're still a failure. I remember one time my kids' dad had helped them make an eggmobile for the school egg race when I was away for work, and you'd have thought he'd come up with a cure for thrush by the praise he got for doing it. It's like when people say it's nice that a dad 'babysits' so his partner can go out for the evening. I remember when my kids' dad moved out, many a person told me it was nice of him to let me keep the house. It was *my* house. Years later, I was sitting next to a high-profile divorce lawyer at a dinner, and when they heard I'd never been married, they told me to make damn sure I got married next time around.

'Why?' I asked.

'So if it goes pear-shaped next time, you're not left without a claim to his money,' they answered.

It didn't occur to them that one reason I don't want to get married is so a new partner doesn't have a claim on mine.

The empty nest thing creeps up on you. Sometimes when I see a parent of a young baby, I want to go up to them and say: 'Hold them close, because all this will be gone in the blink of an eye, and that person you loved so much you wanted to have a baby with them may not even be in your life anymore, and your baby will have left home, and you'll be worrying about whether they're eating the right food, and are they going to have their hearts broken, and have they taken ketamine?'

But instead I say, 'Aw, how old?'

The days go slow and the years go fast.

Then and now

The phrase 'empty nest' was coined by the American writer Dorothy Canfield Fisher in her book *Mothers and Children* in 1914, but didn't become part of modern parlance until the 1970s. It is not a new phenomenon; in fact, one could argue that it's got a bit out of hand. We're seeing the first generation of kids each of whose new school years were marked on social media with a doorstep photo in their school uniform. There's a parental rumpus each time a Gen Z or Gen Alpha reaches a milestone: first word, first step, first breadstick stuck down the sofa, first school play, first sports day, first partner, first time they say, 'Can you stop posting every fucking thing I do on Facebook?'

These are 'sharents': parents who post incessantly about their kids, their lives enmeshed, seeking vicarious thrills from their kids going to Glastonbury, or posting pictures of them going there with them. The separating and letting-go process that is fundamental to growing up grows murkier by the year, not helped by the fact that, financially, people now can't finally leave home until many years later than we once did. The average age for moving out in the UK is now twenty-five years old, with Londoners leaving home on average five years later than the rest of the country. If the trend continues, soon enough they'll never leave home, and it'll be the parents who move out, evicted by desperation or death. Parents are meant to feel the pain and loss of individuation, although I'm not sure Boomer parents did. When I left home in the eighties, there was little more than a cheery wave off at my halls of residence and a 'See you at Christmas! And remember, if you need anything – money, moral support, anything at all – don't call us!' No one expected us to be in touch, and at ten pence per three-minute call from a phone box, our separation was absolute. For sharents, however, when kids leave home, it's like someone's died. When her youngest left for college last year, Gwyneth Paltrow said it gave her a 'nervous breakdown'.[23] Gordon Ramsay was so 'gutted' when his son Jack went to uni that he sat on his bed and put on a pair of his pants.[24] All the celebs have been talking about it: Michelle Pfeiffer, Elizabeth Hurley, Rob Lowe.

I belong to the helicopter-parent generation: those who circle above, managing everything. We pre-date the snow-plough parents, who clear all obstacles before kids even reach them. I will admit to the odd sharent tendency (see

Chapter 5). But whatever kind of parent I am, I see the kids moving out as a continuation of our relationship rather than the end of it. And it has created space for an exciting new relationship to emerge: my relationship with myself.

Three little words

I asked people on social media to sum up in three words what 'empty nest' means to them, and here are some of the themes that came up (most frequently mentioned first):

> **emptiness and loneliness** (*hole in heart, a hollow silence, heart-wrenching emptiness*)
>
> **new beginnings and fresh starts** (*a new chapter, my next phase, time to live, space for me*)
>
> **tidy house and full fridge** (*full fridge sadness, house stays clean, tidy kitchen surfaces, hello clean flat*)
>
> **mixed feelings** (*bittersweet boring freedom, heartbreaking then liberating, proud but lonely, happiest saddest feeling, finally but sad, so now what?*)

HERE ENDETH THE MANIFESTO

kids coming back (*ours have returned, they come back, they will return, you back already?*)

circle of life (*given them wings, grown and flown, re-feather the nest, successful birdlauncher*)

pets (*get a dog, more cats now, replace with dachshunds, dog is bored*)

rekindling relationships (*blossom of marriage, restarting my relationship, fancy my husband, time to reconnect, fancy a fck?*)

grandchildren (*waiting for grandchildren, future beautiful grandchildren*)

dancing naked (*let go now, time to celebrate, forget body tyranny, get baps out, bath Enya wine*)

Someone asked if they could have five words: 'No fake tan loo seat' – then added how much they miss it. Someone else: 'DINNER'S READY! . . . Oh.' That last one resonated. I could hardly do the online grocery shopping for a bit after my youngest left because of all the now-redundant favourites that would come up. That said, if I never see another raisin box or breadstick in my life, it won't be too soon (although I'm not impartial to a Babybel).

Who we were always destined to be

We think we're so different, that we'll never be old or middle-aged, yet here we are. And it's OK. We're not the same as our mothers or grandmothers, and our children and grandchildren won't be the same as us. American activist Lilly Ledbetter, who died last year at the age of eighty-six, was in her sixties when she inspired the Fair Pay Act, having successfully sued her employer Goodyear after finding out she was paid $6,500 less than the lowest-paid man working at the same level. Last year, Manette Baillie became the oldest skydiver in Britain after she jumped out of a plane at the age of 102; for her hundredth birthday, she had driven a Ferrari around Silverstone at 130mph. I reckon the person jumping out of the plane with her would have been shitting themselves in case this is what did for her. She was spurred on to do it by a friend's eighty-five-year-old father who had skydived, thinking if an eighty-five-year-old man could do it, so could she. US designer Iris Apfel died last year aged 102. Her mantra? 'More is more, and less is a bore.' She was a self-proclaimed 'geriatric starlet' who aspired to be the oldest living teenager (and there I was thinking that was the last comedian I dated).

I worked with a thirty-year-old comic across some Scottish gigs a few weekends ago, and on hearing that my grandparents lived until their late nineties, she said: 'That's great, you've probably got a few years left.' That came on top of waking up the morning before I left to find my cat trying to eat my hair, like those cats who eat their owners – only I'm not dead yet. I'm younger than Lilly Ledbetter was when she sparked the Fair Pay Act, and just over half the age of skydiving Manette Baillie. Women in their fifties are reinventing, dancing, speaking, writing, singing, shouting, modelling, painting, saying yes, saying no, running marathons and running for President of the United States. A little more than a century after women were risking their lives and their liberty for our right to vote, the mantra of 'deeds not words' still fits today – or perhaps it's more 'deeds *and* words'. Midlife women, doing what we want to do, saying what we want to say, and being who we were always destined to be.

Lonely as a cloud

Ever since watching Andrew Haigh's *All of Us Strangers*, when I hear the word 'loneliness', I think of that desolate London tower block, housing the solitary souls of the characters played by Paul Mescal and Andrew Scott. Those scenes were shot in a new residential tower in Stratford in East London – it was hard to find a location that would grant permission for their real estate to be used as a symbol for modern-day loneliness and despair.

When my kids' dad moved out, I hadn't banked on how alone you can feel even though you're still sharing your home with two other people – albeit little people who go to bed at seven-thirty (let's pretend I had everything under control and that's true). I got two cats, ostensibly for the kids but really because I needed their beating hearts to fill the vacuum of those uninhabited evenings. Two decades on, those cats are gone (dead), the kids are gone (alive) and this is the first time I've lived alone. I went from my family home to uni, then to house shares, to live-in boyfriends, to kids. It hit me like a brick a few weeks into my fully empty nest that what I was feeling was loneliness, and I was full of shame about it. When Esther Rantzen's husband Desmond Wilcox died, she went public about her own struggle with loneliness, which inspired her to set up the Silver Line. At the time, she said that she had plenty of people to do something with, but no one to do nothing with. I've grown to love my own space and company, but it still feels odd sometimes when I open the door and there's no one there. I said that to a friend once, and she said: 'You're there.'

Bollocks. That's why I got a dog.

It was the right thing for me and my kids' dad not to stay together, but I regret how blasé I was in my twenties about the stability and normality of what we had – the effortlessness, the good fit, the overarching sense of being partners in crime. One thing I've never taken for granted is having had kids with him. It must be hard if you end up hating your kids' other parent because you'll keep seeing little bits of them in the children as they grow up. I see it in how my two look, in their capacity for creativity and languages, their intellect, their love of Lego and their Dutch passports – all of which remind me just how grateful I am that we had kids together (especially the passports). I was in my early thirties when we split up, and I naively assumed another life partner would appear on the scene soon enough. With that in mind, I threw myself into what would turn out to be more than two decades of serial monogamy – or dating car crashes, depending who you ask. Kids' dad aside, my most defining break-ups happened thirty years apart.

Pain has a sell-by date

I was with my first boyfriend from fourteen to sixteen; let's call him Toby. We were both into drama (the subject, not the activity, although a bit of both), and our last production before sixth form was *Sweeney Todd*. He was cast as Sweeney, I as Mrs Lovett. Rehearsals were going swimmingly, especially the breaks spent smoking Rothmans and snogging by the bins. Then, one afternoon, as we walked out of the school gates, he finished with me out of the blue. A week later, my broken heart was topped off with glandular fever – an extra bitter blow to contract 'kissing disease' just when you have no one to kiss. Grounded at a vital stage in rehearsals, someone else stepped in as Mrs Lovett. That someone also became Toby's new girlfriend. I remember my mum saying to me at the time that it was puppy love, that I'd look back on it years down the line and see it for what it was. Forty years on, I still feel the reverberation of that first heartbreak; I think you always do. I found him on Facebook a while back, hoping he'd look like Ed Balls, but he looks more like Mark Ruffalo. I didn't get as far as finding out if he'd ended up with Mrs Lovett, or was the father of baby Lovetts.

Maya Angelou famously said: 'When someone shows you who they are, believe them the first time.' Fast-forward almost exactly thirty years, and on my forty-fourth birthday, the love of my life, who I'd been with for a couple of years, woke up with me, gave me my presents and, after I'd opened them, kept looking at me weirdly. Before I had time to ask what was up, he took a deep breath and said: 'I don't want to do this anymore.'

'Crap birthday prank,' I thought.

But he went on: 'I don't love you enough. I don't want you enough.'

He just kept repeating those same words, no further explanation offered, as I struggled to take it in. A week earlier, he'd taken me to Ireland as an early birthday present, all loved up – or so I'd thought. I couldn't fathom it, not least because one of his presents to me was tickets to a performance of *The Book of Mormon* three months hence. Two hours later he was gone, and I never saw him again. It turned out his capacity for love was greatly enhanced by the age of the person he was loving. My brother broke it to me a few weeks later that he'd seen my ex had changed his status on Facebook to 'in a relationship' (what was he, fifteen?). I went on to his Facebook page to see who he was in a relationship with, and my brother and I both hit upon her cover photo at exactly the same time: a woman in a string bikini, standing by a waterfall wearing a big-brimmed hat. 'She looks really boring,' my brother said. She didn't – it was a waterfall in Guatemala – but thank you, my bro. It was someone from his work, twenty-five years younger than him. (For anyone who doesn't believe in karma, one year later he was a sixty-year-old, living in Croydon with a one-year-old. Namaste.) When he left, I was a single mum to a thirteen-year-old and a fifteen-year-old. And it was my birthday! I didn't fall apart – not on the outside, at least – and I do know this: if he hadn't left, I'd never have run my first marathon; and I'd never have done my first gig.

Flying solo

By the time my eldest moved out, I was single, a Kentish Town Komodo. Komodo dragons are among the ultimate independent female animals, because they reproduce and raise offspring with no male contribution whatsoever, not even mating. This is not misandry but parthenogenesis, also favoured by the glorious mayfly. I haven't managed to pull off parthenogenesis, but I am flying as solo as a Cape honey bee (another parthenogenesist).

I had always hated being single, which tended to lead to me dating the wrong people, until last year, at fifty-five, a switch tripped. My head space up to that point had been overcrowded with people I'd dated, mainly men. Spanning four decades, there's always been at least one person with squatter's rights in my cranium, and I've taken them with me everywhere: uninvited brain guests. The thing about travel is that you can move around all you like, but you're still there, along with your increasing quantity of baggage.

I've been defined, destabilised and debilitated by relationships and break-ups to the point where it's felt like a dirty secret, so opposed is it to my beliefs and behaviours in all other areas of my life. At the start of 2024, after a year that saw not just one but two disastrous relationships, both with comedians – what can I tell you? We're a terrible bet – I experienced a shift so significant it felt almost molecular, as if I'd woken up from a forty-year reverie, only unlike Snow White, the last thing I wanted was seven little guys hanging out with me. At the time of writing, I'm over a year into being happily and mindfully single. I won't go as far as saying 'self-partnered' like Emma Watson did that time in *Vogue*[25] – and anyway, then she changed her mind. It doesn't matter whether you're single, married, a couple, a throuple or whatever the hell takes your fancy; it's about the motivation for it, and patterns that accompany it. Not being OK with myself made me ask way too much of everyone else, and pretty much guaranteed I wasn't going to find the very thing I was looking for. I don't know how you learn to be with someone unless you know how to be alone.

Choosing the bear

Margaret Atwood – 'Men are afraid that women will laugh at them. Women are afraid that men will kill them.'

I can't write this book without mentioning 'choose the bear' – the fact that most women, faced with the choice between encountering a man or a bear while unarmed and alone in the woods, would choose the bear. We know the bear might kill us, but that's all it will do. It won't degrade or torment us or make us feel worthless. It won't coerce us because it 'loves us too much' or control us or cut us off from the people who do love us. It might un-alive us, but it won't make us wish we weren't alive.

I don't think there are many bears in Kentish Town – not even down the road at London Zoo anymore. The nearest I've come to meeting one was in that how-to-handle-dangerous-animals leaflet at Yosemite.

I have, just for now, hit a wall in terms of dating men. Dating is hard at the best of times, and being a woman in your fifties isn't the best of times, with suitors expecting us to be grateful for the opportunity, like candidates on *The Apprentice*. It's not just the people we go on dates with, it comes from the people around us, too, and from within ourselves. When we tell you we're single, you don't need to feel sorry for us or assume it's because we can't find anyone – and you definitely don't need to say, 'It's never too late,' because until you said that, we never thought it was. From Jane Austen to Bridget Jones and everything in between and since, we've been fed the line that the pinnacle of a woman's happiness is finding the right man. Someone asked me about my 'other half' last night; I think I'm a whole person.

My daughter told me there are advertised singles hours in Madrid supermarkets, and if you put a pineapple upside down in your basket, it's a sign you're looking for love. (Elsewhere, it's a symbol for swingers – perhaps that's the reason Tesco isn't running with it as a campaign.) For something shorter term, you choose a perishable item, like a lettuce; for something long-term, it's canned goods. I don't know what happens if you're just in there, oblivious, wanting a salad because it's a hot day – suddenly lots of Spaniards offering sex, I suppose. And who knows what you get for tinned pineapple. Dating goals for me: find a relationship that lasts longer than a pineapple.

I've never been married, which technically makes me a 'spinster'. That word, now thankfully retired from government legalese, is laden with judgement and misogyny, yet the number of women living this way is increasing. Sometimes living alone is lonely, but there's nothing lonelier than sharing your home and your bed with someone you don't want to be with; rather an empty nest than a nest with a couple-not-speaking-at-a-hotel-breakfast vibe. I'm choosing to stay single until I find a person worth not staying single for. It's not that I'm not excited about romance and sex and all that is yet to come, but I'm equally excited about finding clothes made of natural fibres with proper pockets. My dating life was always foiled by low self-esteem; now it's foiled by having some.

Everything is connected

As I have become both more and less visible to the world, the world has become increasingly visible to me. I moved to London in the eighties for university and, apart from my couple of years in Amsterdam, have been here ever since, so it's inevitably a city laden with associations.

My last serious relationship was with someone where the slight fly in the ointment wasn't that he was shagging someone younger at work, but that a few weeks into seeing each other, he was diagnosed with head and neck cancer. He went through a horrific period of life-altering treatment, and I spent much of it by his side. It was an odd honeymoon period, our sleepovers in University College Hospital London, him in urgent care, me on a plastic chair. His treatment was on the fourteenth floor, with panoramic views across the capital, and I watched many a sun set above the London skyline as he fell into another morphine-induced sleep, my memories dotted across the horizon like a menopausal charm bracelet.

It was 1993 when I met my kids' dad, at the time living in a tiny Warren Street flat that he shared with one friend and many cockroaches. Thirty years later, almost to the day, I was sitting in the UCLH hospital café, looking out at Warren Street station, when I realised I could see his old front door; it was even the same colour. The past in front of me, and what I thought was my future behind. Cancer boyfriend and I (he doesn't have cancer anymore, having pulled off a medical opinion-defying recovery) didn't split up because he was ill – nor, surprisingly, did we split up when one night, sitting on his hospital bed, we played 'Which celebrity would you want a free pass to be able to sleep with if you got the chance?' (My options for him were Julianne Moore, Jennifer Garner, Susan Sarandon, Michelle Obama and Jo Whiley, and he made the mistake of answering). We split up because if I'd been OK with being single, we'd never have got together in the first place. Finally, finally, *finally*, lesson learned.

I walk on Hampstead Heath most days, and when I look out across that spectacular and much-used-in-movies view from Parliament Hill, I see ghosts in all directions. Soon after my kids had left home, I went to a spot where I used to take them for picnics – big mistake – and, looking down at the playground where we had spent hundreds of hours, I could almost see and hear the childhood versions of them. Everywhere I go in this city has a memory of something – an amazing kiss, a break-up (break-ups outnumbering the amazing kisses, with some overlap), buildings I've worked in, homes I've lived in, hospitals I've given birth in, cafés I've laughed in, cinemas I've cried in, venues I've performed in and shops I've bought stuff in – stuff that looked far worse at home than it did in the changing room, that I didn't need anyway, and I never got round to taking back. Some places, like Euston station, have so many associations I've almost stopped taking the train.

Everything is connected.

It takes a village

You don't usually have much choice about your kids moving out. When they do, it's not without cause for celebration, partly because they're ready and able to move on to the next thing, and partly because by that time, the only thing everyone's agreeing on is the fact that there's a reason why adult humans and their offspring don't share living space forever. There is a powerful instinct to defy and to separate on their part, and a wish for them to learn that fridges don't fill from the back on yours. Yes, you pine for them when they're gone, but my top tip if you're struggling is . . . have them back home for a bit.

When they go, suddenly your domestic life is no longer a team sport. Geese are right up there when it comes to teamwork. They fly in V formation so they can see more than just the bird in front, but also so they can create lift for their pals as they flap their wings, resulting in the flock as a whole flying with less effort. They take turns in leading and, if a goose gets injured, two other geese fall out of formation and stay behind until it can fly again; then they work together to catch up with the flock. There's even a theory that the loud honking you hear when geese are flying is their way of shouting encouragement to each other on long flights.

We all need people to honk encouragement at us – not scaffolders, ideally, but family, friends, random people on dog walks and strangers we get talking to in queues or on long journeys. A friend's mum used to say that friendships are for a reason, for a season, or for life. I'm very thankful for the lifers I have around me, especially as I never really had close female friends until I was in my thirties. Whether it was the boys'-school experience or something else a psychoanalyst would have little trouble unearthing, my close friendships were always with men, often tipping into romance. Now I can't fathom how I managed without close female allyship and I hold my friends very dear, even the one who thought my online date was at the Royal Free Hospital. As Beyoncé once said: '[There] is nothing like a conversation with a woman that understands you. I grow so much from those conversations.'[26]

It takes a village to get us through midlife. This weekend, I was at a friend's memorial and turned up alone, aware that others would be there with partners or kids or both, and not sure of my tribe. I walked up the pub stairs and saw my tribe – women, many of whom have known each other for decades. Kids and partners have left, new kids and partners have arrived; some people, including Mon, who we were there for, we have lost for good. Yet there we were, the rest of us, together, still standing, and laughing and crying. Then, just as I was basking in a warm North London glow of love, gratitude and remembrance, the friend who was due to give the speech got a migraine and handed me a piece of paper.

'Why me?' I asked.

'Because you tell jokes for a living,' she answered, 'so this will be easy for you.'

I'm not sure how easy it was, doing a remembrance speech with three minutes' notice – I'm back home now, and it's all a bit of a blur. I know it ended on a song, and that I don't and can't sing. Nor do I drink, but thankfully others do. All friends matter, but there's something particularly powerful about female-centric gatherings. Female bonobo groups share food, groom one another and look out for each other – like the sleepover scene in *Grease*, only hairier – and they also band together to protect themselves from male aggression. I wish I'd had more women with whom to link arms while I was hiking my way to the summit of corporate life.

Claim your space

My friend Julie talks about the need to free up your metaphorical parking space. Whatever or whoever has parked in it – job, partner, friend who's not really a friend – if they're there, there's no space for anyone or anything else to come in and park. Our parking spaces get freed up in midlife, as parts of us and our families drive off, which brings with it pain and grief and turbulence, but also frees up the space for something new to drive in.

One of the things that was juggernauting across my parking space was my corporate job. After a speech at the NEC Birmingham, I was going up an escalator and there were photos of a forest from floor to ceiling on the man-made walls. I guess it was to make you feel as if you were walking through the trees, but all it made me think of was how much I yearned to be in an actual forest. How much was I willing to pay not to be stuck in that synthetic world anymore? That was the question. I've always told my kids that no amount of money will make you happy, but that not having enough money will make you unhappy. I met with my financial advisor before pulling the corporate ripcord, and we took the view that I could probably keep the right side of unhappy, which was more than I'd managed in the few years leading up to that point. Once you know that time is worth more than money, you can't unknow it.

When you stop and think about it, what, of all the things you're fretting about today, will matter when you're in your rocking chair at the end of your days? The *New York Times* bestselling book *Swedish Death Cleaning* explains the Swedish philosophy of clearing out your house well ahead of your death, and midlife is an opportunity to get your house in order, sorting out your crap while you're still alive to benefit from the catharsis. I've sorted out the odd cupboard or two, had the front of the house painted for the first time since my twenty-five-year-old was a baby, and had the rotting garden shed replaced. Drawers have been emptied and paper shredded, and along the way I've been taking a bit of a life inventory.

Experiences that have shaped me:

goats sucking my hair (page 130)

my knickers getting twisted on a monkey swing (page 130)

playing the piano for the first time (page 48)

my brother nearly dying when we were kids (page 47)

getting to drama school and realising I couldn't act (page 54)

vibratorgate (page 118)

losing my grandmother (to death, not down the shops) (page 102)

splitting up with my kids' dad (page 139)

having a neurotypical and a neurodivergent child (see Chapter 5 and page 287)

Things I'm glad I said yes to:

a charity parachute jump

moving to Amsterdam

doing my first stand-up gig

getting a dog

Things I'm glad I said no to:

dieting

dating apps

sunbeds

my day job

Things I wish I'd said no to:

drugs

shitty boyfriends

perms

more shitty boyfriends

HERE ENDETH THE MANIFESTO

Super cally fragile lipstick

I dug out the transcript for my stand-up show *Super Cally Fragile Lipstick* when I was writing this chapter, and realised I'd forgotten the ending:

> 'Maybe there is no greater personality disorder than having an ordered personality, especially if you're trying to be a balanced have-it-all twenty-first century woman. If you have to be all things to all people, that has to include being allowed to fail. If I were to talk about all the things I've done in my life, it would sound like a brag, but actually it's a coping mechanism, an incessant need to inject increasing highs to avoid at all costs the dreaded crash – drink, corporate accolades, drugs, skydiving, single parenthood, marathon-running, stand-up comedy, numerous reckless liaisons along the way – until there's literally nothing left . . . And then the crash. And when it comes, you wonder, "How am I going to survive this?" And it's then you look back at your life. Because it will have happened to you before, and you came out the other side. For me . . . I was thirteen, summer term, school play, 1982, *Grease the Musical*. My parents were both teachers at my school – an all-boys school – and I didn't get the female lead. I stood on that stage an overweight, ginger, knock-kneed, bespectacled T-Bird, and that was my crash. I stood there thinking this cannot ever get any worse – a room full of strangers, and they're all looking at me. And they're laughing.'

On those final words, the lights went hard out to black, and there I was in a room full of strangers, all looking at me – and laughing.

Maybe the show wasn't as bad as I thought; maybe it just fell short of what my perfectionism demanded. Things change. I love the premise: super + fragile = a life full of contradictions, fractures and polarity. Neuroplasticity involves the brain rewiring itself over time, deleting the connections that have become redundant and strengthening the ones that haven't. Life experience determines how recently connections have been used, and as we change, so do our neural pathways. I'm still as fragile as I am super, but now it feels like nothing but a strength. Menoplasticity.

Tracey Emin described men as peaking in their forties, while 'women just tend to come and come and come and come and come, so as a woman, you carry on coming all your life until you're old'. Amen, sister.

Lessons from a neurotypical daughter

After a chapter dedicated to lessons from my son, where does my daughter come into it? The answer is, everywhere. It can't have been easy, growing up alongside a sibling with such a singular focus on animals. For all the hours I spent traipsing around the world chronicling monkeys and apes, she spent many of them doing the same, when she might have preferred to prioritise chronicling the clothing rails of Primark over primates. My plan was to end the book with a battle cry for fearlessly celebrating all that is to come without so much as a backward glance, but today I can't stop crying because my daughter flew back to Madrid yesterday after two months back home. I was away for a couple of days when she left (work, not an argument), and when I got home there was a bunch of sunflowers and a little card thanking me for our time together over the summer. Today I'm struggling so hard with my empty nest that I'm finding it hard to write about empty nests, but experience tells me that by the weekend it will all feel different, and that as the sunflowers die, I will be coming back to life.

You love your children equally, but differently, not least because they tend to be quite different. My daughter runs a tight domestic ship, and it's thanks to her that we don't have any condiments with sell-by dates from before she was born. At her instigation, we set aside a weekend this summer to clear out my closets together, weighing up which of my nineties and noughties clothes she wanted to appropriate, sell or give to charity. I expected to feel twinges of sadness, but as I looked at each item, I remembered the stories it would have if it could talk (it would go for a lot more on Vinted if it could talk), and felt at peace with the fact that each garment has lived its life with me to the full. The parties, the dates, the work trips, the early pregnancies, the pregnancies, the post-pregnancies, the holidays, the weddings, the funerals. Watching her try on some of the clothes, sending pictures of herself to her mates saying she looked like Rachel in *Friends*, and knowing she'll create her own stories in them felt exactly right – although if I'd heard 'Wait, you used to fit into this?' one more time that day, *she* was going to the charity shop too.

When she left home, it was the little daily interactions I missed: chatting while we were taking off our make-up, holding her socked feet on the sofa while watching telly, curling up in chairs side by side reading. We have new rituals now, like reading the same book so we can talk about it together. We were reading *Songbirds* by Christy Lefteri last year, and on a FaceTime call we got out our books to compare where we each were – same chapter, same page, same paragraph, such is our mother–daughter synchronicity. We are linked through many things, beyond the fact that I gave birth to her: books, clothes, travel, dogs, music, and dating the wrong people.

Every day I miss her. I especially love it when she's back and her friends come over. The last time a bunch of them were back around our kitchen table, it was as if the intervening years hadn't happened, except now one's a maths teacher, one works for a charity and one's a designer. I said: 'I just can't believe it! I remember when you were this high,' and stopped just short of saying, 'I remember wiping your bottom,' which would have been weird, as these were friends from secondary school.

A few people have pointed out to me that getting a dog is an empty-nest cliché, and absolutely it is. I had to find a new baby, and the new baby is Jeff. I heard at the weekend that the daughter of a friend who I've known since we had our babies together is pregnant. I got momentary grandparent envy and called my daughter. Her response: 'Is that why you're calling? You can't just order a grandkid. It's not Deliveroo.'

I had a dream the other night where she was six again, dressed in the favourite corduroy skirt and welly boots she used to wear, sitting on her favourite step. I woke up and it was so vivid, I reached out to touch her. That little girl is gone; in her place is an incredible woman from whom I learn daily how to live my life. I am in awe of her capacity to travel to different places and still know who she is, to speak different languages, to make friends and go solo into the unknown, to talk openly about how she's feeling and strike a balance between resilience and asking for help, to tell me that of course I should wear a bikini, because I'm her mum and I'm beautiful and she's proud of me – sometimes expressed as: 'Mum, there are people who look way worse than you on this beach.'

On one train journey to Edinburgh, we ended up sitting opposite a woman in her eighties, and next to her a mother with a baby girl. The baby got passed around between us, and the conversation meandered across the five generations of females (the baby's contributions needed work). I hope I'm lucky enough to know my daughter when she's my age. I'll remind her of the time we'd been shopping for six hours during a heatwave, and I said I needed to sit down for a minute with a hot flush – and she told me it was all in my head.

She's just started out working in the film and TV industry, despite my best efforts to put her off. I'm out, she's in, and I couldn't be happier for her. Thank you, Ella, for putting up with your brother's primate obsession, and for putting up with me.

Pick your legacy

It's been brilliant, writing this book. I've learned loads about keeping my cool and maintaining equilibrium, and I hope it's helped you too. It was a big moment when I did the final spell-check before sending it to my editor; then autocorrect wouldn't let me have 'perimenopause', and I nearly lost my shit. Being a woman in midlife isn't redemptive – it is full of pain and loss, of sweat and tears. Above all, it isn't one-size-fits-all. Finding our voices has, for many of us, been a hard-won battle, so we may as well get out of our own way and use them. As Picasso said: 'It takes a long time to become young.'

If you look at your grown children and they're better people than you, you've done your job. But the concept of an empty nest relates to more than parenting. It's about life phase, age, possibility, and the footprint we want to leave behind when the noise and clutter is gone. I love a good cemetery, and not long ago I came across these words on a London tombstone: 'Award-winning Businessman.'

He had died aged forty-two. If I could pick my legacy, it would have nothing to do with my life in the boardroom. Perhaps it would be me calling for change in the way we talk about and treat midlife women – and their daughters, mothers, sisters and friends – and how we treat ourselves.

Many comedians are the love children of ego and self-doubt, secretly scared that if we get too settled and happy, it might take the edge off how funny we are; luckily for most of us, that's a way off being a problem. Midlife women have earned the right to blaze our own trails, rather than tiptoeing on the edges of other people's; far better to have our own imperfect stories than someone else's perfect one. I'm still working on my happy ending, but like a wise old orca, I know where the salmon are.

DO TRY THIS AT HOME

These are a few of my favourite things

After coaching or training sessions, I would ask people to write down three things they were going to commit to doing, sometimes using these categories as thought-starters:

> red: stop doing
>
> amber: keep doing
>
> green: start doing

You've got to the end of the book (for which, thank you), and if we were in a room together now, I'd ask you to pick your three things. As of today, mine are:

> Stop looking at puppies online.
>
> Keep going with the piano.
>
> Start writing book number two!

What are yours?

Not dead yet

Midlife is a good moment to have a bit of a not-dead-yet springclean. I decided to switch out our old banger of a piano for something more tuneful recently, and had not anticipated how much saying goodbye to the old one would hurt. I'd bought it in Amsterdam almost exactly thirty years earlier, and it had travelled with us to various

London homes. It was the piano the kids learned to play on. I made a little Insta film about it, and played its swansong (Abba's 'Slipping Through My Fingers' – not a dry eye in the lounge). Marie Kondo suggests discarding things with gratitude; at this midpoint, we get to live in a new skin and can be thankful for the old one we've left behind. Your task, then, is to pick a thing – a tangible, material thing you don't need anymore. Now thank it, in whatever way feels appropriate, like my last tune on the piano, before deciding on its new home (even if that home is at the bottom of a bin, although ideally there'll be a more creative or sustainable place).

Don't let yesterday take up too much of today

Having thanked and recycled something physical, it's good to do the same for something more ethereal: a resentment you've been holding on to, a fixation with an ex, a regret about something you wish you'd done differently, or hadn't done at all.

Take a moment to write down whatever it is, or was, and how you felt or feel when you think about it. Now acknowledge how it served you to keep feeling like that, and why it's been hard to let it go, and write that down too. Next, thank it out loud (you haven't got this far in the book without being willing to be a knob), and tell it the time has come for it to be ejected from your life. And now wave it goodbye, this thing you cannot see and no longer want or need, noticing how you feel, in mind and body.

Unleashing the power of midlife involves nothing if not knowing what to consign to history; only then can the future be unlocked.

LAST WORDS

Having asked every podcast guest the same three questions, it's about time I answered them myself. So here goes.

My favourite joke:

> 'When I first said I wanted to be a comedian, everybody laughed. They're not laughing now.' – Bob Monkhouse

My life advice:

> The older you get, the less you know. And moisturise your neck.

And my namaste motherf*cking moment:

> Once upon a time, I had dinner with an eighty-one-year-old woman. She told me that, at forty-five, I wasn't too old to reinvent. Two weeks later, she died; two weeks after that, my reinvention began.

Acknowledgements

Firstly, thank you to my body for plunging me into hormonal disarray so extreme that radical reinvention was the only way out, and to the midlife sisterhood for keeping me treading the path to freedom.

To Claire Paterson Conrad at Janklow & Nesbit for taking a punt on me and having the vision to turn scruffy dreams into slick reality.

To Oliver Burkeman, without whom I would not have met Claire.

To my genius editor Lindsey Evans and outstanding publicist Louise Swannell at Headline Books – you both had me at cinnamon buns.

To Tara O'Sullivan, Kathy Callesen, Marta Juncosa, Louise Rothwell, Jill Cole and the rest of the Headline team.

To Chris Lincé for the beautiful cover design and illustrations throughout.

To Wilf Dickie for the text design, Jason Cox for the technical illustrations, and Ruth Ellis for the index.

To Hannah Layton and Izzy Whitaker at Intertalent for their cheerleading, championing and cheerfulness.

To Mike Hanson at Pod People Productions for being the best namaste motherf*cking producer on the planet, and to all our podcast guests.

To Hannah Black for helping me know the world needed this book and that I should be the person to write it.

To Jake for the animal magic, the dog-sitting and teaching me how to be a mum.

To Ella for putting up with being told we look like each other and for showing me how to be a feminist in three languages.

To Mum and Dad for being there from the very first second of this namaste motherf*cking journey.

To my bro for helping me to trust the process and setting me up with a MacBook so I had one less excuse not to get it underway.

To my blended family, who shall remain nameless but know who they are and how much they mean.

To my grandmother Margaret Beaton for being an orca way ahead of her time.

To Charlotte for sticking with me through shit, sheepskins and shenanigans.

To Natasha for showing me how to walk the hardest of steps with faith, grace and dignity.

To Julie for being the wisest woman in town and helping me free up a much-needed parking space.

To Sarah for being the best, and the worst, wing woman.

To Angela Barnes for the ginger fringe-offs, hospital vigils and iced buns.

To Richard Osman for the words that helped make this happen.

To Neil Delamere for believing in me more than I did.

To Laura and Ben for showing me it is possible to find love (and do aerobics) in midlife.

To Averil for letting me be your roommate; I love you to the moon and back.

To Alistair McGowan for getting me back into playing the piano and to Jessica Drake for patiently showing me how.

To John Lloyd for taking a punt on me, and to Juliette Squair for introducing me to John Lloyd.

To Grainne Maguire for being a very funny motherf*cker and for opening a door.

To Regina for keeping the door ajar.

To Dr Benji Waterhouse for your time and wisdom, when it wasn't like you didn't have other things to do.

To Dusty Miller for being the first person to read and love the book and for the megaphone with which you've shouted about it since.

To Deb for the loan of the suit and the love on the school run.

To Natasha Pszenicki and Eve Coles for bringing the cover to life.

To Anna Potts for the effort that makes it all look effortless.

To Jeremy Kynaston for showing me how to be a good goose – the world was better with you in it – and to Serena Gordon and the Hoffman team.

To Yoda.

To Jeff.

To the late, great namaste motherf*cking Joan Rivers.

References

1. Austin, Nicola. 'Invisibility is officially the top super power according to Brits'. wehaveahulk.co.uk, 17 September 2020. (https://wehaveahulk.co.uk/invisibility-is-officially-the-top-super-power-according-to-brits/)
2. Johnson, Sarah. 'WHO declares loneliness a "global public health concern"'. *Guardian*, 16 November 2023.
3. *The Law Society Gazette*. 'Woman make up 37% of law firm partners, new SRA figures show'. lawgazette.co.uk, 13 December 2023. (https://www.lawgazette.co.uk/practice/women-make-up-37-of-law-firm-partners-new-sra-figures-show/5118209.article)
4. Clance, Pauline Rose, and Imes, Suzanne. 'The Impostor Phenomenon in High Achieving Women: Dynamics and Therapeutic Intervention'. Georgia State University. (https://www.paulineroseclance.com/pdf/ip_high_achieving_women.pdf)
5. Siegel-Itzkovich, Judy. 'Why males have lower-pitched voices – study'. *Jerusalem Post*, 18 July 2023. (https://www.jpost.com/science/article-750506)
6. Elephant in the Valley. (www.elephantinthevalley.com)
7. TUC. 'Equal pay day 2024 – tackling the gender pay gap'. tuc.org.uk, 21 February 2024. (https://www.tuc.org.uk/research-analysis/reports/equal-pay-day-2024-tackling-gender-pay-gap#footnote6_gx5523t)
8. Jones, Alan. 'Gender pay gap widens "dramatically" after women have children – TUC'. *Standard*, 23 February 2023. (https://www.standard.co.uk/business/business-news/gender-pay-gap-widens-dramatically-after-women-have-children-tuc-b1062445.html)
9. Royal College of Psychiatrists. 'Hundreds more psychiatric beds needed to help end practice of sending patients hundreds of miles for treatment, says RCPsych'. rcpsych.ac.uk, 5 November 2019. (https://www.rcpsych.ac.uk/improving-care/ccqi/ccqi-news/detail/2019/11/05/hundreds-more-psychiatric-beds-needed-to-help-

end-practice-of-sending-patients-hundreds-of-miles-for-treatment-says-rcpsych)

10 The King's Fund. 'Mental health 360: acute mental health care for adults'. kingsfund.org.uk, 21 February 2024. (https://www.kingsfund.org.uk/insight-and-analysis/long-reads/mental-health-360-acute-mental-health-care-adults)

11 Russell, Helen. 'The culture cure: how prescription art is lifting people out of depression'. *Guardian*, 31 July 2019. (https://www.theguardian.com/world/2019/jul/31/upside-denmark-culture-mental-health-singing-theatre)

12 Launay, Jacques. 'Choir singing improves health, happiness – and is the perfect icebreaker'. (https://www.ox.ac.uk/research/choir-singing-improves-health-happiness---and-perfect-icebreaker)

13 Blanchflower, D. G., and Oswald, A. J. 'Is well-being U-shaped over the life cycle?' *Soc Sci Med*, April 2008. 66(8):1733–49.

14 'Music takes 13 minutes to "release sadness" and 9 to make you happy, according to new study'. Classic FM, 18 September 2023. (https://www.classicfm.com/music-news/music-to-release-sadness-and-feel-happier-study/)

15 Logan, Brian. 'Crowd work is the hottest thing in standup comedy – and not everybody is laughing'. *Guardian*, 24 June 2024. (https://www.theguardian.com/commentisfree/article/2024/jun/24/standup-comedy-comedians-audience-interaction)

16 Guzmán, Pilar. 'Reinventing midlife'. oprahdaily.com, 19 January 2024. (https://www.oprahdaily.com/life/health/a45779948/reinventing-midlife-chip-conley/)

17 Bain & Company press release: 'Older workers will fill 150 million more jobs globally by 2030'. bain.com, 13 July 2023. (https://www.bain.com/about/media-center/press-releases/2023/older-workers-will-fill-150-million-more-jobs-globally-by-2030-exceeding-a-quarter-of-the-workforce-in-high-income-countries/)

18 Scoop press release: 'One in 12 women resign during menopause and it's time organisations do better'. scoop.co.nz, 21 February 2024. (https://www.scoop.co.nz/stories/BU2402/S00192/one-in-12-women-resign-during-menopause-and-it-s-time-organisations-do-better.htm?from-mobile=bottom-link-01)

19. Tatum, Megan. 'Without support, many menopausal workers are quitting their jobs'. BBC, 9 April 2024. (https://www.bbc.com/worklife/article/20240408-menopause-women-job-quits)
20. Ballard, Jamie. 'Women are more likely than men to say they're a people-pleaser, and many dislike being seen as one'. yougov.com, 22 August 2022. (https://today.yougov.com/society/articles/43498-women-more-likely-men-people-pleasing-poll)
21. Workaholics Anonymous. 'The twenty questions: How do I know if I'm a workaholic?' workaholics-anonymous.org. (https://workaholics-anonymous.org/literature/for-meetings/twenty-questions/)
22. Andy F. 'The alcoholic – An egomaniac with an inferiority complex'. AA for Agnostics, 26 October 2022. (https://aaforagnostics.com/blog/the-alcoholic-an-egomaniac-with-an-inferiority-complex/)
23. Najib, Shafiq. 'Gwyneth Paltrow talks "grief and sadness" as an empty nester: "It's evolving"'. ABC News, 23 October 2024. (https://abcnews.go.com/GMA/Family/gwyneth-paltrow-talks-grief-sadness-empty-nester-evolving/story?id=115048016)
24. Sporn, Natasha. 'Gordon Ramsay reveals he wore his son's underwear after dropping him off at university'. *Standard*, 24 October 2018. (https://www.standard.co.uk/culture/tvfilm/gordon-ramsay-reveals-he-wore-his-sons-underwear-after-dropping-him-off-at-university-a3970581.html)
25. Lees, Paris. 'From the Archive: Emma Watson on transcending child stardom'. *Vogue*, 15 April 2022. (https://www.vogue.co.uk/news/article/emma-watson-on-fame-activism-little-women)
26. Gray, Emma. 'Beyonce documentary quotes: Lessons we learned from "Life is But a Dream"'. Huffington Post, 17 February 2013. (https://www.huffingtonpost.co.uk/entry/beyonce-documentary-quotes-lessons-from-life-is-but-a-dream_n_2697739)

Index

acceptance *see* self-acceptance
addiction 113, 163, 195–196, 222
adolescence
   animals 266
   gerontolesence 37
adrenaline 103, 113, 195
adulting 260
adventurers, female 21
aeroplanes
   crying 103
   painted pink 13
   shitting yourself on 76, 256–257
age/ageing
   attractiveness 245–247
   celebrating 260
   freedom and expectations 260
   gerontolesence 37
   inevitability 272–273
   invisibility 23–24
   power 154
   privilege of 257, 273
agency
   being heard 80–81, 94
   reframing 40–41
   understanding situations 40
   vulnerability and strength 40
aggression 96–97, 116
Air Guitar World Championships 14
Akana, Anna 257
All of Us Strangers 274
allies 59, 60–61, 85, 282–283
Amazon toilet breaks 198–199
ambition
   beyond your comfort zone 181
   dreaming big 37–38, 158, 179–180
   learning from failure 234
   putting the work in 158–159, 188
ambiverts 77
amygdala hijack 114, 124
Anderson, Clive 110
Angelou, Maya 65, 276
anger 116
animals
   Beaton's childhood 129–130
   cartoons 132
   collective group names 56
   eye contact 105–106
   invisibility 14
   jokes 72, 146, 210
   learning 212
   parenting 44, 52–53, 277
   polygyny 80
   pregnancy 78
   sex 12, 74, 137–138, 184, 244–245
   social structures 132, 133, 134, 152, 154, 258, 266, 283
   wisdom 154
antelopes 244
apes 134
Apfel, Iris 273
apologising, don't 42
Arquette, Patricia 34–35
assertiveness, not aggressiveness 96–97
assimilation 55
attractiveness and age 245–247
Atwood, Margaret 278
authenticity 89–90, 91
autism 133, 134

Baillie, Manette 273
balance
   dictionary definition 184
   having it all, not 286
   yes and no 185–186, 193, 204–205, 210
Barbary macaques 74
barbershops 106
Barnes, Angela 181, 252
BBC, Director-General appointments 59
bears, choosing 278–279
Beaton, Cally
   childhood 4–5, 45–49, 67, 120, 129–130, 172, 286
   comedy career 16, 17, 22–23, 123, 153–154
   corporate career 14–15, 35–36, 54–55, 57–58, 78, 135, 166, 187–188, 197, 284
   dating and relationship experiences 275–278, 280–281
   degree studies 53–54
   fails to recognise A-listers 16–17
   family 17–18
   first joke 47

Beaton, Cally (*cont.*)
   Invisible solo show 5
   life inventory 284–285
   mental health 18–19, 110
   motherhood 129–131, 134–135, 268
   piano playing 48, 172–173, 224, 292–293
   public speaking 36, 63–64, 78, 87, 89–90, 283
   sales experience 167–168
   single parenthood 57, 139, 274–275
   Super Cally Fragile Lipstick solo show 18, 93, 286–287
Beaton, Ella 133–134, 287–290
Beaton, Jake 6, 7, 129, 132–133, 134, 138–139, 146–147, 247
beauty
   age 245–247
   anti-ageing products 259
   comparing with others 249–250
   personal choice on products and treatments 248–249
Bechdel test 83
Beckett, Samuel 227
being 255–256
being heard *see* voice
Bell, Alex 80, 146
belonging
   assimilation 55
   collective group names 56
   dictionary definition 44
   impostor syndrome 61–67, 68–69, 72
   networking 69–70
   not fitting in 49
   self-acceptance 43
   tribalism 50
Benjamin, Jonny 108, 239
Bennett, Scott 225
Beyoncé 282
Bigelow, Katherine 35
bilingualism 107
bipolar disorder 19
birth stories 81
birthday break-ups 276–277
bison 133
Blanchflower, David 123
Bletchley Park 31
boardrooms *see* work/workplace
bonobos 118, 128, 134, 137–138, 152, 266, 283
Bottley, Kate 226
boundaries, setting 193–194
Bowie, David 66, 256
Bowman, Edith 83
brain
   amygdala hijack 114, 124
   human growth 266
   neuroplasticity 287
   two halves connected 121
brain fog 164–165
bravery 75–76, 84, 163
breathing 124
Bridges, Kevin 158
Brown, Brené 43, 220
Brownlee, Alistair 174, 228–229
Burdess, Abigail 193
Burkeman, Oliver 196, 203, 222
Burnham, Bo 118
butterflies, camouflage 14
Byrne, Ed 229
Byrne, Jason 210

camouflage 13–14, 49
Campion, Jane 35
Cannes 15, 76
car crashes 21–22
career changes 17, 162–163
Carlton Television 54–55
Carr, Jimmy 227
Carradine, David 233–234
cartoons 132
Cassidy, Kira 154
cats, blinking 106
Cavell, Edith 32–33
Chaney, Ashley 252–253
change
   10 per cent shift 208
   acceptance 110, 223
   breaking through, not giving up 239
   claiming space 284
   menopause 153, 164
   opportunity 39, 268
   Serenity Prayer 255–256
   starting small 169, 176–178
   uncertainty 174
   versions of self 65–66
   see also reinvention
chaos 169
Chapman, Tom 106
Cher 188
childhood, length of 266
children's television 53–54
chimpanzees 128, 134, 266
chlamydia 53
choose the bear 278–279
Churchill, Sarah 32
Churchill, Winston 88
Clance, Pauline Rose 62
Cleese, John 201, 202
Clinton, Hillary 91
clitoral massage 117
clownfish 132, 253
clubs, private 55
coaching 7, 65, 121, 208–209

Coles, Richard 102, 126, 210
Collins, Joan 174
Collins, Pauline 259
comedy
   bad gigs 213, 215–217, 233
   crowd-pleasing 186
   crowd work 157
   dying onstage 79
   female stereotypes 37, 52, 93
   flow 225
   gender imbalance 66
   haters 231–232
   hecklers 230
   power of play 118–119, 120
   stage fright 113–114
   timing 92–93
   working new material 200–201
comfort zone, moving beyond 181
communication
   big and small chunkers 142–144
   eye contact 105
   first impressions 86–87
   sideways conversations 105–107, 125
   with strangers 107–108
   see also voice
competence 224–226
compliments 238
Confucius 181
connections
   memories 280–281
   neuroplasticity 287
Connolly, Billy 4, 87
content creation 156
control freaks 255–256
conversations, difficult 95–96
cortisol 103, 195
Covey, Stephen 189–190, 207
Covid-19 pandemic 108, 121
creativity
   learning new things 171–173
   power of play 121, 201
Criado-Perez, Caroline 4
crisis 267–268
crocodile tears 100
crowd-pleasing 85–88
Cryer, Barry 126, 239
crying 100, 101–102, 103–105, 116, 123
culture
   Cally's culture vitamins 125
   courses for depression 122
Curb Your Enthusiasm 261
curiosity 136–137, 141–142

dance 94, 214–215
dating
   break-ups 275–277
   ghosting 1–2
   Joan Rivers on 15
   society comments on 'the whole package' 250–251
   supermarket goods 279
Davies, Andrew 54
dead leaf butterfly 14
deadlines 219–220
Dean, Emily 108–109
death
   grief 102–103
   inevitability 257, 267
decision making
   awareness of death 257
   balancing yes and no 185–186, 193, 204–205, 210
   choose which hill to die on 188–191
   doing the difficult thing first 196
   Eisenhower Principle 207–208
   emotions 198
   get out of the weeds 195–198
   people-pleasing 186–187, 192–193
   personal values 251
   productivity 189–191
   taking time to think 200–203
   yes, if 205
   you can't boil the ocean 192–194
Dench, Judi 254
Dent, Susie 135
depression 18–19, 122
design, man's world 4
Dickens, Charles 99
difference
   accepting diversity 140
   empathy 137
   not judging 134–135
dirty weekends 19–20
distraction 195, 196–197, 203
diversity 140
DNA, primates 128
dogs 105, 289
dolphins 118, 134
domestic labour 30
dopamine 195
dragonflies 12
dreams 38
Dutton, Kevin 181, 188

Earl, David 72
Eclair, Jenny 42
Edwards, Tracy 61, 255
Einstein, Albert 135
'Elephant in the Valley' survey 82–83
elephants 134, 152, 154
Eliot, T. S. 126
Ellis, Havelock 117
emails, responding 197–198
Emin, Tracey 287

emotions
  amygdala hijack 114
  avoiding 116
  decision making 198
  dictionary definition 100
  leaning into and noticing 104, 122–124, 236–237
  mindfulness 112
  society expectations 116
empathy 100, 137
empty, dictionary definition 266
empty-nest syndrome
  animal kingdom reality 266
  celebrating 281–282
  experience in three words 271–272
  having them come back and visit 287–290
  initial crying 139–140
  modern versions 270
  origin of phrase 269
  speed of arrival 17–18, 269
Ephron, Nora 104, 151
eulogy, write your own 261
Evaristo, Bernadine 246
expert syndrome 63
explorers, female 21
extroversion 77
eye contact 105–106

failure
  failing better 226–230, 236
  having it all, not 286
  learning from 212, 213–214, 216–217, 234, 239
  not having it all 268–269
Fair Pay Act 272–273
Fairburn, Rachel 146
feminism
  animal lessons 6, 7, 132–134
  The Guilty Feminist 247–248
  microfeminism 252–254, 261–262
Ferriss, Tim 191
Fey, Tina 34–35, 66
fight-or-flight response 113, 114
films, cartoon animals 132
filmstars 16, 34–35
first impressions 86–87
Fisher, Dorothy Canfield 269
flamenco dancing 94
flowers 23
flying and crying 103–104
FOMO 205
footballers 119
Ford, Henry 183
Forde, Matt 204
Fostekew, Jess 26
Foster, Jodie 246

Frances-White, Deborah 247–248
frogs, camouflage 14
Frostrup, Mariella 37
Fry, Helen 31–32, 88
fulfilment 34

Gadd, Richard 215
Garmus, Bonnie 28
G.A.S. (general adaptation syndrome) 112–113
geeks 135
geese 282
Generation Beta 135
George, Hannah 239
gerontolesence 37
ghosting 1–2
Gilbert, Elizabeth 203
giraffes 78
Gladwell, Malcolm 159
glass ceiling and broken rung 58–59
glass frog 14
Glass, Philip 233
Glenn, Taylor 146, 239
glow, dictionary definition 244
glowing up 246, 250
Godliman, Kerry 42, 181
Goleman, Daniel 114
Gordon, Bryony 38, 98, 188, 214, 222
gorillas 106
Gorman, Amanda 73
grandmother hypothesis 169
grandparents 102–103
Granville, Mortimer 117
gratitude journaling 71
grief 102–103, 126
Groskop, Viv 72, 91
guitars, invisible 14
Guru-Murthy, Krishnan 263
gut instinct 168–169

Haigh, Andrew 274
hair, wanted and unwanted 153
Hamm, John 16
happiness 122–123
Harris, Kamala 246
hate, compared to intense dislike 50–51
hate crimes 51–52
having it all, not 268–269, 286
Hayward, Sally-Anne 233
Hazarika, Ayesha 36, 84, 181
hecklers 230
helicopter-parents 270
Hellnar, Iceland 21–22
Hemmingway, Wayne 165
Hierarchy of Needs (Maslow) 49–50, 103
Higson, Charlie 146
Hoffman, Bob 119

Hoffman Process 119–120
Hollywood 34–35, 83
homeworking 199–200
HOPE acronym 109
Hopper, Grace 35
Horace 215
hormones
  crying 103
  multitasking 195
  stress 113
hot flushes 259
housework/domestic labour 30
HRT 29, 32, 110, 115
human brain size 266
human states 254–255
Hume, Anna 53–54
hyenas 134
hysterectomies 34
hysteria 116–117, 118

Iceland, being dumped and car crashes 20–22
identity 165–166
idiosyncrasy 80
Imes, Suzanne 62
impostor syndrome 61–67, 68–69, 72
Ince, Robin 218
Indian grass mantis 14
inner critic 63, 218, 220, 223
Instagram 246
Intelligence services 31–33
International Women's Week 58
introversion 77
invisibility
  being underestimated 35–37
  camouflage 13–14
  dictionary definition 12
  ghosting 2
  hide-and-seek 4–5
  Hollywood 35–36
  men 23–24
  raging against 29–31
  reinvention 159–160
  secret agents 31–33
  sexism 26–29
  signs of 24–26
  superpower 5, 23, 37
  weight 26
invisible ink, semen as 13
iPhones 257
irrelevance 159
isms 31

Jackman, Hugh 227
Jeffers, Susan 98
Jentz and Murphy Technique 136
JOMO 205–206

Jones, Rosie 42
Jordan, Michael 214
journaling 71, 120

Keaveny, Shaun 168–169
Kemsley, Harriet 216
kindness 70–71
King, Martin Luther, Jr 79
knickers, tangled in swings 130
knitting secret agents 88
Komodo dragons 277
Kondo, Marie 293
Kristofferson, Kris 218
kulturvitaminer 122

Lamott, Anne 220
lanterfanten 235, 262
Laybourn, Neil 108, 109–110, 239
leadership or teamwork 61
learning
  creativity 171–173
  from failure 212, 213–214, 216–217, 234, 239
Ledbetter, Lilly 272
Lederer, Helen 224
legacy, choosing yours 290–291
lemurs 132, 134
Lennox, Annie 89
Lessing, Doris 259
Lette, Kathy 16–17
letting go 233–235, 256, 262, 293
Lexx, Laura 72
life advice last words 42, 72, 98, 126, 146–147, 181, 210, 239, 263, 294
lightning fanny 259
liminality 164, 267
lions 184–185
listening
  active 105–108, 144
  silence 92
literature, invisibility 13
Live at the Apollo 23
Lloyd, John 75, 122
Logan, Brian 157
loneliness 57, 274
Lordan, Grace 34, 198
loss 108–110
Louis-Dreyfus, Julia 34–35
Lyons, Zoe 201

macaques 74
MacFarlane, Robert 267
maiden names 254–255
making the edit 75, 76–77, 94
mansplaining 56, 83, 171
manspreading 194
marathon running 202–203, 258

marginalisation 52, 81–83
Margoyles, Miriam 210, 251
masking 19, 76
Maslow, Abraham 49–50, 103
maternity pay/leave 131, 198
matriarchies 134, 137–138, 152
mayflies 277
McCaffrey, Paul 120
McCall, Davina 29, 115
McCarthy, Mike 109
McGowan, Alistair 172
Meaden, Deborah 34, 228
meaning in life 34
meditation 111–112
meerkats 134
memorial services 283
memories and connection 280–281
men
    barbershops suicide prevention 106
    invisibility 23–24, 27
    role models 55
    what they think about 55
menopause
    career changes 17
    grandmother hypothesis 169
    heating bills 259
    HRT 29, 32, 110, 115
    hysterectomies 34
    symptoms 105
    word origin 153
mental health 18–19, 109–110, 122
mentoring 135, 144–145
Michelangelo 234
microaggressions 82
microfeminism 252–254, 261–262
Millican, Sarah 158, 217
Milner, Peter 195
mindfulness 110, 111–112, 124, 201
mini-breaks 19–21
Minogue, Kylie 17
Mirren, Helen 35
Mirza, Shazia 98, 239, 263
misdiagnosis, medical 3–4, 19, 80–81
misogyny
    medical 3–4, 19, 80–81
    spinsters 279
Moix, Yann 5
Monkhouse, Bob 294
Montaigne, Michel de 65
moose 52–53
Morris, Jackie 267
motherhood
    returning to work 131–132
    unconditional love 268
motivation, carrot or stick 198–200
mountaineering 21, 229
MTV 57–58, 130–131, 155–156, 168

multitasking 195
Munro bagging 229
Murphy, Colin 255
Murphy, Jerome 136
Murray, Al 169–170
music 48, 125, 155, 172, 218
Myers–Briggs Type Indicator 77

Namaste Motherf*ckers podcast 7–8
names, birth, not maiden 254–255
needs
    Hierarchy of Needs (Maslow) 49–50, 103
    people-pleasing 186–187, 192–193
negativity bias 230–231
networking
    boardroom careers 76
    finding support 40, 69–70
    see also support network
Neuro-Linguistic Programming 136, 141–142
neurodivergency 133, 134, 137, 140
neuroplasticity 287
Newman, Catherine 265
Nielsen, Mikael Odder 122

obsolescence 162
octopuses 245
Olds, James 195
opportunity and change 39, 268
orcas 152, 169
Osman, Richard 64
Oswald, Andrew 123
owls 146

pain, good and bad 229
Pal, Anuvab 22–23
Paltrow, Gwyneth 270
panel shows 75
parenting
    animal examples 44, 52–53, 277
    current versions of overparenting 269–271
    single parents 57, 139, 274–275
    successful job 290
    see also empty-nest syndrome
Pareto principle 208
parking spaces, metaphorical 283–284
Parris, Rachel 158
parthenogenesis 277
passive-aggressiveness 116, 252
patriarchy 29, 38, 58, 79, 254
pay gap 30, 83–84
pee in swimming pools 14
pen names 21
penis fencing 138
penis snakes 129

people-pleasing 186–187, 192–193
perfect, dictionary definition 212
perfectionism
  acceptance 223, 226
  competence 224–226
  failing better 226–230, 236
  fear of failure 220, 222, 227
  having it all, not 268–269, 286
  impostor syndrome 62
  inner critic 218, 220, 223
  letting go 233–235, 238, 256, 262
  negativity bias 230–231
  noticing emotions 236–237
  workaholics 221–223
performance bias 59
perimenopause 19, 105, 259
Perry, Grayson 263
Perry, Philippa 98, 246
Perry, Rich 181
personality tests 77
perspective, others 136–137, 141–142
Peters, Steven 114
Peterson, Jordan 203
Phillip, Steve 109
Phillips, Sally 263
Philo 70
Picasso 290
pineapples 279
pink, aeroplanes 13
Pink, Roxanne 223
Plath, Sylvia 218
Plato 61–62, 70, 92, 116
play, power of 118–119, 120–121
playing dead 12
podcast, *Namaste Motherf**ckers* 7–8
Poehler, Amy 76
polar bears 52–53
polygyny 80
Porter, Lucy 126
positivity 71, 97, 205
power, age 154
pregnancy
  birth stories 81
  giraffes 78
  society comments on bodies 249
Pregnant Then Screwed 84
prejudice 136–137
prescription shortages 115
presentation skills 88–89
Price, Katie 81
primates
  DNA 128
  social structures 134
principles, living life by 251
privilege 52
procrastination 195, 196–197, 203, 219
productivity
  carrot or stick 198–200
  deadlines 219–220
  decision making 189–191
  doing the difficult thing first 196
  Eisenhower Principle 207–208
  procrastination 195, 196–197, 203, 219
  turning up 203–204
promiscuity 184–185
public speaking
  authenticity 89–90, 91
  fear 78
  female stereotypes 36
  first impressions 86–87
  impostor syndrome 63–64
  perfectionism 223–224
  preparation 89, 91–92
  presentation skills 88–89
  remembrance speeches 283
  silence 92
  see also voice
purpose, sense of 165, 166, 174, 178–179

QI 75
queenagers 37
questions, asking stupid ones 136

Radiguès, Thérèse de 33
Ramsay, Gordon 270
Rantzen, Esther 274
Rauch, Jonathan 123
Read-Wilson, Tom 80
reality TV 31
red-necked phalarope 134
Reddy, Helen 2
'Reference Midlife Woman' 4
reframing 40–41
reinvention
  10 per cent shift 208
  career changes 17, 162–163
  Chip's perspective 159
  dictionary definition 152
  identity 165–166
  invisibility 159–160
  menopause 153, 164
  midlife experience in three words 159–161, 165
  side hustles 169–171, 176–178
  workplace changes 162
relationships
  break-ups 275–277
  separation 139, 274–275
religion 256
remembrance speeches 283
reverse mentoring 135, 144–145
Reykjavík 20–21
Rivers, Joan 15–16, 98, 243, 263, 294

Robinson, Ellie 226
Rogers, Ginger 78
roles and support network 39–40
running 202–203, 258
Russell, Bertrand 63
Russell, Helen 126

sadness 101–102, 126
Salah Effect 51–52
Schumer, Amy 34–35
seahorses 44
Seasick Steve 255
secret agents
   knitting 88
   use of semen 13
   women 31–33
Seinfeld, Jerry 78–79
self-acceptance
   belonging 43
   inner critic 63
   not comparing 67
   part of change process 110, 223
   Susan Jeffers on 98
   Taylor Glenn on 146
   Toni Tone on 232
   versions of self 65–66
self-sabotage 61
self-shielding 82
self-soothing 110
Selye, Hans 112
semen as invisible ink 13
sensory overload 113
serenity 111
Serenity Prayer 255–256
Seth, Anil 172
sex
   antelopes 244
   Barbary macaques 74
   bonobos 137–138
   dragonflies 12
   lions 184
   octopuses 245
sex-changes, clownfish 253
sexism
   invisibility 26–29
   society assumptions 31
sharents 270
Shirley Valentine 259
shitting yourself on aeroplanes 76, 256–257
shoes, walking in 4
shoplifting 25
side hustles 169–171, 176–178
sideways conversations 105–107
silence 92, 144
Silicon Valley 82–83
Silver Line 274

Sinatra, Frank 6
singledom 277–278, 279–280
six-second rule 124
skydiving 113, 163, 273
Skynner, Robin 201
Smith, Arthur 126
Smith-Cumming, Mansfield 13
Smith, Patti 218
Snow, Jon 79
snowplough parents 270
snowstorms and car crashes 21–22
social media 156, 157–158, 196
society
   animal social structures 132, 133, 134, 152, 154, 258, 266, 283
   assumptions about women 29–31, 245–246, 249, 250–251, 269
   vocal pitch and assumptions 79–80
spellcheck 290
spiderwebs 23
spies 31
spirituality 256
spitfires 13
spotted hyenas 134
stage fright 113–114
stamina 78
states of being 255
stereotypes
   age and youth 135
   comedy 37, 52, 93
   defying 29–30
stress
   amygdala hijack 114, 124
   physical response 112–113
stress-busting 97
suicide prevention 106, 108
suicide rates 2, 109
superpower 5
superpowers 23, 37
support network 39–40, 60–61, 69–70, 85, 282–283
survival strategies as hindrances 255
Sutton, Chris 191
swifts 267
swimming pools, pee in 14

takeaways
   10 per cent shift 208
   be kind 70–71
   build your own spy network 39–40
   Cally's culture vitamins 125
   commit to three things 292
   difficult conversations 95–96
   (don't) talk to the hand 142–144
   dreaming big 179–180
   Eisenhower Principle 207–208
   failing better 236

finding purpose 178–179
impostor to disruptor 68–69
letting go 262, 293
microfeminism 261–262
networking 69–70
not-dead-yet springclean 292–293
perceptual positions 141–142
reframing 40–41
reverse mentoring 144–145
self-coaching 208–209
side to main hustle 176–178
sideways conversations 125
speaking out 96–97
stop, look, learn 40
stress-busting 97
swimming in compliments 238
unhijacking your amygdala 124
walking through treacle 236–237
when I grow up 261
tattoos 254
Taylor, George 117
teamwork or leadership 61
teenagers
   acceptance of behaviour 63
   reverse mentoring 144–145
   screentime 106–107
   sideways conversations 107
The Baton of Hope 109
The Golden Girls 259
The Guilty Feminist podcast 247–248
therapy
   Hoffman Process 119–120
   therapist called Yoda 115–116
thrush 53
TikTok 252–253
time, worth more than money 284
Tone, Toni 210, 232
tortoises 53
tradespeople 26, 81
tribalism 50–51
tummies 249–250
Twain, Mark 89

uncertainty 156, 174

van Dyke, Henry 227
Vanzant, Iyanla 250
vegetables 42
ViacomCBS 15, 135
vibrators 117–118
Vietnamese mossy frog 14
viewpoints, others 136–137, 141–142
Vincent, Norah 55
visibility, selective 23
voice
   agency 80–81
   being heard 75

bravery 75–76, 84–85
dictionary definition 73
difficult conversations 95–96
first impressions 86–87
pitch and assumptions 79–80
speaking out 83, 96–97
see also public speaking
Voltaire 156
vulnerability 40, 89–90, 119

Walker, Johnnie 233–234
Wallace, Danny 185
Walsh, Seann 173
Warhol, Andy 60–61
Wark, Kirsty 34, 60, 200
Waterhouse, Benji 239
Watson, Emma 278
WD40 257–258
Wei Ji 267–268
weight and invisibility 26
Wells, H. G. 11
wheel of life 176–178
When Harry Met Sally 104
Whitlock, Matt 90
Wilkinson, Joe 72
Williams, Matthew 50–51, 137
Winslet, Kate 35
wisdom
   age 154
   gut instinct 168–169
Wolf, Naomi 246
wolves 154
women
   invisibility 24
   social expectations 29–31
work/workplace
   ageing workforce 162
   being someone people want to work with 252, 263
   carrot or stick 198–200
   diversity 140
   'Elephant in the Valley' survey 82–83
   glass ceiling and broken rung 58–59
   homeworking 199–200
   invisibility and sexism 26, 28–29
   mentoring 135, 145
   new leaders and change 135–136
   pay gap 30, 83–84, 272
   performance bias 59
   promotion 166–167
   sense of purpose 165, 174
   side hustles 169–171, 176–178
   women lost from 59–60, 163
workaholics 221–223
Workman, Fanny Bullock 21

Yoda therapist 115–116

RAISING READERS
Books Build Bright Futures

Dear Reader,

We'd love your attention for one more page to tell you about the crisis in children's reading, and what we can all do.

Studies have shown that reading for fun is the **single biggest predictor of a child's future success** – more than family circumstance, parents' educational background or income. It improves academic results, mental health, wealth, communication skills and ambition.

The number of children reading for fun is in rapid decline. Young people have a lot of competition for their time, and a worryingly high number do not have a single book at home.

Our business works extensively with schools, libraries and literacy charities, but here are some ways we can all raise more readers:

- Reading to children for just 10 minutes a day makes a difference
- Don't give up if your children aren't regular readers – there will be books for them!
- Visit bookshops and libraries to get recommendations
- Encourage them to listen to audiobooks
- Support school libraries
- Give books as gifts

Thank you for reading.
www.JoinRaisingReaders.com